Cabrini
adored by its residents but downed by
outsiders
needing to recognize and realize and open their
eyes wider.
Our neighborhood is not just gangbangin', drug dealin'
and full of negativity
it has after-school programs, softball teams and other
extracurricular activities.

You've got boxing classes at Seward Park and tutoring at
C.C., CYCLE and the rest
Every now and then there's a block party where
they're bumpin' all the slow jams,
jukin' it in the rows, reds, whites and what's left.

Bein' raised by yo building and tryin' to be
tru 2 yourself,
even thugs and gangsters throwin' parties 4 moms on
Mother's Day
still thugish but with affection, touching parents
deeply.

This is what makes Cabrini...Cabrini, not just the buildings
but the people.
Like a big family that watches over everyone,
tryin' to get through.

We've been given our bad name,
and we deserve it a bit,
but most of us are here makin' the best of it.

— Bradore *"Hush"* Thompson-17

Cabrini GREEN

in WORds + PICture.

COMPOSED By: DAvid T wHitaker
WORds: CAbrini greeN residents
PICtures: BLAir JeNSEN
DesigN: hArk DESign
PUBLisher: W3 CHicAgo
          in AffiliAtioN witH LPC group

©

Cover by John Bistolfo @ Bark Design

Text designed and typeset by Bark Design

Printed and bound by Courier

Published by W3 Chicago in affiliation with LPC Group

Author royalties for **Cabrini-Green: In Words and Pictures**
are being donated to Cabrini Connections. Cabrini Connections
is a grassroots, nonprofit, tutor/mentor organization connecting
ideas, programs and people to help at-risk kids have brighter
futures. For more information about Cabrini Connections, see
the website at www.tutormentorconnection.org.

ISBN: 0-942986-79-2

Editorial Sales Rights and Permission Inquiries should be
addressed to:
W3 Chicago, c/o LPC Group
1436 West Randolph Street
Chicago, IL 60607

Email: pfp@lpcgroup.com

Manufactured in the United States of America
1 3 5 7 9 10 8 6 4 2

Substantial discounts on bulk quantities of W3 Chicago books
are available to corporations, professional associations and other
organizations. If you are in the USA or Canada, phone the LPC
Group. Attn: Special Sales Dept. for details — 800.626.4330 or
fax 800.334.3892.

☾

INTROduction

After years of stubborn resistance to a high-profile redevelopment plan, a distinct Chicago landmark is slowly disappearing

Sitting in the heart of downtown, the high-rise buildings of the Cabrini-Green housing development have long been a conspicuous element of the city's broad-shouldered landscape. Once thought of as a model for public housing, the complex has since been declared a failure and routinely referred to as notorious, infamous and destined for the wrecking ball. Amid tempered cries of protest and determined promises of progress, the transformation has begun.

In light of what may have caused its gradual demise and what will ultimately come to replace Cabrini-Green, it seems timely to consider the legacy of what is perhaps the most widely recognized housing development in the world. Local and federal politicians, urban planners, sociologists, architects and even long-time Chicagoans who have thought better of traveling through this chronically depressed neighborhood may have already drawn their own conclusions.

In recent years, highly publicized tragedies — like the murder of a young boy on his way to school and the sexual assault of a young girl in one of the development's buildings — have served as corroboration to those who view Cabrini-Green as a sad and dangerous place spoiled with poverty, crime, violence, drugs and gangs. And, certainly, the headlines didn't begin there.

In 1968, in the wake of the assassination of Rev. Martin Luther King Jr., rioting in and around Cabrini-Green destroyed area businesses. In 1970, two Chicago police officers were shot and killed in a neighborhood park. Gang warfare in the early '80s was the apparent motive for a Chicago mayor to briefly take up residence in one of the high-rise buildings.

While no one can deny the pain that's been dealt and endured here, it can be argued that the community has been classified all too easily by live reports from the scene. The lens of the media has, on occasion, gazed beyond the sensational and offered a more balanced glimpse of the area, but the milder sides of the community have generally emanated from unique sources or have been spawned by individual achievement.

In the 1960s, local heroes Curtis Mayfield and Jerry Butler — and before them, Ramsey Lewis — preserved the area's hard-working image when they reached legendary status in the music industry. In the '70s, a popular, nationally-televised comedy series based its weekly satire on the everyday lives of Cabrini-Green residents. In the late '80s, a celebrated book chronicled the author's experience as a volunteer coach for the neighborhood's now defunct Little League Baseball organization and, in the mid-90s, Cabrini-Green served as the modest backdrop for a nationally-acclaimed film documentary on a young basketball prospect. In the meantime, two men who grew up here distinguished themselves as savvy Chicago politicians.

These men serve as a powerful reminder that, while many have considered Cabrini-Green a neighborhood to avoid, others have simply called it home. What will come of the area's memory for the people who have lived here, raised families here and perhaps even planned to die here? Those who know this neighborhood best have been heard from the least.

Through extensive interviews with long-time residents — from mothers and fathers to grandparents and teenagers — this book casts an intimate history of the place and its people. Crafted from their stories and experiences, this unique retrospective examines the true legend of Cabrini-Green, aiming to capture a firsthand perspective of its lasting identity before it goes the way of so many other communities that once claimed this harried plot of land.

The area's long tradition of transient poverty began when German immigrants first settled here in the 1840s. These early farmers soon expanded into goods and services and their settlements were said to have slowly grown into an urban neighborhood. Capitalizing on their newly acquired trades, these immigrants moved on to greater opportunities.

The Germans were replaced on the land by new arrivals from Ireland. When the Great Chicago Fire of 1871 leveled the city, Swedish immigrants moved in and rebuilt the area, but they too eventually moved on to other parts of the city.

The Sicilians were the next group to inhabit what was still considered an indigent enclave. The community was apparently run by a powerful few. A spot close to where Oak and Cleveland streets now meet became known as "death corner," because of the number of murders that were said to take place there during this time. With more than 3,500 families crowded into frame and brick tenements, what was commonly referred to as "Little Sicily" was quickly re-dubbed, "Little Hell."

When World War I broke out, African-Americans surged out of the South to northern cities like Chicago in search of jobs created by the country's growing defense industry. By 1930, there were at least 280,000 African-American people living in Chicago, but most of them were relegated to the South Side of the city.

In 1937, the Chicago Housing Authority (CHA) was created to begin dealing with the problems of the city's impoverished neighborhoods, which were brought on by a combination of the Depression and this great migration. As more African-Americans poured in, they were slowly beginning to move to other parts of Chicago. Because of the social climate of the time, however, they were steered to the most rundown areas. One of those areas was the immigrant community of the Near North Side, where Italians remained the great majority.

On this site, the CHA began building 581 two-story and three-story townhouse units meant to serve as temporary housing for working-class veterans of World War II and their families. The CHA stipulated that the homes be opened to 75% white and 25% black families in an effort to make the new development a model for integrated public housing. Sitting on the southern edge of what is now a 70-acre complex, the Frances Cabrini Homes, more commonly referred to as "the row houses," were dedicated in 1942.

While not all of the families that began moving into the row houses, or Cabrini Homes, toward the end of 1942 were African-American, the population was once again turning over. Italian families slowly began moving out. Within ten years, the majority of families living in this area was African-American.

Today, more than 98% of the people living in Cabrini-Green are African-American, and the row houses now constitute one of three distinct neighborhoods that make up the community. In 1958, in an attempt to meet growing demands for low-income housing, the CHA added 15 high-rises made of red-brick infill and exposed concrete frames — increasing the size of the development to 2,056 units and, at that time, making it the country's largest public housing complex. Although officially called The Cabrini Extension, Cabrini residents have long referred to the red-brick high-rises as, simply, "the reds." The William Green Homes, better known as "the whites," were built in 1962, bringing another 1,096 units in eight more buildings.

While these three developments intertwine to form the larger community, each has also managed to maintain a particular independence within Cabrini-Green. Parks, streets, schools and especially gangs have determined loose boundaries. Still, the common bond among residents of the row houses, reds and whites is obvious, cemented in part by the more clearly defined physical and economic barriers that until recently seemed to isolate Cabrini-Green from its affluent neighbors — namely, the Gold Coast, Lincoln Park and Old Town.

Together, the complex contains close to 3,200 units. Its population is said to have reached up to 20,000. At last count, there were fewer than 6,000 residents living here. The CHA has already demolished two high-rise buildings and closed three others. The fate of the existing high-rises remains in doubt.

The larger plan, though still being negotiated, is to transform the development into a series of neighborhoods made up of townhomes housing low to middle-income families. The CHA has made overtures that housing opportunities in this area will be made available to about 30% of current residents. As for the remaining residents, the CHA has committed to aiding their relocation efforts.

Though Cabrini-Green may be slowly disappearing, it will carry on in the memories of those who lived here. Rather than focusing

solely on its destruction or reconstruction, this book looks back on the life and times of Cabrini-Green through their eyes and in their own words.

Accompanied by present-day photography and archival pictures that help chart Cabrini-Green's 58-year history, those who have made a life here share both the tranquil and painful sides of the book's central character, unmasking common misconceptions and revealing its many, often contrasting, faces.

They know it as a place where parents celebrate a child's graduation, where neighbors meet for backyard barbecues, where teenagers play pick-up basketball games and study together at after-school programs. And, they know all too well of the poverty, crime, violence and drugs that have deeply settled into the community's fabric. They know it's a place recognized by its problems and doomed by its presence.

In the pages ahead, residents of various ages serve as expert guides leading readers on a walking tour not only through the row houses, the reds and the whites, but through their own lives. One neighborhood at a time, one generation at a time, one person at a time, they tell a story that's never been told...the story of Cabrini-Green from the inside out.

part I THE eARLy days
1942 68

"Hey, Mother Vassar!"

shouts a young female who can be seen passing through the walkway outside a garden apartment at 814 N. Hudson Street. Sitting at her kitchen table, Alamer Lee Vassar **smiles** brightly, glances toward her weary screen door and in a syrupy voice responds, "Hey, baby."

At 75, Mother Vassar, as she's known in her neighborhood, never had any children of her own, but she gained the reputation of looking out for those around her. While she has lived in this one-bedroom apartment for close to 20 years, it can be said she has been here since the beginning.

In 1942, at age 17, Alamer Lee Vassar left her home in rural Mississippi and hopped a train for Chicago, where her husband, a military officer, was stationed. The first apartment building she moved into, at 1230 N. Larrabee Street, was not yet considered public housing, and the historically impoverished area surrounding it was not yet known as Cabrini-Green.

Just a few blocks south of her, however, the Chicago Housing Authority (CHA) was preparing to unveil a collection of two-story and three-story buildings meant to house the families of those working in the country's defense industry, along with a certain number of low income families. Touted in some circles as a model for racially integrated public housing, it attracted a significant number of prospective inhabitants. The first families moved in August 1, 1942, though the community wasn't officially dedicated until 1943.

The Frances Cabrini Homes were named in honor of St. Frances Xavier Cabrini, a Catholic nun who dedicated her life to work among the poor and imprisoned. Because each building contains a string of modest apartment units, this neighborhood was quickly referred to as, "the row houses."

Mother Vassar moved into the row house neighborhood shortly after the Cabrini Homes opened and not long after her divorce. In the last 50 years, she has lived at several row house addresses. In that time, little has changed, and everything has changed.

Carrying on its hardscrabble tradition, the neighborhood still exhibits the character of a humble, urban village. The row house buildings are huddled together on narrow, tree-lined streets, and laid out like a set of carefully arranged Lego blocks. The slim, flat rooftops of the two-story buildings are expertly aligned with each other and strategically parallel to the more stout three-story buildings that run the perimeter of the site.

Sitting on land that's been depressed approximately four feet below street level, the two-story buildings are made up only of duplex apartments. The three-story buildings were constructed at street level and contain both duplex and garden apartments. Every row house apartment has its own private entrance and a small yard.

Courtesy: Chicago Housing Authority

For decades, the row houses have essentially hid in the shadows of the more contemporary, more visible red-brick high-rises that sprung up around them in the mid-50s, and the imposing white high-rises, or William Green Homes, that were added in the early '60s. The gradual surge of city development on all sides has only made the entrenched neighborhood even more inconspicuous to those on the outside looking in.

After years of housing generations of families, the sandy brick exterior of these rapidly aging structures have long faded to a pale hue, their foundations show signs of fatigue and many interior walls are scarred with hairline cracks. Though time has punished the row house neighborhood, it still maintains a simple charm when compared with the distressed high-rises that loom above it. No matter how the larger community's history will read or where it will end, it is here that it all began.

Mother Vassar isn't the only one who claims witness to the birth of Cabrini-Green. Ms. Lillian Davis Swope wasn't quite ten when curiosity spurred her to walk one block — from Sedgwick Street, where she lived in a tenement house with her family, over to Hudson — for a peek inside one of the newly constructed but still uninhabited Cabrini Homes. She moved over to the row houses when she was 17, and her family eventually grew to include five children. She has lived in an apartment on Oak Street for close to 50 years. She is well-known in the neighborhood for her untiring work with community organizations.

Few may realize that jazz legend Ramsey Lewis spent the early part of his youth in the Cabrini Homes. He remembers his first piano lesson at Wayman Church, which is still an anchor in the community. For many years, Mr. Lewis has worked with young people of Cabrini-Green through a variety of organizations. He's also been known to return to his old elementary school, Edward Jenner, to perform a holiday concert for the students and staff.

Ms. Arzula Ivy remembers the early days of the row houses as well. Like Mother Vassar, Ms. Ivy is 75 years old, originally from Mississippi and one of 16 children. She too resides in the row houses, where she has raised three children. Her children and grandchildren still live in the community.

Ms. Marjorie Davis also raised three children in the row house neighborhood after growing up here herself. Her mother, Ms. Inez Gamble, 72, lived in the row houses on and off for 30 years before moving to the city's South Side.

At 65, Ms. Margaret Wilson and her husband have lived in the row houses close to 40 years. She has raised five children and her community involvement has included everything from PTA president to assistant precinct captain. She currently works for 27th Ward Alderman Walter Burnett, who also grew up in the row houses.

It's been 14 years since Ms. Zora Washington, 55, and her husband moved out of the row house neighborhood where she lived for 30 years. While raising five kids, she worked at Edward Jenner school for 17 years. She continues to work in the community, at Schiller school, and continues to refer to her old neighborhood as home.

Sitting at her kitchen table, Mother Vassar admits that looking back is not always easy. Interwoven in her memories of the past are lingering reminders of pain and struggle. Like the others, however, it's the places, people and promise of the neighborhood that most easily come to mind.

Mother Vassar: I came to Chicago in 1942. I moved into a building at 1230 North Larrabee on October 2nd of that year. There wasn't no projects here then and my husband was in the service. That's what brought us up here from Mississippi. I got a job and went to work. Back then they would beg you when you walked out the door, sayin', "Do you wanna work for me, do you wanna work for me?"

It was beautiful down here. They used to have this festival and parade in the summer, and they had these lights that run from Chicago [Avenue] all the way up to North, and we used to sit out in front of 1230 and look at the people drivin' by and parkin' their cars – whites and colored peoples at that time – and everything was lovely, I mean beautiful. And the kids, they'd go around the corner, over on Scott Street, to this park that had a swimming pool and places to play inside and out. All the kids from Scott, Larrabee and Division streets, that's where they'd go, and we'd go and sit on the benches in the park in the summer.

Lillian Davis Swope: I remember when they built these and I was quite young and nosy, so I went in and looked at them. I said that I was going to move in here someday. I lived across the street, in the tenement houses that were there then. And I went to [Edward] Jenner school.

I moved into the row houses in 1952, when I was 17. I had got married and my husband was a veteran, and that gave me priority. I moved into 926 North Hudson, and as my family grew, that made me eligible for this apartment on Oak.

People were excited at the beginning, but mainly they built the row houses because we had a lot of veterans that was stationed nearby – like at Fort Sheridan and Great Lakes – and they were attending school. But they had families, and no place for their families to stay. So, President Roosevelt decided that they would build these apartments so that they would have a place to stay....It was all nationalities here back then.

Now, in order to move into the row houses – it was like, white, black, white, black in every other apartment – and a black individual could not move into the row houses unless a black moved out, or if you were white, a white would have to move out. That's how it worked, but there wasn't no black and white issues at that particular time. We would visit one another, drink coffee together, we had Bible classes together.

Jenner school was predominately white, and the education was much better. You felt comfortable. I had no problems and the Italians and the Irish, they had no problem. In fact, when I was young their children could spend the night at my house, and I could spend the night at their home.

Ramsey Lewis: It was my parents, my older sister and I. We lived in the row houses at 904 or 907 N. Cleveland, I'm not sure, but I went to Schiller school first and then to Jenner for fourth, fifth and sixth grade. One thing I distinctly remember is that it was a predominantly Italian neighborhood at that time. We had two of the largest Catholic churches in the city in St. Philip Benizi's and St. Dominic's, and I certainly remember the feasts they put on once or twice a year.

I remember we had a great amount of pride in our neighborhood and our homes. We were quite proud of the flowers in the front and the vegetable gardens and grass in the back....My memories of the row houses are really all positive. We were church-going people and I had to do all the usual things every other kid had to do. I had to do my homework. I had to go to piano practice. I had to have a part-time job, all the things everybody else had to do. In grammar school I worked up at Harry's drug store, and later a friend of mine got me a job at Superior Engraving Co., which was down near Superior and Wells and Franklin...and for a while I did deliver papers downtown because I remember those mornings at 4 a.m., standing on the corner waiting for the bus.

Inez Gamble: When I moved over here [in 1952], it was like family, like one big family. And people were more interested in keeping everything up. We used to win prizes on how you kept your home and your yards and things like that, ya know, and you didn't have to worry about the children like you do now. They didn't have all this gang violence and stuff, ya know. We had all kind of activities over here for the children...and they used to block the streets off for dancing and, this was like the early '50s.

Arzula Ivy: I moved to the row houses in July, 1954, and it was very nice in here. My husband was in the service so we found out we could move over here from the South Side and it was beautiful. It was mixed at that time but we had no problems with none of 'em. Everybody was just nice.

I had two kids, Gene and Clemon. No, I had Cheryl too by then and I raised all three of them here in this house, right here, all by myself. Me and my husband separated, but I just stayed here and raised them.

Down on Hudson Street there was apartment buildings and tenement houses, this was before they tore them down to build the high-rises, and they went clean down to Division. There was stores over on Larrabee, like Pioneer Meat Market and Big Frank's and Del Farms, and they had restaurants and everything.

Margaret Wilson: Oh, I remember Del Farms, and on down Larrabee you had Pioneers and then I think it was Krogers. We had the A&P up on Clybourn, Greenman's store was at Franklin and Oak, Harry's drug store was on Oak and Larrabee and then the cleaners was right next door to that, and everybody knew everybody in this community.

Inez Gamble: We used to go up to [Montgomery] Wards and shop in the basement. We didn't have to go downtown, 'cause we could get what we wanted right here in the neighborhood. There was all kinds of shops up on Larrabee Street at that time, and this was before the high-rises were built 'cause there was still lots of Italians living around here, and I remember that Pioneers Meat Market up there on Larrabee was run by a man named Mike and he was Italian. Yeah, but we didn't have no problems as far as any kind of racism or anything, it was just an everyday normal thing, no trouble at all.

Oh [*laughing*], but there was this old candy store up on Oak Street, and what was the name of that man that owned it? Yeah, Phil. Phil knew me real well. He would always cheat my kids outta their change, and I wouldn't care if I was in the bathroom washing my hair, I'd wrap a towel around my head and march up to the store and he'd say, you mean to tell me you gonna come in here and raise all that sand over two cents? I'd say, yeah, if you wanna keep it I am. Every time my kids come in here you wanna short change 'em [*laughing*], and every time you do I'm gonna come up here and see you.

Ramsey Lewis

Ramsey Lewis: When I was four years old my dad came home and told my sister she was gonna be a piano player. He told her she was going to take piano lessons over at Wayman Church, that was our church. Well, I heard that and got awful jealous. I started complaining to my dad, saying I want to play piano too, but he told me he could only afford to have one of us take lessons....I kept it up, and on the day of her lesson, my dad said to me, you can go too.

I could not have been happier, until I learned what piano lessons were all about, and that there was a golden ruler involved. If you didn't hit the right keys, you got hit by that ruler. Shortly after that first lesson I remember saying, forget about it, Dad. Of course, he said, oh no, you wanted to play piano and now you're gonna stick with it. Well, I did and I must have progressed pretty well because about two years later the teacher, her name was Ernistine Bruce, she came to my parents and said, Mr. and Mrs. Lewis, your daughter is a very bright and talented young lady, but I don't think her talent is in the piano. But your son, she said, he is very skilled at the piano. And then she told them to consider getting me more lessons and taking this more seriously.

Those were the worst words I could have heard....I was still only five or six years old and it was rough because when other kids were playing baseball I was at piano practice. I stuck with it and by the time I was nine I joined the church choir at Wayman and was playing at the services.

Mother Vassar: There was a lot of white people here in the row houses in those days but even then the kids would all come to my door, and whatever they wanted I had it for them. But I didn't have no pickers or choosers. I would tell them all, I say I love you, but I don't play. They'd come to Mother Vassar's house when they couldn't go nowhere else. They'd come by for some candy and just say hello and when they ask me where I get that smile, I tell 'em it musta' come from Jesus.

I always had love and concern with other peoples, old and younger, 'cause that's how my mother raised me, so I'd look out for them. When I lived in 1230 we had an evangelist move in next door to us and her name was Mother Moses and, oh, she was beautiful. She lived in the upstairs and downstairs was where she had her church. Every Sunday we'd go down to the church, and I'd sing at all the funerals [*laughing*]. I'm still singin' and I'm 75.

Inez Gamble: We came over here because we were looking for what would be my first apartment. We had lived in the basement of a house at about 54th and Drexel on the South Side. I think it just had one little bedroom and anyway, we finally got an apartment in the row houses, and you would of thought we'd bought a home. We had our own bathroom and everything. We were so excited. The kids could go out and play and everybody was, ya know, just, like I said, like a family.

They even had a $3 fine for littering back then. I remember one time the kids put the garbage out and then later someone found a letter with my name on it lying in the street, and boy I wanted to kill them boys 'cause that was a $3 fine.

Arzula Ivy: People did look out for one another, and we could go to the store and leave our doors open or our windows up and nobody would come in here.

I had a vegetable garden in the front yard and people would come by and look at it and even take pictures of it. It was beautiful. I had a fence around it and I had cabbage and collard greens, and string beans and onions and it was real pretty.

The CHA (Chicago Housing Authority) would always be out there cleanin' up. When you threw paper on the ground or garbage and stuff, they'd charge you for it, but now you can throw all the garbage out there you want and they won't charge you nothin'.

Marjorie Davis: You didn't even have to lock your doors, and you could sleep in your backyard if you wanted. Everything was more kept up. Windows were shiny, they scrubbed their stoops, they kept their yards clean, their houses clean. Everything was spick-and-span, and we won awards for these yards.

Ramsey Lewis: It wasn't until I was in college that I realized I was from what others might consider a "poor" family, as far as money was concerned. But growing up in Cabrini I never wanted for anything. We had clothes to go to church in, we had clothes to go to school in and clothes to play in. We had bikes and skates and sleds. I do remember my dad was strict, he was very strict...but we were God-fearing, law-abiding people, and that's how we lived.

Zora Washington: When it was warm out you could lock your screen door and leave your big door open and go to sleep. There was a family that lived next to us on the corner right there at Locust and Cleveland. We called her Miss Mary. She had a grandson, Roger, and I can't think of the girl's name, but she had a little bit more than the rest of us did and she used to have parties in her backyard and they would have their chairs out there and barbecue and play music and stuff, and they would actually sleep outside all night long...all night. And, at that time when they had the

MARjorie DAVis

poles up in the back yard, you could leave your laundry hanging up all night long. Now? No. [*laughing*] Now, you better not be out, let alone your laundry.

Ramsey Lewis: Of the guys I ran with as a kid, two or three of them were white guys and two or three were black guys. I didn't realize there was anything unusual about the fact that our neighborhood was mixed. We had moved from the South Side when I was very young up to the North Side and that's just how it was....Looking back, my parents didn't raise us to look for the differences in people. But, I do remember coming home one day and asking my mom or dad why some kids were calling me nigger, so that did

happen, but the way my parents explained it to me just made me feel sorry for the ones who had said it. There really wasn't much more than a push or shove that came between us kids back then.

Lillian Davis Swope: When I moved over here I felt we just needed someone to come in and just do something for the children. The kids did have Lower North Center, and they still do. At that time it was located on Locust and Orleans. And Ms. Margaret Smith, she still is over there now, but after school she would have the children in the little storefront and we would have activities like playing checkers and things.

And that was nice, but I decided I wanted to start a majorette group, and a drum and bugle corps. Materials for the drum and bugle corps was not available, so we turned that into the young boys in the community just doing steps – just anything that they made up, they did it – and then the young ladies went the same way. We did have an idea what a majorette would be like and because funds wasn't available, I took it upon myself, with the help of other mothers that had children in the group, and we made their outfits. The parents bought the young ladies boots, so, we had a group.

Margaret Wilson: When we came over here from the South Side in the early '60s, I found it to be a quite interesting and family-oriented community. It appeared to me that everybody over here had Mayor Daley's telephone number. I mean they were the most politically sophisticated people I'd ever seen...'cause I remember thinking, how do all these people know so much about politics, and the mayor, and people like George Dunn?

The people were very interested in their community, in what was going on. They had a say so, ya know, in how the politicians were voting on issues that concerned this community. I was in awe, I was really in awe when I came over here.

They had so many programs for children and families, particularly over at the Lower North Center. They didn't just have programs for kids, but for the moms too. That's how I first got involved in the community.

Zora Washington: I was about 12 years old when we moved over here from 16th and Springfield. The day we moved and we saw where we were moving, we were really excited because it was more or less like having your own home. We had a front and back door, we had a yard, upstairs and downstairs. We lived on Cleveland, 922 North Cleveland.

There were six of us, four girls and two boys and just my mom. My mother is more of a keep-to-herself kind of woman – and in some cases I am, too – but she did make friends and get involved in some community things.

I do remember when I was a kid I got on the girl's...it was like a girl's drill team with Lillian Swope. Her name wasn't Swope then, but Lillian Davis. She talked my mother into making the little majorette skirts and outfits. My mother was a sewer so she did get involved like that. She also helped out with the block parties.

In fact I was talking to my husband not too long ago about those block club parties we used to have when we was kids – dancing in the street. It was usually organized by streets, but, of course, kids came from all over in the area.

And at that time we had the church, not St. Dominic's but St. Philip Benizi. St. Philip's is no longer there but it sat at the end of Cambridge and Oak streets where the empty lot is now. They did those summer feasts. That was a good time. It was a parade thing. It went down I think it was Oak Street and around some kind of way – maybe down Oak and somehow they got to Division and then came down Larrabee. That's where everything was stationed, the concession stands and the rides and things. It was a mini carnival. I remember once my husband got on the tilt-a-whirl and I had to hold him [*laughing*]. The feast was a religious thing, but I wasn't Catholic so it had no bearing on me whatsoever. It was just a fun time.

Margaret Wilson: The churches were also very much a part of the community. If there was an issue the church would often call the meetings to help resolve whatever community issues were going on. There was St. Dominic's and St. Joseph's and St. Matthew's and Holy Family.

Someone over at Holy Family church was involved in moving families from Cabrini to Indiana in the late 60s. I knew some of those families. My best girlfriend's mother went out there and I remember visiting there once...and she has a daughter that's still down there and I think they're all doin' pretty well.

But we became very involved with the Catholic church, St. Philip Benizi's. My sons became involved with the scouting, and my daughters became involved with the girl scouts.

St. Philip's had the feasts every year and they'd shoot off fire-crackers, and the first time I heard it I thought they were bombs. I just moved over here and had five little children and I thought, my Lord, it must be world war three [*laughing*]. I got all my children and I grabbed the phone and we went into the closet and I called my dad and told him there was some kind of war going on outside and that he should call the police and come and get us. The kids were screamin' but trying to peek out the window, the little baby was crying....When it finally stopped we peered and peaked outside the door and life was so normal [*laughing*] and I asked my neighbors, "Did you hear those bombs?" They said, "Bombs?" Those were M-80s or whatever they were for the church celebration.

Ramsey Lewis: My life was pretty structured as a kid. At 11 years old I started at the Chicago Musical College, so I didn't hang out in the neighborhood as much as other kids. But music was always there. With the neighborhood being interracial there was always talk about different kinds of music. I was exposed to all kinds of music – jazz, pop, R&B, blues – especially in high school. My dad never said, don't listen to Frank Sinatra because he's white or anything like that. He brought Art Tatum's music into the house and all sorts of stuff but at the time I was so into gospel and classical music that I didn't appreciate it until later.

Whenever I could, though, I would go play baseball with my friends. I remember playing a lot of baseball over at Seward Park. I was on a team called the Lodgers and our rival was a team named the Northwinds. They came down from further up on the North Side.

Lillian Davis Swope: We had a lot of things goin' on over here. We had Ramsey Lewis and we had Curtis Mayfield. I used to let Curtis practice his music in my house when I lived down on Hudson. I knowed all of them, Jerry Butler too. I had to finally take Curtis over to Seward Park, and got the park to give him a room because my house wasn't conducive for him to practice in.

Margaret Wilson: Curtis Mayfield and Jerry Butler were a little before our time. We came over here after they had become the Impressions, I think. The guy who was still around was Major Lance, the one who did "Monkey Time." I believe he also died recently. He died before Curtis did, but Major Lance used to work at Harry's drug store up at Oak and Larrabee, [*laughing*] and he used to aggravate me so bad when I'd come in there.

Zora Washington: I was raised by a very strict woman and I was older so I had a lot of responsibility as a child. Also I really didn't get to go out that much. My younger sister went more places than I because she was a little sneaky Pete. Now don't get me wrong, I did my little sneaking stuff too, like going to the dances in the basement [of the red buildings] and stuff like that. This was later, when they built the red high-rises. I think Curtis Mayfield played at some of them, which were usually held in the 911-929 building.

And Curtis lived close to me when I was young. In fact, his sister, Carolyn, was in the drum majorettes with us, so she was one of the kids that my mother made the skirt for. She used to come to my house. As far as dealing with Curtis, he was not my speed. As a kid, he just wasn't it [*laughing*]. As I got older, yes, I grew to appreciate his music, but as a girl, noooo.

Lillian DAVis Swope

Arzula Ivy: There was lots of jobs but I wasn't workin' at the time 'cause I was on public aid and my kids was small. One day I said I'm gonna go to school and get my grades up and get me a job and go to work. There was an aid place, I think at 419 Oak Street, and I went up and asked them would they pay for me to go to school and they said, well yes, we'll pay for you, give you some tokens and different things, and I started school down on Washington Street.

I finished school and then I got me a job at the Playskool factory, which was down at 1750 North Lawndale, I think, and that was where they made the toys.

I always took my kids to the shows up north or to the park or over to that Riverview [amusement park]. I'd get off of work on Friday and we'd go up to Riverview on Friday night and then again on Sunday, that's what we did.

Zora Washington

Zora Washington: For high school I went to Washburne – it wasn't Cooley High yet, it was Washburne. It was a mixed school. There were whites, blacks, Hispanics. In fact, children from across the city came to Washburne. It was a trade school. And that's where you learned, at least that's where I learned about prejudice. It was subtle and it included the teachers.

I never will forget getting mistaken for a friend I had who didn't go to school very often. I was tall, but I wasn't fat – I was just a big kid – and my friend was short and heavy. My teacher sent me home one day with a note to my mother asking my mother to come to school. I thought I was going to die, and when my mother came up to school, she told my mother I had been out of school for five consecutive days.

I had to convince this woman to go through her records and that's when she really found out that it wasn't me who had been absent, but my friend. To me, as a kid, the message was, all black people look alike. That was the feeling that I got from that because there was too much difference in us. I mean how could she? I'm tall, she's short, she's wide, I'm slim. How could you make a mistake like that?

Margaret Wilson: Transportation was so good around here we must have had three or four buses that could take you downtown anytime. So in the early days I didn't feel a boundary to the community. And the more I got involved, I went to more and more meetings all over the area. We went to community meetings in Lincoln Park, we went to meetings downtown, we went to meetings on the Gold Coast...and all these meetings had something to do with Cabrini or the North Side that people were bringing attention to. So at that time I didn't feel like Cabrini was separated from the rest of the area at all.

Ramsey Lewis: Now, when I got to [William H.] Wells High School, which was a predominantly white school, race was a bigger problem. I guess the white kids couldn't figure out why these black kids from Cabrini were coming all the way over to Augusta and Ashland, so that caused some tension....I really didn't notice much of it myself because I was so busy playing piano, and by that time I was performing at assemblies and things, but sophomore year word had got around about a big rumble...and the talk was that all the black kids were gonna get their asses kicked. A lot of the kids from Cabrini walked to school, through different neighborhoods, so this put a scare into everybody. Well for weeks there was so much talk going back and forth about this is gonna happen and that's gonna happen that word reached down to the South Side. At the time, there were a lot of tough black gangs on the South Side...so on the day this big rumble was supposed to take place, all these gangs drove up to Wells high school in cars, and all day long they sort of patrolled the streets. It was pretty amazing, and there was no problem that day.

Inez Gamble: In fact, there wasn't but one time that I felt something, like, race related in all my time here, it was on the Larrabee bus. I went to sit down by this lady and, well, it was almost unbelievable because [*laughing*] I had been around here all these years. This had to be about '54 or '55. I sit down by this old lady – I guess she must have been around the age I am now – and she told me, oh, go to the back of the bus. What do I know about goin' to the back of the bus? I was born here. I looked at her and I said, "You know what, you just better be glad that I'm me, because if I was somebody else, you would get hurt on this bus." A friend of mine was on the bus and thought I was gonna haul off and hit this woman. I got so upset, when the bus turned the corner up here on Chicago Avenue and got to Wells, I had to get off. I came back home cryin'. I was that mad.

Margaret Wilson: Like I said, we attended St. Philip's church and that's where my sons went to school, 'cause it was right up the street at Cambridge and Oak. It was a great big church and it was beautiful. When the Italians left [this community] they took it with them...brick by brick. They may have took it back to Italy, I don't know. The church was closing and it was our church, and they took that church brick by brick. Those of us who attended were in shock, we had never heard of anybody taking the church... but it was very traumatic. That last Sunday, we went to church and they had their Italian garb on – I guess they were Knights of Columbus or something because they had their swords and stuff – and that was the last Mass, and they said the Mass in Italian. We were just in a state of shock.

Ramsey Lewis: See, when you live in Cabrini, you can only make so much money. I think it was my sophomore year, and my dad must have hit that number 'cause we were told we had to move. We didn't move far though, but up to 1142 N. Orleans. In fact, that was the last building to be torn down to make way for the new park [in front of the Seward Park fieldhouse]. So, I was long gone before the red buildings started to go up.

Inez Gamble: It was around 1958 when they built them projects, the red buildings, and ya know, it really didn't start changing around here until they had all those doggone high rises up. We were half scared to walk through there for fear someone was gonna shoot down at you from off of one a them ramps. It wasn't good 'cause they was packed in like sardines, ya know. That many people piled up on top of each other, that's not good.

Marjorie Davis: They stopped screening people like they used to [when the high-rises went up], and by the time all the kids from the South Side and the West Side got together it was a dangerous piece of mess over here 'cause they wasn't good for each other....A lot of them I grew up with. I had a lot of friends in those buildings, but after a lot of the changes I wouldn't go up in them. Yeah, the real mistake happened when they built those high-rises.

Arzula Ivy: When they were movin' into the red buildings, most of them people were on public aid, and along that time they were lettin' them in here when they were 18.... Yeah, I don't go up that way, I used to but now I wouldn't dare...and then things were startin' to change and people weren't working as much as they did before and some people started to move out.

Lillian Davis Swope: I remember when the red buildings were coming up, people were very excited but also a little concerned because it would mean many more people over here. I think the Italians had some political connections because I remember a lot of them moved into the 500-502 building...that was considered the integrated building. But that didn't last very long.

Margaret Wilson: Dr. King came to St. Matthew's Church in 1966, I believe, and I was there but didn't get a chance to say anything to him but hello. I remember when Bobby Kennedy came through here. My youngest son talked to him, but I think with Dr. King it was a quick visit and then they were gone.

And, of course, I'll always remember the day he was killed. It was just pandemonium....I was at work in the [red high-rise building] at 1161 North Larrabee. I worked for the Chicago Committee on Urban Opportunity then, which is now the Department of Human Services. I remember we were watching it all on television and the West Side really went up right away. When the shooting started here we were up under the desks in a hurry.

Zora Washington: When Martin Luther King got killed, it was a Friday and I was at home cleaning. That was my Friday ritual – cleaning while listening to Ray Charles and Nancy Wilson. I remember someone knocking on my door but they were gone by the time I got there. Then my oldest son, Jerome, came home and I sent him to the store to get some milk. The store was over there on Oak – it was like a drugstore – on Oak Street close to Larrabee....Anyway he came back crying, "Ma, they're tearing up the store." And I'm saying, boy, you're lying. You just don't want to go to the store. Now get out of here. I didn't have on the TV, I didn't have on the radio, so I really didn't know what was going on...and here I was trying to throw my son out the door to go to a store that was getting torn down, ripped off and all that kind of stuff. It was really a terrible time, it really was.

I remember later on that night, my friend's brother knocked on the door and he brought some food in and I'm saying, "Fred, where did you get this from?" He says from the store where everybody else is getting some. He says I got some and I thought I'd give you and Jack some. And I think my husband said that one of his friends had asked him to go out with him that night and he declined. He wouldn't do it, but it was a rough time.

Lillian Davis Swope: I never will forget when Dr. King was assassinated. A truck came through here – right down Oak Street – and it was loaded with pineapples. The young men actually pulled those drivers out of those trucks, and emptied the truck and just took all the man's stuff out and they was beating him so bad that they almost killed him. And all the pineapples, people was grabbing them, and taking them...and it was a lot of fighting going on.

I was right out front watching this and I was thinking that the cleaners was owned by Italians, and the drugstore, it was owned by a Jew. And, I went down to them and told them that I thought they should close up, because there was rioting going on. They were both at the corner of Oak and Larrabee. I think they

thought they could stay, and wasn't nothing gonna happen to them because they had been in the community so long. But, no, they had to go, too. So they closed and left and the businesses were destroyed.

And I happened to go into a store about six months ago, on Lake Street and Wells, and the fella that had owned that drugstore [on Oak and Larrabee], was behind the counter. I hadn't seen him since and I didn't know that I was going into his store, you know. He stopped everybody in his store to tell them that I had saved his life once.

Mother Vassar: It was in an uproar when Martin Luther King died, but I just kept prayin'. Things happened so fast, and people turned to who they could turn to, they'd go to get a bag of food and clothes at places like the Goodwill and you could tell things weren't like they were when I first moved here. At that time I moved to 1309 Cleveland, and the neighborhood had changed pretty good. There were some whites but not like before.

Inez Gamble: Back then it was real nice until those riots. That's when all them businesses got burnt up. Really and truly, I think the Italians were ready to move out of here anyway, because it was becoming predominantly black, and they were ready to move. But a lot of those businesses up and down Larrabee didn't go 'til then.

Zora Washington: Del Farms grocery store was wrecked and at that time we didn't have a car, so that meant we had to get the bus — we had five children — and we had to get the bus, go up on North Avenue to the grocery store and come back with food on the bus. And the neighborhood looked, it just, it really made you want to cry. It did because you knew the neighborhood that you lived in, and that black people had torn it up and the powers that be were not going to fix it up. You knew that...it was a scary time, it gave you a scary feeling.

How could you help not being depressed? It was like we lost hope. The person that could do it for us was gone. It was a terrible time. Those stores never came back. There used to be a store on Chicago Avenue across from Wards, Big Frank's. Then you had like a small department store on Oak and Franklin called Greenman's. It was where you could go at the last minute and get your daughter a pair of gloves...and some hair ribbon or something like that.

You felt isolated because you had nowhere to go. Anything that you wanted, you had to drive or get a bus out of your neighborhood.

Lillian Davis Swope: After that people was just trying to get it together, and hoping that nothing like that happened again....It was a tough time then because we had established relationships, like with the store owner, and the cleaners, the drugstore. Pioneers was destroyed. Del Farms, they didn't stay. It just seemed like everybody who had those businesses lost interest. I guess they say, "If you all don't want nothing, we gonna make sure you all don't have nothing."

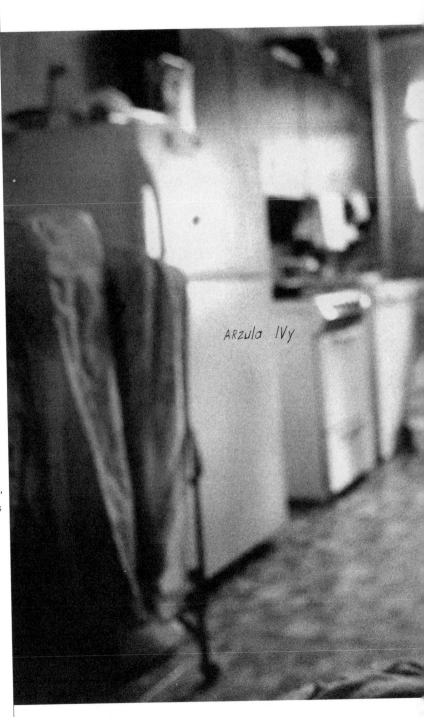

Arzula Ivy

Arzula Ivy: That's when it got real bad, when they killed Martin Luther King. That's when it got real rough, they come all down here tearin' up and we had a lot of stores on Oak Street and they tore all that up, burnt it up and I think they hurt some peoples too, but I stayed inside 'cause I got scared. It started to change right behind that.

All the young people were going to work and then boom, all this changed and, I mean, it shoulda' been gettin' better but it just got worse. After that, they never did build it back up. I reckon they say they wasn't gonna be bothered, so everything was torn down, and now if you have to go to a drug store you have to go so far....Yeah, it was better a long time ago when there was Jews and Germans and Italians and all that. It was just beautiful in here and I can't believe it because Dr. King was trying to get everything straightened out and then all this happened.

After it changed, ya know, I started to move two or three times [*laughing*], but I said, naw, I'm gonna wait and see what happens in here. All three of my kids stayed here when they got grown, and I seen all of them get married...and I just wasn't gonna leave them.

chapter TWO

Rise of the REDS

Courtesy: Chicago Housing Authority

high-rises. Above the entrance to 911, in red spray paint, it reads, "Camp Ball," another name for the building, this one tagged by the gangs. In 1951, Rochelle Satchell was born in an A-frame house located approximately where 911 now stands. Today, the 911 building is her office, and raising families is her life's work.

In the side room on the building's ground floor, the kids have pulled off their jackets and settled into one activity or another. Three girls huddle around a toy kitchenette in the corner, two boys sit in cafeteria-type chairs and talk at a table and two girls and a boy shuffle through movie tapes in a small cabinet. Bright sunlight pours through a row of windows, throwing a spotlight on cinder-block walls that have been painted blue and decorated with drawings of animals, buildings and people. This after-school session is just one facet of a program Ms. Satchell designed, through the Winfield Moody Health Center, to help meet the needs of adolescent mothers in the community.

In her previous post at Winfield Moody, Ms. Satchell's primary role as a counselor was to make home visits to pregnant teens and young mothers. In 1984, she approached her boss about doing more. When he asked what she had in mind, Ms. Satchell outlined her idea. "I told him I wanted to open up a center for young parents, so they can come and not only learn about how to take care of their baby, but so they can learn how to cook and clean and plan and budget...because when I was growing up this is the component that was missing. And it was still missing." After securing space from the CHA, the program was up and running by the end of the year. The teen parenting program later expanded to include after-school activities for kids and college prepatory classes for adolescents.

Shortly after her birth, Ms. Satchell's parents moved their family over to the row house neighborhood. Just a few years

"C'mon now, you all know where you're supposed to be." The booming voice of Rochelle Satchell ricochets through the open hallway of the red-brick high-rise building known as 911. Her command startles a handful of elementary school kids wrapped in colorful, puffy coats. "Let's get moving," she demands, but each child is already marching quietly into a side room on the building's ground floor.

The official address of this twin structure is 911-923 N. Sedgwick, but the building doesn't actually sit on a street. There are no curbs or sidewalks. Instead its doors open up on a lagoon of cloudy asphalt. The opposite end of this vast parking lot meets the backside of two more red-brick

later the deteriorating tenement buildings to the north were being razed to make room for the development's high-rise expansion, officially called the Cabrini Extension.

Completed in 1958, the Cabrini Extension consisted of fifteen buildings of seven, ten and nineteen stories designed to house 7,000 residents. Made of red-brick infill and exposed concrete frames, they are rectangular with one or two perpendicular wings at the rear of each building. At the time, adding 1,925 units to the row houses total of 581 made it the largest public housing development ever constructed in Chicago.

In 1949, the director of the CHA, Elizabeth Wood, described the plan to bring high-rises to public housing as a way to create "islands in a wilderness of slums." She advocated rerouting streets and constructing blocks of high-rise buildings that would redefine urban neighborhoods. With more African-Americans migrating to Chicago from the South in the late '40s and early '50s, designers of the Cabrini Extension thought high-rises would provide an economical solution to a shortage of housing for the poor. More than $200,000 was spent on landscaping the area with trees, shrubs and grass. When the buildings opened, lawns covered 17 acres of the extension's 35-acre site.

You can still find a plant, some trees and even a healthy patch of grass sprinkled around the red-brick high-rises of Cabrini-Green. But, in listening to those who remember the early days of the neighborhood, it's nothing like it used to be.

Ms. Satchell remembers the green grass and the way it seemed to glow under the gaze of the deep red high-rises. She remembers the way the sun sparkled off the windows of those brand new buildings. She remembers the excitement of taking an elevator to the top floor of one building so she could get a better view of the others, and the city beyond them.

She also remembers Jerry Butler, a neighborhood kid who grew up to become a musician and a distinguished member of the Rock 'n Roll Hall of Fame. At the time, Mr. Butler lived just north of the newly constructed red buildings until his family moved into one of them in the mid-50s. He and a few friends started a band that later became the Impressions. Joined by a kid from the row houses named Curtis Mayfield, the Impressions skyrocketed to the top of the music industry. Mr. Butler and Mr. Mayfield went on to successful solo careers. Today, Mr. Butler serves as a Cook County Commissioner in Chicago and continues to work with young people in the community.

At 80, Ms. Viola Holmes says she has enough memories of Cabrini-Green to span a lifetime. She too lived in the area before ground was broken on the red buildings. She moved into the reds in the late '50s but also lived in one of the white buildings for a time. She has raised three children in this community, but for many years her work took her to the North Shore. She has lived in her current apartment, a red-brick high-rise at 1121 N. Larrabee Street, for more than 20 years. "They say they're gonna tear it down," she says. "But I don't want to go no where else."

Ms. Henry Johns is known as "Miss Hen" in and around the building at 1015 N. Larrabee. She moved into the high-rises in 1957 and, at 68, has seen the community at its best and worst. Her ten kids are grown, and many still live in Cabrini-Green. These days she watches over all of the children in the building, as well as her many grandchildren.

When her family moved into the high-rises, Ms. Paulette Simpson was just a girl. It was 1958 and the buildings, she says, "were perfect." Her childhood was a happy one but, at 52, Ms. Simpson is troubled by the changes she's witnessed over the years. Like her mother before her, she works as an administrator at Holy Family Lutheran Church. The church sits on the corner of Hobbie and Larrabee streets, right next door to the building she's lived in for more than 20 years.

Before leaving the community last year, Ms. Marsha Crosby had lived in Cabrini-Green since she was seven. She says the childhood she remembers is far different than the one her son experienced, which is why she took advantage of an opportunity to move. Still, she says she will always have fond memories of her early years in the community and, now that she lives just north of the development, she holds out great hope for its future.

In the decorated side room on the ground floor of 911, Ms. Satchell sits at a long table next to three children who have decided which animated movie the group should watch. Although her work brings her back every day, Ms. Satchell also moved out of Cabrini-Green when the opportunity presented itself. An increase in rent and a son continually approached by gangs, she says, was the last straw. But her commitment remains.

Looking back on her life in Cabrini, she says, can be difficult. Like the others, memories of a pleasant childhood or carefree adolescent years are forever tied with the painful recollections of April, 1968. Still, the good times are not forgotten.

Rochelle Satchell: I remember the Martin Luther King riots because that was a real nightmare. I mean trucks that normally came through here, people were snatched out of 'em. White people were being beaten with bricks. It was sad. If you ask somebody why are they doing it, they couldn't tell you. It was just on TV and they had no reason to do it. We were on an island, it was different than the rest of public housing 'cause whenever you went outside this community, nobody even knew about Cabrini-Green 'cause nothin' ever happened over here until then. The whole thing was really senseless.

We weren't worried about nobody harming us, it was just a shock. It was emotional, but it was more emotional for the girls. Then later on that night, people were just talking about the looting they had done and what they had gotten out of it.

But, days after, when you talked about all the people that was hurt and they showed pictures of what had happened, a lot of people regretted what they did. But they couldn't go back in time....In a lot of ways, it's never been the same around here.

Henry Johns: Oh, it was great when we first got here. I was born in Arkansas and moved to Chicago in 1951. They were building the red high-rises when we arrived, and in '57 we moved into the 1117-1119 [Sedgwick] building, which is now gone. That was the best home we had had since I had been around. I was around thirty something and my kids went to Jenner, Cooley and Waller...all good schools. In our building, there were maybe one or two families of Puerto Ricans and a couple of white people when we first moved in. But it was a mixed neighborhood and everybody got along.

I came up from Arkansas because I wanted to try different work. When I was growin' up back in the 40s we lived on a farm and we had to pick cotton and chop cotton and all that, so I decided I was gonna try something different....It was exciting coming to a big city, and makin' a real paycheck. Rent always had been high...so I had said this is gonna be our home until we're able to buy one.

Jerry Butler: When the red high-rises were being built, the initial reactions was, wow, this is gonna be great. And I think in its embryonic stages, it was great. It was a mixed community with all types of blue collar workers. We had bus drivers and plumbers and sanitation workers.

I really grew up in the area. My family's first apartment was at 942 North Sedgwick, and this was about 1949, so at that time the Mother Cabrini Homes - which are the low-rise row houses - were the only part of Cabrini. It wasn't until 1956 that we moved into 1117 North Cleveland, which were the red high-rises. But even before that, while I lived up on Sedgwick, I hung out on Hudson, Oak Street and Larrabee....That's where all the kids were.

Rochelle Satchell

Rochelle Satchell: My earliest memory is 1955. The milkman. I used to run downstairs to wait to get the milk. We used to get it delivered in the bottles. On Saturdays, we would get chocolate milk in the bottles. My mother and dad both come from here, and I grew up in the row houses and moved into the red high-rises when I got older.

Before the high-rises went up there was a lot of old buildings here, but they were getting real run down. A lot of Italians lived in them....If you looked at the row houses at the time, they looked fresh and pretty and then you looked at the surrounding buildings and it was just – they were time to go.

So it was a time of transition. The Italian families began to move out, but the row houses were still mixed. They had Jewish families, Italian families, Spanish families. You were really mixed there, so it wasn't about color...and we bought into their holidays. The fiesta was an Italian fiesta that they had every year and we would look forward to that. Then they had the floats that went through the community and they would have it from Chicago Avenue all the way down to Larrabee and Division, and they would have rides at the carnival and lobsters and things. I mean we looked forward to that every year.

Viola Holmes: I lived up on Vine Street, where the white buildings are now. It was mostly Italian people at the time but everybody was friendly.

We had street cars, just like the train but a street car and there was nothin' but houses over here, and family people. They did have juke houses up and down Larrabee where you could go and do your thing. Everybody had fun. I lived at Orchard Street and Division for a little while and then I moved into the first red building they built. I lived on the 13th floor of the building that Mayor Jane Byrne stayed in later on, 1150 Sedgwick.

They say I was born in 1919....I was born in Arkansas and I wanted to come to Chicago. I was a grown woman and wanted to live where I wanted to live...and my father moved up here with his second wife, and I wanted to see him. He was a farmer. My dad was a good guy, and my mother died when I was about six years old. So I moved here and I got a job working for a lady in Wilmette....I worked all my life.

Rochelle Satchell: The first red building that went up was 939, but a fire broke out, so they had to take that construction and work at 911. That's how they had 911 the first building. And it was great. We were really waiting for it. It was different. They laid the flowers and the grass and it was simply gorgeous. It was people of all colors moving in....The elevators was really exciting.

Mr. Elax Taylor at 911 Hudson. I remember him moving in first. I remember that because he had a lot of boys. We were in the row houses at 926 and 911 was like adjacent to that. They moved in and then it was like the trucks were pulling up from everywhere. And cars, a lot of people had cars moving stuff in. It was just...it was a day. We were excited about who else was moving in and seeing if they got any boys.

Henry Johns: I was on the 15th floor and had no problem 'cause the elevator worked just like any other elevator. Nobody would stop 'em or hold 'em, and no kids could ride the elevator by their self....If my kid was caught doing something wrong around the building in those days, the janitor would bring them up and say, Miss Hen – that's what they call me – your son was caught breaking a limb off of the trees and shrubs....I would take my son in the house and thank the janitor, but now the janitor [*laughing*] better not knock on the door and tell on peoples' kids, he'd get hollered at and cussed out and everything...but we all used to work together and we kept it beautiful all the way.

Viola Holmes: I thought I was livin' in heaven. It was beautiful. I'm not kidding, it was beautiful. They got 1150 boarded up now. They say it's comin' down...but everybody was excited about it. We had a big playground for the kids to play in during the day and all the grown folks would take over in the night time and set out there in the back. We'd have our little drinks and stuff and there wasn't no glass or trash left around for the kids to get into. I'd have my little fun out there and go to bed and then go to work.

I had two kids. I'm 14 years older than my daughter and then 16 years older than my son. Later I adopted my cousin's baby and raised him here in 1117.

Like I said, I worked up north in the suburbs, in Wilmette and in Northfield. I worked for families, took care of the kids. I raised all kinds of babies. I took the train and the buses to get up there. After my husband and I got divorced, my kids would go with me to work. I never worked for no family where my kids couldn't go...so they grew up where I worked at, in the suburbs.

Paulette Simpson: I was born in Tennessee and lived on the West Side when I was real young, then we came here in January of 1958. I was ten, but about a year before that I came over here with my girlfriend, who had an auntie that lived over in 939 or something. But I remember walking through 500-502, which they were building at the time, so when I learned we were moving over here I remembered and told my mother....It was an exciting time, and it was amazing to see something that tall because I was just used to houses.

Viola Holmes: From Division all the way down to Oak Street and all around here, they used to have everything...all the stores and festivals and fruit markets, and all this around here was houses. Montgomery Wards was down there then and they'd block off Division Street and I think they would do it twice a year. I can't recall what it was but they had things for kids and horses and all that. It was just like a parade, and this is where they'd set up and have food and everything. You took a dollar and you could buy a whole lotta stuff. The summer time always had stuff going on. That was back when summer was summer.

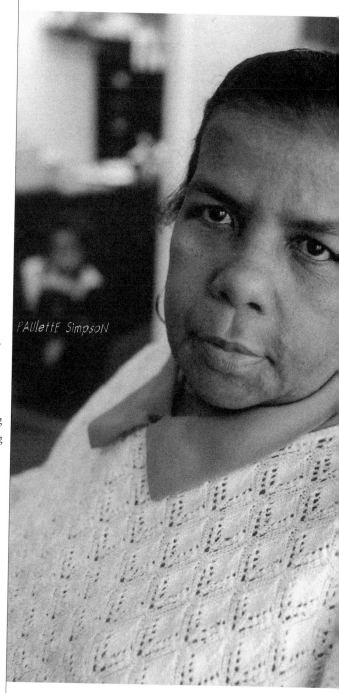

PAUlettE SimpsoN

Jerry Butler: It was the row houses that was basically an Italian neighborhood. There were Black and Irish and others, but never enough of one group for there to be any racial tensions. It was a pretty good mix and it was really a wonderful time because each year the Italians of St. Dominic's would throw a big festival right by Jenner school there. There was food and games and entertainment...it was really a wonderful time.

Rochelle Satchell: The management was all white men and they were respectful to the people, but still they would follow the guidelines that the Chicago Housing Authority had. You couldn't have a piece of paper with your name on it outside the building. Everybody took care of everybody. You never had to lock your doors. You never had fear of anybody just coming out. You never felt like they were going to do any harm...and the buildings were very well kept.

Very early in the morning, I used to like to get up because I would always like to see people in a rush coming out of the buildings. They were working men. I seen more fathers and mothers then. We had great respect for our elders. We weren't allowed to talk back to adults. Respect was just a known thing. It was just really nice.

I mean the kids were playing in the hallways everywhere. You could smell the fresh units when you walked up and down the steps in the morning. The elevator was fresh. You never smelled urine, never smelled raw garbage. I mean they were burning it at that time, early in the morning or late at night....You always knew who managed the building, because basically it was janitors who lived on the first floor in the building and he was on 24-hour call. It was like his presence was always there, so you knew you couldn't mess it up.

Paulette Simpson: I went to Jenner, my auntie went to Jenner... and she's 87. That school goes way back. It says right on the building, 1907.

But we had white girlfriends. There were some white girls that lived in our building and one lived across the street, but they all moved sometime in the '60s. I wonder what happened to them.

There was a couple of grocery stores in the neighborhood, Pioneers and Del Farms, and some liquor stores. Pioneers, I think, was owned by an Italian family. A lot of people from the neighborhood worked in Del Farms, and the black-owned store was called Jets. A lot of people worked in there too. It was convenient to have all those stores around.

Rochelle Satchell: I went to Jenner, and I would say it's a landmark. I know sometimes things are better torn down, they cost more to renovate it or to restore, but I see it as being a landmark. What can I say. It's a lot of memories, you know. It's like when we had homecoming, it was not only blacks that attended that homecoming, it was all nationalities that attended that homecoming and that's a memory. Everybody remembers their first experience in school, and it was good memories.

In fact, my turning point in life was at Jenner school...in the sixth grade. I had a behavior problem. I liked to get in trouble, and it was because I couldn't read that well, and the sixth grade teacher, Ms. Sherill, wasn't going to tolerate me misbehaving and she used to make me write on the board. One year she told the whole class she was going to fail me. Everybody looked at me and I broke out and I ran across the street and I told my mother. She came up there and the teacher told her what happened, and my mom took me home and she whipped me too. From that day on, I had to stay after school every day and Ms. Sherill worked with me until I improved my reading. That's why I work with kids today that have behavior problems, because sometimes it's due to not being able to comprehend.

Jerry Butler: I went to Washburne school, which was at Sedgwick and Division. Most of the white kids who went there came from the Northwest Side or the suburbs because that was one of the good trade schools....Anyway we'd be playing our music and white guys would come up and ask what we're listening to. Today they call it crossover, but music really, ya know, is universal.

Ramsey Lewis had already moved out and was makin' it big with the Ramsey Lewis Trio, but I had all kinds of role models growing up. There were a lot of men in the community at that time and there was Mr. Evans. He coached the baseball team and he'd round up the kids and take us over to the lot where we'd play ball...and there was a policeman, I remember, who was a great role model for all the kids, because there weren't a lot of black policemen at that time....Back then, there was no such thing as a black fireman.

Marsha Crosby: Well I moved in Cabrini when I was seven years old with my mom, my sister, two brothers and my father, and that had to be the late-50s or something like that. My father was working and mom, she was staying at home with the kids.

I don't remember too much, but I know my parents had been looking for a larger apartment...just trying to find a decent place to live with enough room. I guess somebody told them about the Chicago Housing Authority and they put in an application. They were just beginning to build Cabrini, because the white projects weren't up yet and only half of the red projects were built. So somehow we got into 1157 and I don't even think it was all the way full. We was one of the first families to move over there.

It was so very, very nice. I mean, everything, they had such structure about it. It was like the family would get fined if their children are caught walking on the grass and everything. We were just like free to be outside to play, no problems. It was just great. In fact, when I first moved in Cabrini, it was like interracial because we moved next door to a Hispanic family...this is 1157 North Cleveland, which is gone now. Yeah, it's gone now. But I look back and there are a lot of a good memories for me as a child growing in Cabrini.

Paulette Simpson: My mother was the second person to move into 502. The elevator excited me and everything was perfect. If you had a problem with anything in your house, CHA was out there within 24 hours or less. They were on top of everything then.

Henry Johns

I went to Jenner school. I played out in the playground. I went to Lower North Center to take dancing classes, and I used to go to Stanton Park for swimming.

Henry Johns: There was a pool behind 939 Hudson for a long while. The hole's still there, but they had to close the pool one year. People would mess it up at night, put glass in it or something, and it just wasn't safe for the kids. But we still had one pool over at Stanton Park, which is behind 630 Evergreen.

There were a lot of things we could do around here. We would go to Lincoln Park and, ya know, take the kids in baby buggies and walk there and come back. All the time I used to take my kids up to Riverview [amusement park]. It's been gone a long time now, but when my kids would graduate from school, that's where they'd go to celebrate. The number ten bus would take you right there, no problem....There was the 911 Hudson basement parties, and Lower North Center was really good then. They had roller skating over by 1119, and on the black top we'd have music goin' and roller skating set up right on the black top.

Marsha Crosby: I didn't know too much about the row houses coming up as a kid. I didn't really venture down that way, so I really didn't know too much about the row houses.

My first two years I did was at Waller, now they call it Lincoln Park High School. I did my first two years there and when I got in my junior year, I decided I wanted to transfer to Cooley. It was called Washburne before it became Cooley. I had my parents thinking, it'll be much easier because it was so close. You won't have to pay car fare or anything, but I also had personal reasons. I graduated from Cooley Vocational High School and I majored in business education. Being in college wasn't stressed so much as it is now, but by it being a vocational high school I majored in business education and I was able to get a good job when I got out of high school because they taught you all the business skills and everything like that.

So I have good memories of going to high school, basketball games and homecoming games and everything and I don't remember any violence or anything bad happening in high school, like killings and muggings and stuff like that. High school was just a great time for me. In fact, my whole childhood and teenage years at Cabrini was great.

Like I said, mostly all the families were two parent families and I remember going to Wayman Church over there with my mom. You know how parents sacrifice for their kids, she always made sure that we had church clothes....We had a lot of different activities within the church. This one lady, she took up a lot of time with us. She was in the choir and she would give us piano lessons. She lived at 500 Oak and I don't know if she's alive today, but she was the type of person like, when you may not want to go to your parents with certain things, well, we could go up to her with any problems we had....She was charging us for piano lessons like three dollars, two dollars or something. We'd go over there and she got us on the road to playing the piano, which I dropped [*laughing*]. But my brother, it worked out well for him because he does everything. He's a musician and he's very talented, very talented.

Jerry Butler: At that time they had all kinds of organized activities for the kids, both through Stanton Park and Seward Park. I mean there was Boy Scout troops and wood carving classes and things where you could learn how to make toys. And there was baseball. We played baseball all the time.

But by '57 I had graduated high school and was beginning my music career. There were a lot of bands I played with early on, and it was the Roosters that later became the Impressions.

Curtis [Mayfield] lived in the row houses but I didn't meet him in the neighborhood, I met Curtis through the Northern Jubilee Gospel Choir.

Our band used to practice over at Seward Park, and there was an old wino that hung around there by the name of Doug...and he could play the guitar like you wouldn't believe. He had this old beat-up guitar, but man could he play it. He was phenomenal. Me and Curtis would just sit and listen to him play all day, and I think it was from him that Curtis picked up a lot of his stuff.

We played the basement parties they used to have in the red buildings and we played over at Lower North Center...any place we were allowed to play, we would.

I was at Curtis' funeral and I was thinkin' that in another two years Curtis and I would have known each other for 50 years [laughing]. That's longer than I've known some family members.

Rochelle Satchell: Every high-rise building had a Laundromat in the basement and a big space for activities. So everything went on down there. Every day there was something going on. You could go dance in one building and skate in another. You could go practice if you wanted to be in a singing group...and we used to watch Curtis Mayfield and Jerry Butler down there before they got started. They used to practice in 1121 Larrabee basement and then they also used to practice at their apartment, I think. We would go down there and peek at them practicing not knowing they would ever be famous, but it sounded good.

Paulette Simpson: When I got to be 13 or 14, we'd go to the beach a lot. I rode the bus and my friends walked. I said, I'm not walking. There was plenty to do, ya know, we went to the Lincoln Park Zoo, we had parties in the basements of the buildings, we'd skate, we'd go to St. Joseph's and skate....We went to Riverview two or three times a month. We'd also have our own block parties, and I remember I would shop downtown a lot on North Avenue It was really a normal childhood.

Viola Holmes: I used to walk all the way downtown all the time, or just take the Larrabee bus when it used to come up here. Ain't been no bus on this street for ten years [laughing], but you can still get downtown and go to Marshall Field's if you want.

Jerry Butler: I shrink away from saying music was part of the black community because it makes it sound like it wasn't part of any other community, but music was always there for us. It was part of the neighborhood. We grew up singing. My mom was always singing around the house...and the first place kids went was church. What do they do in church? Sing songs. In fact, I met my wife through a singing group at my church.

One of the reasons Curtis and I became leaders of the group was because we were crazy enough to go out looking – we'd go downtown and just start knockin' on doors at studios and record companies [laughing]. We'd say hey, we can sing, you wanna hear us?

The music business wasn't like it is today. Every company had a man that was out lookin' for new talent. We knew this race problem existed, but this was business and often times when it's about making money [laughing], people tend to put their racial feelings aside.

When we recorded "Your Precious Love," we knew it was good because all the kids loved it....Not long after that, my mother had to move. The CHA told her, your son's a famous musician so you aren't poor enough to live here anymore. Now I hadn't made a dime yet, but we had to go because our financial status was about to change dramatically.

Marsha Crosby: We mainly stayed in the neighborhood, but we would also go to the movies and then over by Schiller school they had, on Friday nights they'd have like a skating rink and everybody would get out and go roller skating. Then over at Seward Park they had some activities for kids...but we just mostly hung out in the neighborhood and we did more visiting each other houses and playing on the ramps, opposed to going out and doing anything, ya know, until we got older. Then we would start going to 911 Hudson and 862 Sedgwick to the basement parties [*laughing*]. I think it was from like seven to nine or seven to ten and then we have adult supervision, and they would open up the basement and somebody would spin records and teenagers would go down there and dance and stuff.

Our basement parties were the biggest highlight for me as a kid. I remember walking from 1157, walking toward the field, we was just hoping we'd see the red lights on because if we see the red lights that means [the basement party] was open. We used to be so disappointed [*laughing*] if we didn't see those red lights on. A man by the name of Mr. Elax Taylor used to open that up for the kids, for the teenagers and stuff. They took up a lot of time trying to help stuff and create things for the kids.

When I got old enough so that I could stay out, if I went out partying or something, coming in the building by myself wasn't nothing. I wasn't worried about anybody bothering me or anything. Those things, we didn't have to worry about then. Me and my girlfriend, we was grown and we just liked to sit out in front of the building on nice, summer nights 'til two or three o'clock in the morning, just me and her, just talking about different things. She lived at 1158 Cleveland and she would go on home, and I crossed the street down to 1157 and go up to the second floor and I wasn't watching, ya know, or scared or anything.

Rochelle Satchell: I didn't know what violence was until like I would say the late '60s. There was a shooting and that like shocked the whole area over here. The guy got caught, because we felt like he had messed it up for everybody. Nobody hesitated about telling on him.

But the even worse thing was the Vietnam War. There was a lot of guys died over there and it was like every other day it seems like we were all going to funerals of somebody that we knew was dead. That was like a black flag over the community, because there was a lot of grief stricken families here and it was everybody supporting everybody.

I even remember when Jesse Jackson first came over here in the mid-60s. He was a militant at that time. I think that's before he got married. He had a cousin that stayed at 457 W. Oak and he musta' got wind that Martin Luther King was coming into speak at St. Matthew's, so Jesse came in and he got a lot of guys all riled up.

Marsha Crosby: We grew up in a time when we had more two parent households. Mostly every child had their mother and their father and was trying to make it, opposed to how it is now...and I'm just trying to remember when things changed.

Henry Johns: I think when it really started turning was after Dr. King got killed in '68....I sure didn't see it comin'. It just happened. All our kids were at school and we were afraid. We saw it on TV and we just start runnin' out lookin' for our kids, 'cause some did get hurt up there at Waller school. They start fightin', the white and the black. I guess they was all mad.

Marsha Crosby: During that Martin Luther King riot, I was sick but I remember it was a big riot. On Division they had like a cleaners and they had a drugstore, and they had a little store on the corner and you could just see people just running and just taking stuff and everything. I was looking out the window at this, so you could see it.

They had the National Guard over and everything, and we were put on a curfew. You had to be in by dusk. They just tore up everything, looted and burned up everything. It was just a mess.

Henry Johns: Everything was going on outside. There was shooting, burning, looting, police and the National Guard. They called in the National Guard and that was really scary. They were riding in these jeeps and they got these rifles and they got the knives on the end of the guns, and I just wanted to get my kids inside....With the National Guard and police terrorizing everybody it went on a good three days, and after that the police just start harassing anybody, like they do now...and there'd be shooting. Police would shoot at them, and the boys – that's what I call the [gang members] – they would go on the roof and shoot back at them. We had bullets comin' through our windows...

We weren't even allowed to look out our window. If we look out our window we had a spotlight on us and a gun. We were really afraid for our kids, that's when it really started, 'cause then the young gangs would get guns and we would have to walk the smaller kids to school, ya know, make sure they get to school.

But before all that, this was the best place we could live. It was really great.

Paulette Simpson: I don't think they were that angry, I think they were just greedy...just taking advantage of the situation and being greedy 'cause I don't remember seeing anybody cryin', just bein' wild. Why do you riot, ya know. All our stores were gone after that, and prices went up in the ones left...so you were payin' for what somebody else did.

That was it for Del Farms and Pioneers. A couple months ago you could have walked out there to Elm and Larrabee and see the floor tiles from Pioneers still lying on the ground. They was blue and white....It's been a vacant lot ever since.

Henry Johns: The police never did get any better around here. Even today, it's like, we can be back there asleep and if we don't come and open that door when they knockin', they got that hammer and they'll knock your door down. For nothin', they just lookin' for someone. Then they go all over your house without any such warrant or anything...and if you any kind of young person they be kickin' 'em around and throwin' them around. They say they lookin' for gang bangers. Well, don't no gang members live here, but they just do it anyway.

It's the same way with the ambulance. They say, if you not dyin' we not comin', you better call the privates. Well, I don't know if I'm dying or not. Now I don't know who answers that 911, but that's the word they give you, if you not dyin', we not comin'.

Rochelle Satchell: After the riots, there was a lot of things just burned down. It didn't affect the housing here. It didn't affect them physically, but mentally they were affected. It affected everybody here. Not only was it the prices going up, it was the fear now. We were surrounded by whites and now you had to go to shop outside the community and what was going to happen.

It was whites all around out there, all around on the streets. In here there was still some, but it was very few. It was like in the early 60s, the Italians began to transition out. You could visually see them moving out and what you seen was people moving out and minority and blacks coming in. It was Hispanics and blacks. You could see the transition, and the riots were the icing on the cake. The few families that was still here, they left.

chapter THREE
Bright WHITES Form Green

Yusufu Lonell Mosely **knows exactly** where he was the day Dr. Martin Luther King, Jr., was shot and killed in Memphis. He was watching television in his family's home on Chicago's South Side. But, shortly after hearing the tragic news, he went back to his old neighborhood and, as he says, "rioted with everyone else."

Sitting behind his desk at the Winfield Moody Health Center, which is located on Clybourn Street just yards from the Cabrini-Green high-rise building where he once lived, Mr. Mosely admits that at age 47 he's much wiser than he was at 15. But having returned to his neighborhood once again, this time to work as a counselor in the community, he doesn't necessarily apologize for his actions in the wake of Dr. King's murder. "I regret the damage that was done to the community," he says, "but not the rebelliousness. I mean, we were angry and confused and thought, what can we do? They killed this man who taught us to love your enemy. I guess we were thinking, maybe they'll listen to this."

More than 30 years later, Mr. Mosely sees his work as an attempt to help preserve this community. He uses words like inspiration and commitment to describe his ties to

Cabrini-Green. "I've watched someone like Jesse White rise to prominence and continue to give back to the neighborhood, that's inspiring," he insists. "Cabrini-Green is where I spent my formative years, where I learned about things like civil rights and equal opportunity, so I wanted to make a commitment myself to this place and these people... because this is who I am. That's why I'm working here now."

As a counselor, Mr. Mosely serves clients from all parts of Cabrini-Green, not just the white high-rises, or William Green Homes, where he spent much of his youth. He acknowledges that the white high-rises have, at times, seemed somehow cut off from the red buildings and the row houses of Cabrini. He realizes gang turf has had a lot to do with this feeling of separation over the years, but is unsure whether a more subtle rift reaches back to the origins of the white high-rises.

Shortly after construction was completed on the Cabrini Extension, or red high-rises, ground was broken on the William Green Homes. Named after a past president of the American Federation of Labor, the Green Homes were built on the north side of Division Street, with most of the buildings standing to the west of Larrabee Street and east of Halsted.

As the final component of the complex, these white high-rises consisted of 1,096 units in eight buildings, fifteen and sixteen stories tall. Though families began moving into the buildings in 1959, they were not officially dedicated until 1962.

The white high-rises are hulking concrete structures. The ends of each building contain one row of windows surrounded by a solid concrete frame. The front of the buildings are lined with windows, each row of six resting above precast concrete panels. In the rear are exposed hallways, or ramps, that lead to apartments on each floor. These ramps are covered from top to bottom by thick, link fencing.

Like many other developments of the time, the white high-rises are made up of many large apartments concentrated on the lower floors of the buildings. All of the five-bedroom apartments are located in duplex units on the first and second floors. The three- and four-bedroom apartments occupy the third through sixth floors, with the smaller units on the upper floors.

Today, many of the buildings are pocked here and there by soot from small fires. On some higher floors, windows are boarded up or simply left frameless after being vacated. On the ground floor, much like the red high-rises, most of the slots for resident mail boxes hang open and damaged. Graffiti dominates the elevators.

This is not, however, indicative of the appearance of the apartments being occupied in these buildings. Like the rent being charged, this too varies from tenant to tenant. In fact, the interior of the high-rise at 1230 North Burling Street, a building which is now run by tenant management and considered a model in the community, is visibly free of some problems other buildings experience.

Ironically, Mr. Mosely's most distinct recollection of the day, in 1959, when his family moved into apartment 107 in the white high-rise building at 1340 North Larrabee is how sparkling clean everything was. "It was a brand new building," he beams. "It had trees, nice grass and a playground in back, which was something we didn't see on the West Side. It was beautiful."

Ms. Thelma Randolph saw beauty in the buildings as well. As a little girl living in the row houses, she remembers charting the progress of their construction. She begged her mother to move the family to one of those new buildings. When she was in the fifth grade, her family did move to the Green Homes. She has lived in various white high-rise buildings ever since, and has raised three children here. For the last ten years she has served as a parent volunteer at Schiller school. She also works for an after-school tutoring program at the nearby New City YMCA.

Although Ms. Wanda Hopkins no longer lives in the Cabrini-Green neighborhood, she is well-known as a community activist whose work with (PURE) Parents United for Responsible Education keeps her connected with the area's parents and school administrations. She remembers hers was the second family to move into the building at 534 W. Division. They were forced to leave the area in the early '70s, but she returned to the white buildings with her own children in 1976. She says she owes a lot to Cabrini-Green. "I would not be the person I am if I hadn't lived in this community."

Ms. Gloria Crite never lived in the high-rises of Cabrini-Green, but she and many others who were raised in the shadows of these buildings have long considered themselves full members of the community. As she puts it, the high-rises were "a big step up" from where she lived. Since graduating from Bradley University in 1972, she has worked as a teacher and is now assistant principal at Sojourner Truth School on Ogden Ave. Truth serves kindergarten through third graders who live in the white buildings and surrounding area. As one who grew up around rather than in these buildings, and who has taught thousands of young people from Cabrini-Green, Ms. Crite holds a unique perspective on the community's past and present.

Jesse White **never lived in the Cabrini buildings either, but while growing up on Division Street he watched both the red and the white high-rises spring up around him. A noted baseball and basketball star at Waller High School (which later became Lincoln Park High School), he attended Alabama State University on an athletic scholarship. After serving as a paratrooper in World War II, he returned to Chicago to play baseball for the Chicago Cubs. In the off-season, he taught physical education at Jenner school. In 1963, he moved to Schiller school, where he spent the next 26 years. In that time he founded, directed or inspired a slew of extra curricular programs for the young people in the neighborhood. Founded in 1959, the internationally recognized Jesse White Tumbling Team has performed everywhere from the Cabrini row houses to Tokyo, Japan. In 1974, Mr. White was elected State Representative of a district that includes Cabrini-Green. He later served as Cook County Recorder of Deeds, and in 1998 he became the first African-American elected to the office of Illinois Secretary of State. He continues to lead the tumbling team, and remains a fixture in the community.**

Mr. Mosely, despite his participation in the troubles of '68 — which, he insists, may have involved vandalism but did not include violence — clings tight to memories of his early days in Cabrini-Green. He jokes about chipping his tooth on the playground behind Schiller School. In his mind, he retraces the route that led he and his friends to old Riverview amusement park on long summer days. He reflects on the lasting adventures of his first Boy Scout troop, and the fun he shared with his brothers and sisters.

Yusufu Lonell Mosely: There were seven of us, one sister and six brothers. I'm the fourth oldest in the family, and my older sister was married by then so she didn't live with us. I was in fourth grade when we moved in. My mother was on welfare and my biological father was not there. He left when I was 12.

It was an interesting time because the neighborhood was new to all of us....I remember we slept on what they call a roll-away bed. Now they call them futons. I had a brother who slept on the couch....In the white buildings we had a upstairs and a downstairs, and there was a closet big enough to make a bedroom, so we would just take the shelves out of it and make it a bedroom. It was very nice. We had a kitchen with a real stove and all that kind of stuff.

I went to Schiller school and [*laughing*] I remember out on the playground one day there was this girl up on the swing, and I was trying to see up her dress and the swing hit me in the mouth and broke my tooth.

yusufu lonell Mosely

Thelma Randolph: We lived in the row houses first. I watched them build these projects, and then my mom moved into the whites. I was in fifth grade when we moved. Oh, it was very exciting. It was amazing, something to be seen. Matter of fact, we begged our mom to move. "Let's move into them tall buildings over there, Mom." She needed a larger apartment for one thing, and we moved to 714 W. Division.

There was an adjustment because in the row houses it was like a little community, you know, and everybody was like a big family. When we moved over here it was like, it was still a family but it took us a little longer to feel that way.

It was all different races, we was the second black family to move into 714. There was Hispanic, whites and all kinds of races....It was wonderful. We all got along and it was nice.

Jesse White: There were seven of us, four boys and three girls, and my mother and father. My father was born in Missouri. My mother was born in Arkansas. They met in Alton, Illinois, and got married. When I was seven years of age we moved to Chicago from Alton. My family moved to a house at 536 W. Division. It was a predominantly Italian neighborhood but there was a good cross-section of people from other ethnic backgrounds.

When I was growing up I had a lot of role models. I had Claude Walton from Stanton Park, who was my physical education instructor. We had a Warren Chapman who was over at Hudson Playground. He was one individual who helped get me a scholarship to college. Fred Ross taught me there was a lot more within me than I thought...and, of course, my parents.

There was a lot of competition with softball, big-time competition with softball, where guys would get together and establish teams. We'd play at Seward Park or Stanton Park. On the blacktop behind 660 Division they had rollerskating. The lights would come on at night, and the kids would rollerskate. They had a drum and bugle corps. Mr. Wilson, who lived in 1230 Burling [building], he had a beautiful, beautiful drum corps.

In those days when I was coming up we had some tough individuals, but you didn't have gangs. You didn't have drugs. You didn't have disrespect for adults. If you got in trouble at school, the teacher would spank your butt, and when you got home your mother would spank you, or if you got caught out in the neighborhood acting ugly, the neighbor would get you. [People] were watching out for one another.

You could travel anywhere you wanted to travel. There was no such thing as a limitation or a boundary. Wherever you went you were fine....The racial thing was not...that was not the deal. In Cabrini there's never really been a black and white thing, never been a black and white thing where there was hatred in their hearts for white people or other individuals.

Gloria Crite: I never lived in the buildings, but I grew up in the community. We always felt like we lived in Cabrini-Green. I was born over on Hill street just west of Orleans...and then I lived on Orleans Street and Locust, where the St. Luke's Church parking lot is now.

My mother did apply for the housing in those earlier years but for whatever reason we were never accepted. We lived in the poor, really terrible housing nearby. There were five of us and my mom, and we lived in three rooms, a kitchen and two bedrooms really...a dining room we used as a bedroom and then another bedroom. We had to share bathroom facilities with four other families on the floor. It was a big building...and there was lots of things going on in the building. It was the kind of neighborhood you grow up fast in.

So when the high-rises were built it was a big step up for some people to move in the projects versus living in some of the homes that surrounded it. They were really very old and dilapidated and really horrible conditions we had to live in.

Where we lived, it was an "integrated community" because right across the street was where the whites lived, but we were not allowed to intermingle, like we would not go on their side of the street. We would meet in the middle of the street to play, and then we'd go back to our homes on our side, and they'd go to their side. It was just a known thing, you just did not go on their sidewalk. You could play in the middle of the street but you could not go over on the sidewalk.

Wanda Hopkins: We moved here September 1, 1960. We were the second ones in the building at 534 W. Division.

When I moved in it was just so beautiful, the buildings wasn't grayish the way it is now but really the white color, and the apartments were so new, and the floors were shining....I was about four or five. I can remember the white sidewalks and the little chains, you know, the little chains to keep you off the grass. We came from the South Side around 41st and Lake Park, and we moved in here for low income.

Nobody was here, so we really didn't have a lot of people to talk to 'cause we were the second persons in the building. There was only four children in our family. We were able to choose any apartment we wanted and my mother chose 402....She didn't want us to go too high and didn't want to be low.

It was so new and so pretty and the grass was green....My mother says you're really crazy to remember all that, but I look at it now after all these years and I can just remind myself of how it was and I can tell people that this was not the original plan. But I remember other families moving in, and these were all white families, and someone organized the Cub Scouts and the Brownie Scout because I remember I became a Brownie....I remember the Brownie uniform and all that, my brothers were in the Cub Scouts.

Yeah, and we used to live right next door to a white family, I'll never forget, we'd spend the night at each other's house, stuff that you'd never think of would happen back then. I remember Alice and Sally. I lived in 402, they lived in 403. My mother never felt that anything would happen to me when we spent the night at each other's house, and her mother never felt that....It's almost unheard of now. But I keep tellin' people the way it is now was not the original plan, and I just wanted them to know that. I guess that's why I kept it all in my memory.

Gloria Crite: There were gangs as far back as I can remember. As a kid in the late '50s, I remember them and they began to get more assertive. They would beat you but they would not necessarily kill you....In those days they would fight with chains and brass knuckles and those sorts of things. I remember the murders, deaths, fighting and violence, but we were a close knit family and we spent most of our time inside, and when we were outside my mother was always out there to supervise or watch us.

I had two other sisters and two brothers. The brothers had more leeway because they worked at a very early age to help supplement the family. We were raised on welfare, and didn't have a father in the household, so they went out and did shoe shining. Sometimes they would get robbed before they'd get home. They worked down in the LaSalle Street area, it was the affluent area, the Gold Coast, and just coming home from there to the house they would run into problems because they had their shoe shine boxes with them, so people knew they worked and so they became prey.

Jesse White

Jesse White: I've always believed that you should set a good example for our youth. When I was a youngster coming up in the neighborhood, if I was walking down the street and a guy would swear, my brother would grab him and say, I don't want you to swear around my brother. Don't you disrespect my little brother.

Or if guys were out shooting dice, and they'd see Mrs. Jones walk down the street, they'd hide the dice and take their hat off and say, How are you doing, Mrs. Jones? As soon as Mrs. Jones passed they threw the money back down and started shooting dice again. Or when a lady would get on a crowded bus...the young guys would get up and say, Hello, Mrs. Brown, would you like to have my seat? Not today. That's rare.

We even have negative songs out there now where they degrade and demean the female gender...the rap and scratchin' and cussing music. Some of it, if it's done in good taste, I don't have a problem with it, but when it comes to demeaning the female gender or anyone, then it becomes ugly.

Yusufu Lonell Mosely: There were mostly Latinos and blacks in the area at that time, with one or two white families. But, they didn't stay long.

We had a bakery across the street from us and they made fresh bread and stuff....We also went to Sammy's Red Hots down on Division. It's still there, and everybody knew when you'd been to Sammy's because you had to double bag those fries from all the grease.

But we went downtown too. I remember I went downtown with my sister and got my first pizza. We went to Riverview [amusement park] a lot. It was a summer thing. Coca Cola would come around in their delivery trucks and they would give you free tickets to Riverview. We'd take some bus all the way up there...and we'd make sure to avoid the whites who weren't too comfortable with blacks. If we spent the little money we had up there at Riverview, for our way home we'd jump on the back of the trolley cars and hang onto the sign. The trolleys used to come right down Clybourn Street. The conductors, they sat up front, and never really paid attention to little black kids hanging off the back.

Sometimes we'd go on school days, but if you ditched school back then you'd have to go down to Lincoln Park or somewhere because if someone around here saw you they'd grab you and take you home to your mama.

One of the rides was called the parachute, and you could see the parachute from Cabrini. That's how you knew Riverview was still open when you'd see the parachute up there.

Thelma Randolph: Back then the pool at Stanton Park was outside. I would go there a lot but I was also involved in Sunshine Ministries, which was a place where we'd play games and learn about the Bible.

We'd go to Seward Park sometimes, but that was like in the other neighborhood, you know. But basically there was always something to do. We'd walk to the beach, walk to Riverview, walk to the zoo. The milk trucks used to have free tickets to Riverview. You could get in free, and ride the rides if you had a ticket that they used to give us with the milk. They delivered it, and they used to give the kids a whole stack of tickets, and we'd just walk up there. You'd walk up there with your friends, and ride the same ride all day long. We'd also go to Sammy's, they still have the best French fries [*laughing*].

Jesse White: I was a tumbler as a kid, and then I later played baseball and basketball at Waller High School. I was an all-city basketball player for three years. I received a scholarship to Alabama State University in Montgomery, Alabama, and I lived in the same dormitory there with Eugene Sawyer, the former mayor of Chicago. Dr. Martin Luther King, Jr., was my minister and Rev. Ralph Abernathy, another famous civil rights leader, was my fraternity brother.

After [college], I signed a contract with the Chicago Cubs, and four days before I was scheduled to go to spring training I was drafted by Uncle Sam. So instead of going to spring training, I went to basic training, joined the 101st Airborne Division as a paratrooper and jumped out of airplanes for two years with General William Westmoreland. Then, after I got out of the military, I began my baseball career. During the off-season I taught school during the day, worked for the Chicago Park District at Stanton Park in the evenings, and was asked to put on a gym show in December, 1959, at the Rockwell Garden Housing Project. From that came the Jesse White Tumbling Team.

Yusufu Lonell Mosely: My mother was on welfare...and my stepfather couldn't come around because welfare at that time didn't allow the man to be around. The welfare workers would come and check and see if there was a man in the house. They'd check and see if we had a TV, if we had an iron and if we had the utensils that any normal household would have had....They'd cut some of the money if they saw something like that. I remember we had to hide the toaster one time.

Gloria Crite: We had cousins who lived in the row houses and I remember the event they used to have over there. It was a religious thing where people would come out and there was a parade and it was like a feast, but I was young so I can barely remember it.

When we moved to Orleans Street, Orleans was the strip. The Bucket of Blood was on the strip. It was a club and you'd see the guys and the pimps drive up in their convertibles and stuff. They called it the Bucket of Blood because somebody was always

killed. I don't remember if that was actually the name, but that's what everybody called it.

We went to St. Luke's but we also went to every church in the community; Union Baptist, St. Matthew's, Wayman, and then I went to after-school like religious instruction at St. Joseph's and even the Moody Bible Institute. So we weren't members of just one church. My mother believed in exposing us to all different religions. That was also one way of my mom keeping us occupied and off the streets.

Those were difficult times. I think she was getting $75 per month from welfare and that had to go to rent and lights and food, and I can remember her putting the money on the bed and counting it out, and then taking it over to the hardware store. The landlord owned the hardware store.

The landlord was not a good one. He didn't keep the building in good condition, he just collected rent....The lady right next door to us ran a whore house, and her patrons would come in and out, ya know, it was all visible, even as a child you knew what was going on, so we grew up fast.

Jesse White: What was happening then was there was a shortage of adult role models within the family, and the parents would come to me and say, Mr. White, we know that you have love in your heart for our children, and you live in the community. I lived two blocks away from the school where I taught, and that was unheard of back then. I had also graduated from the same school and knew most of the people, so I was looked upon as a father figure, big brother or surrogate father to a lot of kids, and then I was with the young people after school. We had a track and field program and wrestling, volleyball, basketball. I had the drum corps., the largest Boy Scout troop in the nation. So I was doing a lot of things with the kids outside of school. I'd take them to the circus, to the baseball games, football games, to a lot of places that they normally would not have had an opportunity to visit.

These were kids who would come to the park, and I would work with them on tumbling, and they were impressed with my teaching techniques. They were impressed with my ability to perform, and I don't do quite as much as I did or a lot less than I did then because I'm 65 now. I was in my 20's then. So, after the first show was over, and about 350 people were in the audience, I wished the kids well. I told them that was it and the parents were a little upset....What they were really trying to say is, all this time you're teaching these kids how to tumble, and they do a great job, and now that's it? That's a big letdown.

So, later we were approached by other parks and other YMCAs, boys' clubs and youth organizations, and they all asked us to come, and so we would perform for the parks and for the playground and for the YMCA's and the boys' clubs. And then DePaul University

DePaul University asked us to perform at a basketball game. I think they were playing Loyola University. And then Loyola liked us, and they asked us to perform. Then Loyola played Northwestern, and Northwestern liked us, and then it set off a chain reaction. We performed for the Chicago Bulls-Detroit Pistons game. The Detroit Pistons called us, and we went to Detroit to do the Pistons' game. They played the Cleveland Cavaliers. The Cavaliers liked us, and they invited us.

We've been able to perform for all of the NBA teams with the exception of the Lakers....We will do about eight National Football League teams a season, maybe 20 major league and minor league baseball teams, colleges and universities, continental basketball, professional soccer and the list goes on and on.

We've been to Tokyo, Japan, and in February we're going to Hong Kong representing Illinois in the Chinese millennium. We'll be in the parade, and after the parade we will perform about ten times in the various venues within the city.

Wanda Hopkins: I went to the Y, actually it was called the Isham YMCA and it was right up near Division and Clybourn. I'll never forget, I went there almost every day of my life, 'cause my mother worked two jobs, so I went from five years old until I was 16 or so. I eventually worked there.

I knew everybody in the Y. I always went everywhere in the world with Jesse White. He used to call me his "Sweet Wanda," he still calls me "Sweet Wanda." He used to have to take me everywhere because he never knew when my mother was going to be home.

I have really known Mr. White all my life....He knew that my mother was trying hard, she had divorced my father and she was struggling and he just, I guess latched on to me. I was a terrible track runner and he always had me up there with the winners, you know, it was unbelievable. They would get red and blue ribbons, and I would probably get a white or something, and my ribbon was up there just like theirs.

Thelma Randolph: There was eight of us kids and we stayed on the fourth floor. And oh, yes, it was green. I tell people this blacktop out here was all grass, with trees and flowers and didn't nobody pull 'em up and tear 'em out....There was a lot of stores on Larrabee Street. It seemed like every other block was a supermarket, you know, and North Avenue was like a mini shopping mall. It was like a little community. Everybody loved the way it looked and everything.

I remember we used to go the that YMCA, Isham Y....Like I say, back then we had a lot of things to do, a lot of things. There was always a quarter party or after-school programs, especially when I was in high school. We had teen night, and it really was a lot of fun.

Jesse White: I was a public aid recipient for about nine years. I lived in a third floor walk-up apartment in the rear of the building, and I said once my feet become firmly planted on this earth, I was going to do something for someone. Later, I thought about what a wonderful thing it's been to be able to go to college free, to serve in the military, to play baseball for the Cubs. I have to give back. I have to wrap my arms around something that is positive and to make a difference, and that's what I've been doing.

There are a lot of beautiful young people in Cabrini-Green, a lot of wonderful people....With the tumblers we put these young people on airplanes. They'd never flown in an airplane. They never slept in a hotel, never swam in a swimming pool, had never been in a professional arena. Now my kids meet the ball players, get autographs, get souvenirs, can say this weekend I started out on Friday performing in Atlanta, Georgia, and Saturday evening performed in Orlando, Florida, Sunday afternoon performed in Miami, Florida, and here I am back here, and I have $600 in my pocket because I performed six minutes in each city, and I slept in a beautiful hotel, was fed well, visited the cities,

met the athletes, performed in the beautiful arenas. Not very many people can brag like that.

Yusufu Lonell Mosely: Jesse White was the first black teacher I'd ever seen. All my teachers to that point were white. Anyway, he became the gym teacher at Schiller. He had told us he played for the Cubs and he would race us out back. He could out run all of us.

But, the first thing he did, and this is why he is who he is now, he became a community person and he went door to door asking parents if they want their son to be part of the tumbling team, the drill team or the Boy Scouts. I ended up in the Boy Scouts...Troop 146 if I remember.

Wanda Hopkins: I went to Schiller school for a while and then a law passed that all the children that was on Division Street had to go to Jenner school, so they sent us to Jenner. Now my mother tried to protest this, but there wasn't enough people. She had been an activist for I don't know how long. I guess that's why I'm one now....I didn't stay at Jenner long. My mother was not pleased with it, so we went to St. Joseph's on Orleans. I graduated from St. Joseph's. I continued my education in Catholic schools and went to St. Stanislas.

But before that, when my brother was still going to Schiller, someone had thrown a grocery cart over the ramp in one of the building's and he was hurt. That's why the fences on the ramps go all the way to the top now. Back then they just went about half way, but my brother was in hospital treatment for two years.

The city did nothing to help out with my bother's expenses, the CHA did nothing for us....They supported us in no way when it happened.

Yusufu Lonell Mosely: The ramps were open back then. There was no big fence, it was about chest high and I had a friend who would climb over and show how bad he was by just walking down the fence. I said, man you're nuts. One time – they had milk bottles in that day – and one boy threw a milk bottle over off the ramp and it hit a young man in the head and crippled him for life. It hit a young Latino guy who lived in 107. We lived in 108 and we were just playing a little before that happened. I remember that very distinctly.

Thelma Randolph: I think it always was a little different in the red buildings than in the whites. We was on this side of the street, and they was on that. It was just like walking into a new, different place. I went to Cooley High, which was down past the reds on Division, and it just felt like a different place over there.

There's something about the reds, I wouldn't really go in to them. It was like three different neighborhoods; the reds, the whites and row houses. Matter of fact, it's the same way now. It's really like one community with three neighborhoods because it's all considered Cabrini-Green. But people in the whites would holler [*laughing*], "I don't live in the reds," people in the reds say, "I don't live in the rows..." and ya know.

Jesse White: Later on, when I was teaching school, kids had some reluctance about going across Division Street. Division Street was the demarcation line. You can't go across Division Street or you can't go over to Stanton Park to swim in the tank, the swimming pool, because you'd get beaten up. Those lines were drawn because of the gangs. The gangs have done a tremendous amount of harm to our community, to every community.

You have these guys who go off to prison and they come back, and they poison the rest of the community with the gang mentality. The same things that they encountered while they were in prison they brought back.

Yusufu Lonell Mosely: Wells Street was like the dividing line going east and the Ogden Street bridge was up then, and that would run into the white community. Then you had Montgomery Ward further down on Chicago Avenue and the Chicago River just to the west. As a kid, I remember seeing no fishing signs by the river and you'd look down and see dead fish floating on the water, so we knew something wasn't right.

But there were dividing lines and yes, you felt it, you felt it. I experienced it a couple times, when they said that bad word, that "N" word a couple times when I didn't really know what it meant. It was like okay, we don't want to mess with them...and when I got older I realized what they meant by that. So you could feel it. It was definitely felt.

Gloria Crite

Gloria Crite: I attended Waller High School and graduated in 1968. It was a very integrated school at the time, but they would only allow so many blacks from the Cabrini-Green area to even attend Waller. Since my address was not a Cabrini address it was easier for me to get in. A lot of my friends were directed to go to Cooley or Wells high school.

The students who did go to Waller from Cabrini I didn't really associate with them much because I was in more of honors classes and they weren't in them....Some girls I had known had babies before that and didn't even make it to high school. They dropped out. But if you could get into Waller instead of Cooley, then you were in the mix, as they say.

When I did go away to school I realized I was very well prepared, whereas a lot of other students from Chicago Public Schools dropped out their freshman year of college.

Thelma Randolph: My mother always cooked on Sunday but the only real tradition was Christmas. My mother never had a fake tree. She had to get the tallest, biggest, greenest tree. We always had a live tree for Christmas.

We also had the block parties every year, especially up on the blacktop, and roller-skating parties, you know, where you bring your roller-skates and set up music. That's when it was cool back then. You could walk around, you know, sleep outside, on the porch. You didn't have to worry about anything....And I never experienced any racism at all. I didn't go up to Lincoln Park that much, but when I went I never experienced it. My mom must have shielded us from a lot of prejudice. She had to. And I read about Martin Luther King coming to Chicago [in the mid-60s], and how he got treated, but I was young and didn't know what had happened...so [racism] wasn't something I worried about. My mother never raised me that way, ya know, you don't do nothin' to me and everybody'll fine.

Jesse White: When I went back to teach in the neighborhood, it was a viable housing project. There were around about 22,000 people there, a mix of blacks, whites and Hispanics. The Whites gradually moved out, then later on the Hispanics moved out and the community became predominantly black.

You see, twenty-five years ago the Chicago Housing Authority used to inspect the apartments. They knew who was in each apartment, and they made sure that the conditions were habitable. They wanted to make sure that the people who lived there, their name was on the lease, and they made sure that you kept your apartments clean, your stairway and hallway clean. The janitors were on their mark.

And then, all of the sudden things kind of fell apart. The gang bangers came in, and they changed the makeup and the program of public housing like we perceived it to be. They decided that they wanted to run it. They turned the lights off in the hallway, and they used to force people to pay them to get on the elevator. They would practice pharmacy without a license, if you understand what I'm talking about. There was a lot of street pharmacists, hallway pharmacists but, you see, the thing is that you have so many wonderful people who live in those housing projects, but the few have the tendency to give a bad name for the ones who you would not mind having as your neighbor.

Then you had a lot of people who became involved with drugs. They'd bring some beautiful young people into this world, but yet they weren't there to serve as a safety net to make sure these kids would grow tall and straight. They'd send the kids to school and they'd say the school has the sole responsibility of educating our kids. Well, you know and I know that it's a combination of the school, the community and home, but you start at home first.

The bottom line is this; early on [management] was selective about who they would let in, and they would move expeditiously to get rid of the ones who could not live in peace and harmony with the neighbors and friends. That was the way to go, but somewhere down the line those two things stopped working.

Yusufu Lonell Mosely: As I got older I learned about the Civil Rights Movement from a priest who used to be over at St. Matthew's Church. In fact, I remember going to see Martin Luther King speak at St. Matthew's church. It must have been 1966. But the priest at St. Matthew's was Rev. Smith and he was a beacon in the community....Well, he went down South to some [civil rights] convention and I heard about it and tried to convince my mom to let me go. She said no and finally my stepfather said let him go....When I came back I had a consciousness of really everything around me and an explanation for what was happening to me when they used that "N" word. By that time I knew what it meant but the South experience gave it greater emphasis on what they meant when they said that.

At that time, whites were not so bold. They'd say it when they were in a crowd, and we always felt that one brother could beat up ten white guys 'cause we thought we were tough....On the weekends we'd head down Division Street and over to the lake. When we crossed Clark Street we'd always encounter racism. It was never really in an intense way 'til you got to Clark Street. All the shows were down there...and people would let you know you were in the wrong place, calling you nigger real loud.

One time I got accosted, some kid said what are you doing over here, and I said remove your hand from my shirt. This was a young white guy, older than me at the time, and I was 14 or 15. He was taller and more muscular than me and he grabbed me because he couldn't grab the other guy I was with. When he grabbed me I just broke loose from his grip and punched and, of course, when he hit the ground we all jumped on him. After that we went on to the park, where we got stopped by the police and was asked did any of us know the guys who jumped this guy. There he was sitting in the back seat of the cop car lookin' right at me, but he couldn't or wouldn't say it was me. So I felt like I was saved from the wrath of the police that time. I never got arrested for any battles with white people, but I did for stealing bikes up in Lincoln Park.

Gloria Crite: There wasn't too much trouble up at Waller. You went to school and came home. We didn't really hang out up there per se. The kids were pretty friendly. I think the fear and the animosity came after Dr. King's death...but prior to that if there was any at all then it was not that pronounced as far as I was concerned. There was only about three blacks in the honors classes and we were not always in the same classrooms, but we had girls from Egypt and Jewish girls, we were all there. Now, we were never like the kind of friends who go up and spend the night, no, we never did that, but we did get along all right.

Yusufu Lonell Mosely: I lived over in the whites until '67, and then we moved to the reds, to 1160 North Sedgwick, where people tell me Mayor [Jane] Byrne lived when she was over here. Shortly after that my stepfather moved us down to the Roseland neighborhood on the South Side. Like I said, I still came up here a lot to see my friends.

Thelma Randolph: I was in the house watching the news when it came on. I said, "Mom, mom, Martin Luther King got killed." People was runnin' around bustin' in stores and stuff. My mom wouldn't let us out the door. We couldn't go out.

I was hurt that this community just went wacko....That's when all the stores disappeared. They didn't ever rebuild all those stores on Larrabee and the cleaners that was on Division. Everything that was on North Avenue they broke in. They didn't go over the borderline, which was Orleans Street. You don't pass that line, you know. That's the way people used to think, you don't pass that line at Orleans. That's like going up into State and Rush and all that. They didn't go past there. They just tore up their own community.

Yusufu Lonell Mosely: I didn't really know what to do when I heard about Reverend King. I just went outside and looked around at what people were doing. Then I thought of my old neighborhood and I got on the train and headed up here to Cabrini.

I remember walking up from the train and there was a group of people standing in front of a store at Clybourn and Division. There were two cops, detectives, standing in front of the group and they were saying the first person who tries to go into the store is going to jail. Well, a brick flew threw the front window and everybody just pushed past the detectives and went on in. I hooked up with a friend of mine and we did our own thing from there.

People talk about how when the riots took place we burned up our own community, well we couldn't get into anybody else's community. They had cordoned off the Ogden Street bridge over here, and Halsted had a line of police, and there were a lot of stores up on North Avenue so they sealed that off to a great extent....There was a Motorola television station up there then, and that was the dividing line 'cause Motorola was on this side of North Avenue....We eventually did get up to North Avenue and hit some of those stores. We got around the cops by going through alleyways and side streets.

Wanda Hopkins: I remember when it was announced on TV and I was young, but people went crazy. There was a store across the street from us they were just looting and throwing things....I think the store was called Grocery Land and it was where the Winfield Moody Health Center is now. My mother was a very strong mother, she didn't play with that stuff and she didn't let us out during that.

We couldn't believe it and the National Guard, I remember them driving up in tanks. You could see them, like they were going to blow our buildings up. We were thinking that they were going to blow us up.

Oh, God, it lingered on for days. People were very angry, you know, they wanted to kill all white people. I mean it was really something, my mother had to keep stressing to us, "that's not what it's about, that's not what it's about." People were saying stuff, and you would listen, like, you know, why would they have to kill our only black leader? Why would they have to do that, you know, so, it was stressful for the kids.

Gloria Crite: We had a riot in the school, and I was sitting there in the lunchroom at Waller when it happened. Oh, it was like out of the blue, the black students they just started throwing the plates and food and stuff and I escaped out a side window...and after that there became a lot of anger.

Yeah, they just went off...and it was chaos. Classes were canceled the next day and when we did go back the atmosphere was tense. In looking back on it, they didn't send like they do now, professionals who come in to talk to the young people and work through the problems, so we had no group of people to go to to talk about the emotions and the feelings that we had as a result of it. Each young person had to deal with it in their own way, and this is one reason why there was more fear. They didn't know if this was going to happen again. People became more cautious of who they were sitting with, you had to be careful, you had to segregate and separate yourself so you weren't being perceived as part of a certain group.

And then there was another incident where a white boy came in and he shot up the school's auditorium. A black kid had threatened him at the bus stop one day and so he came back to school the following morning with his family's gun. And he just started firing. He was arrested but I don't remember what ever happened to him.

Yusufu Lonell Mosely: I remember going into Del Farms on Larrabee and filling up a bag with stuff, mainly cigarettes, then I heard someone say the cops were comin' and heard a loudspeaker say, "Whoever comes out without receipt will be arrested." I went toward the back of the store and there was a group of people in the freezer, white people too, but there was no way out the back so I just got in line and one by one the cops were checkin' receipts.

When they got to me I said the receipt must be in the bag somewhere. The cop said there's no receipt so you're going to jail, and then some lady, who must have seen me in the back, said, "Oh, no, he was here. I saw him in here before." So I got out of that one.

But, I'm walking down Larrabee and who do I run into but my mother. She came over to visit a friend. She asks me what I'm doing with all those groceries and I say, "Oh, I went shopping for James' mom." James was my friend. My mom looked in the bag and said, she don't smoke. She said get your ass inside.

Thelma Randolph: They were mad because they killed Dr. King, that's the only way I figured people were doing all this stuff. But it was more than that because I remember the National Guards coming in. They came in and there was a curfew. Everybody had to be off the streets, and tanks was going through the streets, guys in army gear, and at night big, bright lights. When they hit your window it would like light up your whole house. So, it was kind of frightening, definitely. The whole thing was sad to me. It was sad to me.

Gloria Crite: After that they began to allow more and more students from Cabrini into the high school and the classes were getting larger each year. Plus, they had closed Cooley, so they needed a place to send the students other than Wells....I graduated in '68 and my sister came out two years later, and by her year it had changed completely. It was white flight, so they had to figure out what to do with all these black folks at Waller high.

That's why they felt they had to change the name of Waller to Lincoln Park a few years later, to make it a fresh start, to start over, and at the same time they began to exclude the students from Cabrini-Green because they built Near North High School and just said let's send them over there. To separate them and divide.

The whites on the other side began to move back in and send their kids to Lincoln Park...then they set it up where you could come from all over the city to attend Lincoln Park, like a magnet school.

Wanda Hopkins: Well, I think that's when everything really went down hill. I don't remember after that the real cleaned up buildings. It looked as though we had messed it up for ourselves by looting, and doing all the things that people were doing, and it felt like people thought we weren't civilized. After that, I felt like management would no longer care for the buildings any more, and so, we had that to deal with.

There was always the gangs, the Cobra Stones and all of that, but I really believe because of the way they did us, the way they didn't care for us anymore that people began to start creating their own gangs, the Black Gangster Disciples and all, because they felt that there was no hope any more.

Nobody cared about us. It just was unbelievable. The buildings were no longer the same, the people that were not of color no longer stayed in the buildings...but they had started to leave I believe in '65, probably around there.

Gloria Crite: I didn't feel it, like a depression, after King was killed. He was dead, we were sad and that was about it. It really didn't impact upon me until I went off to college. We were not a politically minded family. We were not involved in the Civil Rights Movement at all. Our number one concern was survival, and making ends meet and eating, the basic things [*laughing*]. I started working when I was 12. I had to earn money to go to school so I didn't have time to have other concerns like that. I had two jobs by the time I was 13. I worked at the school, and then I worked at a doctor's office after school. I was making money to pay for my bus ride to school. Sometimes I had to make a decision, either I eat today or I ride, 'cause I couldn't do both.

But, my mother made it very plain to all of us that you will go to school and get an education...because her education stopped when she was 12 years old. As a child she was in the South, in Memphis, and she had siblings to support. She had to work in the white peoples' homes to help her family...so she was very persistent about us going to high school and to go on to college. Now, how

we would get to college we had no idea, so we had to keep our academics up and try to earn a scholarship and things....She was very excited when I earned a full academic scholarship to Bradley University....And that's where I became a real militant [*laughing*]. I was a revolutionist....I was also committed to coming back to this community to work, to teach, and that's why I'm here today.

WANda HopkiNS

Wanda Hopkins: Things weren't kept up as well after 1968, but I had heard from my mother that the old Mayor Daley had had a plan, and that the buildings were not working out the way he thought it was. It was supposed to only be a transition, you're not suppose to stay in Cabrini housing developments all your life, ya know, once you make it you're supposed to be able to get out.

That was the point of those buildings, people were not supposed to have generation after generation in the building and he had decided that, 'cause my mother was just the way I am now, she went to find out what people were saying. The mayor wanted to do something different, that the buildings was going to come down, and that was written in the plan 20 years ago, that these buildings would come down and the area would be regentrified. They used different terms at that point, but, now it's really coming to pass.

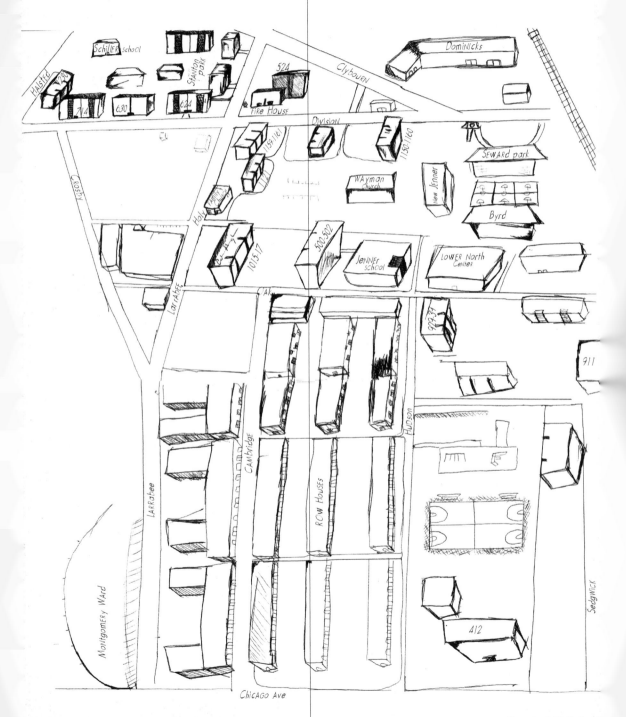

Illustration: Calvin Hughes-18

FIXtures
IN the Community

A dark four-door sedan with municipal plates rolls up in front of Schiller school, the passenger door flips open and out hops **Mr. Jesse White**. A light March snow sprinkles his Navy blue suit as he walks swiftly from the car to the school's front doors. Inside, a few teachers stop to say hello and a group of children camped in a hallway study his familiar face. Mr. White peeks his head in the front office and is met with a handful of surprised smiles. Within minutes, he's being treated like the groom in a receiving line.

It's not everyday that the Illinois Secretary of State visits your school. But at Schiller school the visits from this politician are not all that uncommon, and at this school Jesse White's warm welcome has little to do with his esteemed position as Secretary of State. Here, he's Jesse White the school's former gym teacher, Jesse White the tumbling team coach, Jesse White the neighbor, the former field trip organizer, former military paratrooper, former Chicago Cub, former Boy Scout leader, former head of the drum and bugle corps. Here, he's Jesse White the role model, father figure and friend.

It's safe to say that for the last 40 years Mr. White has served, like Schiller school itself, as a Cabrini-Green institution. In fact, at seven years old, when his family moved to the neighborhood, the white high-rises had not yet been built, but Schiller school had already been serving the community for 50 years.

Named after the famous German author, dramatist and playwright, **Friederich von Schiller School** was built in 1892. In 1961, a new school building was erected at 640 W. Scott Street, and today it is surrounded by the white high-rise buildings that house most of its students. The school serves fourth through sixth grade.

Jesse White isn't the only Schiller graduate to eventually become a teacher at the school. Bernice Thompson also returned to Schiller, where she's worked as a community liaison for more than 33 years.

In 1971, **Sojourner Truth School** was built directly behind Schiller at 1443 Ogden Street. Students from the area attend kindergarten through third grade at Truth before moving on to Schiller. Truth is named after the famous African-American spokeswoman of the 1800s, who rose to prominence fighting for the rights of women and African-Americans.

Edward Jenner Academy of the Arts is another legendary institution of the Cabrini-Green community. Located at 1009 N. Cleveland Street, where the row houses meet the red high-rises of Cabrini, it opened in 1908 and was named for the English physician who developed a vaccine against smallpox in 1796. Covering kindergarten through eighth grade, Jenner has served many generations of young people from this neighborhood. A new Jenner school is nearing completion just to the north of the original building, and students will be attending the new school in the fall of 2000.

To accommodate an increase in population in the area, **Richard E. Byrd Community Academy** was built in 1960. Located just northwest of Jenner at 363 W. Hill Street, it primarily draws pre-kindergarten to eighth grade students from the red high-rise buildings. The school was named after the English explorer who was the first man to fly over the North Pole, in 1925, and the South Pole, in 1929.

Just north of Byrd school, at the corner of Orleans and Division streets, is **Seward Park**. The sturdy brick fieldhouse has been sitting on this site since 1908, when the park was completed. Named after William H. Seward (1801-1872), the Secretary of State during President Abraham Lincoln's administration, the park includes baseball fields, basketball courts and a playground. For decades the fieldhouse entrance faced Elm Street, but Elm Street has been removed in the last year and the park now stretches all the way north to Division. This area has been impressively redesigned into an urban green space that includes iron benches, brick columns, ornate light fixtures and a modern clock tower.

Stanton Park, located among the white high-rise buildings at 618 W. Scott Street, was opened to the public in 1910. Named after Edwin M. Stanton, President Lincoln's Secretary of War, the park included a fieldhouse, playing fields and an outdoor swimming pool. In 1964, the fieldhouse was demolished and replaced with an indoor swimming facility. In 1971, a gymnasium was added to the complex. Like Seward Park, Stanton has for years offered a variety of programming activities to the youth of the area.

Cabrini-Green has always been home to many religious institutions. In the early days, two Catholic churches, St. Philip Benizi and St. Dominic's, were anchors in the community. They both were predominantly Italian parishes. St. Philip's closed in the late 1960s and St. Dominic's in the early '70s, as African-Americans became the great majority in the area.

St. Joseph's Church, the third oldest parish in the Catholic Archdiocese, continues to thrive at 1107 N. Orleans Street, where it has stood since 1878. In fact, St. Joseph's was founded in 1846, but the original church burned in the Chicago Fire of 1871. The school at St. Joseph's, which is attended by many children of Cabrini-Green, serves kindergarten through eighth grade. The church also offers its students after-school programs. Its HighSight program provides scholarships to students to attend quality private high schools in Chicago and works intensively to prepare them for college. Father Sebastian Lewis O.S.B. has led the church since 1960.

Wayman African Methodist Episcopal Church has operated at 509 W. Elm Street since 1893. It too sponsors an after-school program that serves the children of Cabrini-Green. The church also provides day care service to the community and runs a welfare-to-work initiative. Wayman church has always been especially active in the neighborhood and many among its congregation have been attending its services for several decades. Dr. Walter Johnson has served as pastor of the church for the last eight years.

In 1966, the Reverend Dr. Martin Luther King, Jr., paid a visit to Cabrini-Green's **St. Matthew United Methodist Church**, located at 1000 N. Orleans Street. After his speech he led a civil rights march downtown that drew 25,000 supporters. St. Matthew's has been supporting this community since 1916. Today, in addition to regular services, its programming includes Head Start day care, tutoring for sixth through eighth grade, after-school activities for ages 6 to 14, Cub Scout meetings and a food pantry.

Holy Family Lutheran Church sits among the red-brick high-rises at 542 N. Hobbie. Built in 1962, Holy Family has been active in the community from its start. Pastor Charles Infelt, known as "Pastor Chuck" in the neighborhood, remembers organizing baseball games in the fields around the church. He also coached a couple basketball teams before eventually becoming the pastor at Holy Family. Not only has the church offered broad youth programming over the years, its Cabrini Alive project has brought thousands of volunteers to the community to work with residents in cleaning, repairing and revitalizing Cabrini buildings.

Sunshine Gospel Mission has been serving the Cabrini-Green community since the neighborhood was first established. Sunshine itself goes back to 1905, when the Dillon family of Chicago founded the organization in association with the Moody Church. Bill Dillon, Sr., operated the program for decades. Its original home closer to downtown, near Dearborn and Ontario streets, included a homeless shelter, along with its Bible study programming, spiritual retreats and enrichment activities.

Sunshine moved to the Cabrini community in the '70s and is currently located among the row houses at 525 W. Iowa Street.

Interestingly, when Sunshine took children of the neighborhood on camping trips to Michigan in the 1940s and '50s, the children had to be segregated. Despite the fact that these children lived among each other in what was still a racially-mixed Cabrini, state regulations kept white children in one camp and black children in another. To avoid this uncomfortable circumstance, the organization purchased its own camp in 1957. Sunshine continues to offer summer camp and provide church formatted programming. Reverend Dana Thomas has been involved with the organization since 1988.

Lower North Center is another organization that pre-dates Cabrini-Green. Founded more than 60 years ago, it is one of the Chicago Youth Centers. Today it is located in the heart of Cabrini at 1000 N. Sedgwick Street, where it continues to provide young people of the neighborhood with a place to go for recreation, academic support, counseling, leadership skills and more. From Head Start to Career Planning to summer camp, elementary aged children and teenagers have for decades looked to Lower North Center as a second home. Ms. Margaret Smith has served as the matriarch of this Cabrini institution for 40 years.

Since 1963, when the **Community Youth Creative Learning Experience** (better known as CYCLE) was founded in the basement of LaSalle Street Church, this organization has offered community-based education aimed at transforming the lives of children of the Cabrini-Green area and their families. Currently located at 1111 N. Wells Street, CYCLE is nationally-recognized for its innovative approach to youth programming. It offers academic enrichment to elementary and high school students and its services include a GED program, ACT and SAT study workshops and adult literacy classes among others.

In 1965, the Chicago Housing Authority teamed with Montgomery Ward to establish The Montgomery Ward Cabrini-Green Tutoring Program, which matches adult volunteers with grammar school children from the Cabrini neighborhood in one-on-one tutoring. For years the program relied on employees of Montgomery Ward, who volunteered their time with the students. One employee, Daniel Bassill, volunteered to lead the program in 1975. In 1990, the organization incorporated as a separate entity. Today, the **Cabrini-Green Tutoring Program** is housed in the New City YMCA, 1515 N. Halsted Street, and Daniel Bassill is the president and CEO of **Cabrini Connections**, a tutor/mentor organization that serves junior high and high school students of the area.

The **Fellowship of Friends** grew out of the Sunshine Gospel Mission and the **LaSalle Street Young Life** program. Pastor Steve Pedigo, who has worked in Cabrini-Green since 1976, calls it a Quaker church made up of young families. The church was established in 1980 and is currently housed in the old St. Philip Benizi school at 515 W. Oak St., at the corner of Oak and Cambridge. Besides church services, Fellowship of Friends is very involved in youth advocacy for children who are dealing with the court system. Working with pre-school to adult, the church runs an after-school program, holds Bible study classes, organizes field trips and camping trips and offers career and other counseling, all aimed at forging long-term relationships with its congregation.

The **Al Carter Youth Foundation, Winfield-Moody Health Center** and **Cabrini C.A.D.R.E.** are just a few other organizations that have proven to be valuable resources to the people of Cabrini-Green.

part II THE MIDDLE AGES
1968-84?

chapterFOUR

Growin' in a **ROW**

About ten years ago, Rosalind Kirkman-Bey came back home.
After living in Germany, Hawaii, Georgia and Colorado,
she and her three children moved back to the row house
on Cleveland Street where she grew up. "It is ironic," she
says with a smile.

Sitting at her kitchen table, Rosalind admits she has mixed
feelings about living here now. Her former husband's military
duty kept the family on the move. When they divorced, she
felt she had little choice but to return to her mother's house.
When her mother passed away, Rosalind and her children
were compelled to stay.

"I still remember the good times we had growing up here,"
she says. "My brothers and sister lived here, and this house
is still kind of a connection to my mother. Even though the
rest of my family lives outside the community now, everybody
comes here, no matter what, because of my mom. We always
end up back here."

At 33, Rosalind works as a electrical engineer for a company
in Chicago's western suburbs. Her older brother, Richard, is
a chief engineer for the same company. Her oldest child is 14.
"Being a single parent can be difficult,
but I'm doing my best to raise them,
to teach them right from wrong,"
she says. "To me, as long as our communication is there,
we'll be all right."

The experience of living in different cities and countries, Rosalind says, was a good one. "If I could live anywhere I actually would have to pick between Hawaii and Germany. I loved working with the Germans. I used to work in this warehouse and we basically assisted the military during the Saudi Arabia [conflict], working with the plasma and all of that."

In her many travels she was surprised at the number of military people, from various places, who had heard of Cabrini-Green. "There were people from Arizona and Texas, and they had heard of Cabrini-Green. They mostly heard about the negative things," she says. "I would have to let 'em know it wasn't as bad as they thought."

Born and raised in the row house neighborhood, Gerald Washington agrees that it isn't as bad as people think. At 38, he no longer lives in the community, but he works here. He is a program director at Lower North Center, which is part of the Chicago Youth Services network.

Walter Burnett doesn't live in the row houses any longer either, but he represents the community as Alderman of the city's 27th Ward. At 36, he looks back on a childhood of fun and adventure, but he also admits the community's long struggle with poverty, gangs and drugs was evident when he reached his teenage years.

Angie Smith was the second of her mother's four children. Her family moved into the row houses when she was a young girl. Now 33, she and her two children live in a row house of their own. She believes children behave differently today than when she was growing up here. There was much more to do, she says, and everybody seemed to get along.

Having lived in the Cabrini-Green community on and off for 27 years — in the row houses, whites and reds — Anita Walker says that despite troubled times, her family has made the best of it. As a mother of three, her primary focus has been to keep her son from suffering the same fate as her brother.

Though he is a frequent visitor, Richard Parker, Rosalind's 45-year-old brother, moved out of the row house neighborhood not long after high school. He witnessed acts of violence when he was growing up, and says Cabrini-Green has only worsened since he left. He doesn't see much hope for its future.

Meanwhile, Zora Washington and Lillian Davis Swope (who we met in Chapter One) continue to provide insight and inspiration to row house residents, like Rosalind Kirkman-Bey, who came after them.

As for Rosalind, she doesn't know how long she will continue to live in the Cabrini-Green area, but she says this community will always be home to her. "This is where most of my memories are."

Gerald Washington: We lived in a row house over on Cambridge, yeah, 841 North Cambridge, and I remember getting in trouble one time when I was a boy. My grandmother lived across the street on Iowa and I went across the street to get something to eat but I wasn't supposed to cross the street, even though it wasn't a busy street. I was only about six or seven then, but I remember that because that's the only kind of trouble kids would really get in back then.

I had a lot of good times over in this community 'cause there was always something to do. When we were staying on Cleveland, they used to have what they called these block parties, and everybody would come out for it and people would skate, and there would be live music, and we'd have polishes, chicken, hot dogs, hamburgers, and it was like a little carnival on the street and it was real cool and a lot of fun. And every year the Black Rodeo would come to town and set up over on Seward Park, and it was great for us to see all those black cowboys doing their thing. Everybody would come out, and everybody was like one family. It was like the little saying, "it takes a village." I think back then it was holding true for this community, at least in the row houses. I wasn't too familiar with what was going on up on the other end, in the reds or the white projects, as they call them. We really didn't go up there.

Rosalind Kirkman-Bey: We lived in 500 when I was born, in 1966. Then, when I was five we moved to the row houses. It was much neater back then. The residents who lived here took more care with their yard and really watched over their children. I went to Jenner school, and the teachers, ya know, they would work with the kids and the children were willing to learn more....When we were young we used to go to the tutoring program down at Montgomery Ward. Somewhere I have a picture of me with my tutor, but it's been a long time.

For fun we used to go to the Lower North Center. They used to have dance groups there and they used to give d.j. parties and they had different gatherings like that....I used to love going downtown, to Water Tower, to Rush Street, and they used to have a game room called Rubus or something and I believe it was on Rush Street, and I used to love going there....I rarely went to the basement parties because my mom was very strict.

Lillian Davis Swope: After a period of time, public housing was growing predominately all black. So, what they did over here, they'd taken the whites from the row houses, and when they opened up the high-rise building, they said all the whites that lived in the row houses who wanted to could move to 500-502 Oak – what we called it was the integrated building. There was a majority of whites there but the rest of the neighborhood was more black, and they didn't particularly care for that, so they gradually left.

Walter Burnett: My earliest memory about Cabrini is when we first moved there. We actually moved to the white side, 714 North Division. It was a nice building. My mom was a teenager and my dad was 20. My mom and dad knew everybody. Everybody in the building knew everyone. Everyone helped everyone. At that time, I was about five years old, so this is like in 1969. My dad had just landed a truck driver's job with National T, which used to be right over on Larrabee and Hobbie Streets. It was exciting for them. My parents, as I said, they were young. Most of the parents

Rosalind Kirkman-BEy

around there, just like today, were young, you know. They were young and they had their growing pains.

But we weren't there for long. I guess my parents must have had too many kids and the apartment wasn't big enough, so they needed a bigger place. They got a three bedroom down in the row houses, and it was beautiful. I mean it was like we moved to the suburbs. It was so different than the projects, no elevators, none of that stuff. We had grass to play in, we were able to hang our clothes outside...that's how nice it used to be. You could hang your clothes out there and no one would bother them.

Gerald Washington: I have two brothers and two sisters, I'm the fourth. A lot of the people I grew up with didn't have a father. My father was always home and he's still home. He helped raise me. As a matter of fact, that was the person who I was most afraid of growing up...it was always what my father would think or what he would do if I did something wrong. It's not that my father was bad, but he just didn't take no medicine. My mom didn't either. We had this wooden chair and I'd always have to sit in this chair when I was bad and that's where she would whoop me. I used to call it the electric chair.

But, like I said, we used to get into a different kind of trouble than kids today. I can remember our yard, before it got kind of a makeover we didn't have any grass back there, and me and my younger brother and some friends would gather up some dirt and we'd make what we called dirt bombs, and we'd put them in some brown paper bags and we'd throw them over the roof onto the street on the Mohawk side. We'd do little crazy stuff like that....We used to go up under the house, there's like a crawl space, and we'd have a little club house under there where we'd go to just have some conversation and hangout.

When any of us kids really got into it — I remember there were two kids who would always be fightin' about something — but one of the older teens, he had to be about 18 or 19, he had a pair of boxing gloves and whenever we would get into some altercation he would go and get his boxing gloves and let us settle it like that, instead of really fightin' each other. We'd go into the gangway and that would be the boxing ring and we'd go at it, but box, not really try and kill each other.

Angie Smith: We moved in the row houses when I was about 10 or 11. I remember we used to play hide and seek and other games with a group of kids from the neighborhood. I went to Jenner.

I was the second of four kids, two boys and two girls, and I have two kids myself....When I was growin' up my mama had people look out for us when she wasn't around. My mom was a strict person, she always spoke what was on her mind. She'd tell you right from wrong. She would say you got a mind of your own, use it to the best of your knowledge.

On all the holidays everybody would meet up at my grandmother's house on Hudson Street. So I look back on happy memories. In the summer time they used to have movies on the basketball court on Hudson. Right outside, they'd set it up and they'd show movies. And the block parties was always fun, and we still do it on our street.

Richard Parker: We moved here in, I think, '66. I was in kindergarten and I remember when King was assassinated. That's like my first memory because they had set the cleaners on fire at Oak and Larrabee. We stayed at 500 on the 11th floor so we had a chance to watch it all. I remember it because they had tanks out there...going down Oak street. Every night we watched the tanks go down the street. It was kind of fun because you see tanks, something you play with, so for me it was like a big toy.

And I can remember the big snowstorm Chicago had in 1969. It came up to our shoulders. For me, I was just four, so it was way up to my head....We didn't go to school the whole week.

We lived in 500 until '75, and then we moved in the row houses to 832 Cleveland. It was a big change. It was like, ya know when you're kids, it was like we were moving to a house. Moving from the projects, it was like a house atmosphere because we had an

upstairs and downstairs, we had a front yard and back yard. You had more places to run and play hide-and-go-seek.

Walter Burnett: When I moved there, I was so small that I don't remember if it was mixed or not, but peoples' doors would be open all night. They would leave their doors open like if it was real hot outside, they'd leave the back doors open all night, not worry about anything. Folks didn't have bars on their doors like they do nowadays. When we moved there, it was nice. Our biggest activity used to be running around the block, and we would flip on old mattresses.

We would go to the Lower North Center and play kickball, dodge ball, basketball, go camping. They had a lot of activities going on over there. We used to go swimming across from the center, behind the 939 apartments.

And people used to have candy stores. I remember when I was a boy scout, my boy scout leader was Mr. Harvey. Mr. Harvey used to stay down on the 800 block of Cambridge and he used to be the boy scout leader, but he also would sell candy out of his house – snowballs, potato chips, penny candy. A couple of folks used to do that occasionally. Also, there was a lady on Cleveland who used to do that. I forget her name. She started in her house too, but then she bought an old truck and she started doing it out of that old truck, and business grew for her. From that, she ended up buying her a building and moved out of the neighborhood, but she still came over and sold the candy.

Gerald Washington: Al Carter's program was really great back then. He had Al Carter's Olympics and every kid in the community would come out. You'd have close to 1,500 kids involved in all these events out on the dirt behind Seward Park, because there was no grass out in the back at that time...and they had little league baseball and basketball tournaments. There was always something to do.

Anita Walker: I came over here when I was 14...we lived at 544 [Division] for a year and then moved to the row houses. It was peaceful, this was the 1970s. We got a four-bedroom where we were able to forget to lock the door at night, and when we woke up everything was still there. People, ya know, respected what was yours and they didn't trash your area. There was respect for the elders and there was self-respect instilled in the children.

But because we moved over here after the two policemen were killed, it was already taboo to live here. It was just like the West Side projects, but they didn't want to come over to see us because it was Cabrini-Green. That really made me mad, and I'd tell them it's not like that, but they stereotype it and the label gets thrown on everybody....Cabrini, in my opinion, is still no different than some neighborhoods on the West Side, but Cabrini just got a lot of publicity. If there was one killing over here, there were several out West, just not enough for the media to cover it, or a lack of concern.

I guess at times it did feel like it was our own island, but we had to make the best of it. I do remember, when I was very young, my mother saw some guys beating a kid out in a parking lot. She called the police and said, someone's getting beat down here. No one came so she had to call again. Still, nobody came. This had to be about 1971. They were still beating him and, finally, she called and said, a white woman's getting beat over here. Sixteen police cars showed up real quick. Then, they came to our house and told my mama she better not make any more false reports.

Rosalind Kirkman-Bey: I always considered the row houses, the reds and the whites as the same neighborhood. There's still the distinction today between the row houses and the project buildings, but it's really one neighborhood. There wasn't a boundary back then, but everything is like a boundary now. But the way I see it is like, the row houses is a lot different...it's a lot safer to be goin' in the row houses than goin' in the projects. My sister lived in 500-502 [high-rise] and they had experiences where some guys she was dating both had been robbed, but coming in the row houses they never had that. Me personally, I don't like goin' in the projects and unless I really had to I wouldn't

go into the projects. I guess by it being more secluded it's easier for something to happen. In the row houses it's easier to know your neighbors.

Walter Burnett: It's funny, because growing up you didn't really know people who lived outside of the row houses, because you mostly deal with the people you live around....When I got older is when I started knowing people from the other areas.

Zora Washington: I don't think there was any separation between the row houses and the high-rises back then. Even when the William Green's were built, there was no hesitancy about welcoming them in. I think it took the policemen getting killed and then it was like there was a division. How it came up, I don't know, but there was a division. But I don't think we had any real big problems over here until those two policemen got shot (in 1970), and I think that's when everything really turned around.

Lillian Davis Swope: When the high-rises first went up, people thought it was wonderful. But, they soon found out it was a disaster. I, at one time, wanted to move in the high-rise, but it was too many problems. You know, you and I could open our door at the same time and it was too congested. Then the children, the children were doing okay in the play lots and everything, but eventually, you know, if the mother's on the 15th floor and something happened to her child out in the play yard, so, that wasn't kosher, either. And then the elevators, and the playgrounds and things that wasn't kept up like it should of been. And, none of the apartments was kept up like they shoulda' been...you could just see that change. And then they started the gang activities, and kids was fighting amongst themselves, parents fighting amongst themselves.

Zora Washington: There was supposed to be a difference between the row house people, the reds and the whites as they were called. The row house people supposedly were the elite. How did that happen? I have no idea. In fact, [a teacher] at Jenner tried to tell me that there was a difference between the people and I told her no, we were all the same. How could she say that? And besides, she only worked at Jenner, she didn't have a taste of any of the other people around here, but I came to find out she was not alone. Some other people felt the same way.

I have never felt that there was a difference and still I remember my first day working here [at Schiller school]. I worked at Jenner for 17 years and when I came here, my husband told me, he said, "Zora, you cannot go over there. You do not know those people. You can't go over there acting like you did when you worked at Jenner."

So when I came over here I was trying to be a nice Zora. It did not work. It lasted maybe a day and a half...because two little boys called me a "B" and I had never, ever encountered that. I was very angry to say the least. I picked them up by their necks. They were walking on their toes going to the office, and I literally threw them in there to the assistant principal. I told him, look, you tell those children I don't play with kids, and I turned around and I walked out. After I cooled down a little bit I went back to the classroom, I got their names and I went to their houses to talk with their parents. My husband told me, don't you go in no [white] buildings over there....I don't care where you are, what's the difference? I went into the houses when I worked at Jenner, and I go into the houses over here.

Anita Walker: My own childhood was checkered, very checkered... the good, the bad, the good, the bad. I had to grow up fast, I had to adapt to my surroundings. I had to act older, and I had to be more responsible....I was admired and despised at the same time because people thought I talked proper, because I spoke correct English they labeled me as proper-talkin', like I thought I was cute. I never had a lot of friends, but I could get along with anyone who could get along with me.

It wasn't my goal to live in Cabrini-Green. It wasn't my goal to ever have kids [*laughing*]. I came from a family of eight and I couldn't stand children...and when I went to have an abortion when I first got pregnant, I went to a doctor on Division Street and he told me there were people paying him to make it possible

for them to get pregnant. So I said, then take this and give it to them, I don't know what it is to be responsible. And I didn't. I was totally clueless as to what to do for a baby. I hadn't even learned what to do for myself, ya know, I hadn't shopped and done things for myself enough to know what a baby needed. Sure, my mom had children that she kept bringin' in and I had to deal with it growing up, but I didn't like it. I mean, I loved them, but I didn't like the responsibility....The situation was that, my mom was married, he beat her, and I didn't like that, so whatever it took to make it all right, I did. That meant watching the kids.

When I did eventually have my own I didn't get on public aid until 1976, when my third child was born...then I moved to the row houses on my own and had responsibilities.

RICHARD PARKER

Richard Parker: Cabrini really was never as bad as people say it was. But there was times it was violent, like when [*laughing*] I got kidnapped one time. I look back on it now and laugh, it's funny. I was at Jenner, and at that time you could go home for lunch. My mom was very strict, and we was always told at lunch time, come straight home and eat lunch. So me and a friend of mine, Greg, decided we were going to go to the grocery store and buy candy. So we go to the store, right around Oak and Larrabee, that used to be a candy store. We was going into the store and two guys are out front, teenagers, probably about 17 or 18, and one says, are you the guys who was botherin' my dog? We were kids so we just said, yeah, we did, [*laughing*] what about it. So the guy says, oh he's smart, and they say we're gonna get you, and if we catch you we're going to kill you. So we're like ya, ya, ya and running around the cars and kinda laughing. We're kids.

But they actually caught us and took us to **1017** on the fourth floor – they grabbed us and walked us over there. They get us up there and say you guys bothered our dog so we're gonna beat you up or rough you up. They're saying, what should we do with them? One guy says, we should kill them. So we started crying. I'm in fourth grade then, and we're up in this hallway by the elevator, and so one guy says let's suffocate them. The other guy says, no that would take too long. Then the other guy said, let's shoot them. My friend and I, we looked at one another and my friend really started crying, and then I started cryin'. The guy pulled a gun out and he says, well, I only have one bullet. Who am I going to shoot? I said, shoot him [*laughing*]. And, of course, my friend pointed at me, and we were going back forth....And the one guy says, I'll tell you what, let's line them up together, put a gun to their head and shoot both at the same time. So we both got back and in front of each other and we were going back and forth and we was crying and crying and finally one of the neighbors, this lady, came outside and said, what's going on here? We're crying and she says, what are you guys doing with these little kids? And the guys run off.

I went back to school that day and had to tell the teacher I got kidnapped and she said, sure you did. Sure you did.

Lillian Davis Swope: We had what you call the friendly officers, or officer friendly. They were stationed here. They knew me real well, and they used to come by and talk....Well, by the two officers getting killed over there by Seward Park [in 1970], they stopped the friendly officers from coming out in the area. A lot of men had built up confidence in these officers, it was kind of a shame that they had to discontinue that program.

Walter Burnett: My mom actually took me out of Jenner school in the third grade because I had got lost on the camping trip. We went camping, a whole bunch of us and so everybody was like no man, I know my way, it's this way believe me, and so everybody followed them. It was the blind leading the blind and we got lost for the whole day. Then they found us, finally, and we came home and my mom was so mad, she took me out of the school. She took me out of the school and she put me in St. Dominic's for third, fourth and fifth grade. They had a school at that time, so I went there for a couple of years and then they closed down and then I went to Byrd.

Of course, going over to Byrd school I got exposed to a lot of kids from [the red high-rises] like 1150-1160 and 364-365. At that time, 1150-1160 was a bad building. The Stones had that, the El Rukn Stones had moved into that building and they were gang bangers, but they were more business gang bangers. They were more into prostitution. Drugs was not that exposed at that time. More so prostitution and extortion and things like that.

So you started seeing a few things and we started seeing young girls grow up and get fast. Cooley High was still there, they hadn't torn it down yet. But, ya know, it was still nice. It was still a nice neighborhood. People still had respect, even though the guys were doing their little thing, it wasn't all out in the street yet. It was just in their building, so you only knew about it if you heard about it.

Some of the kids were a little tough and bad and they were starting to get worse. Other than that, the majority of the folks were good. All my friends' parents were respectable. A lot of them worked, but if they didn't work they still had decent homes and took care of their families and had good morals and all those good things. The families weren't dysfunctional. The biggest thing around was alcohol at that time. It wasn't as dysfunctional as things are nowadays. It was still a great neighborhood, man. We used to have so much fun.

Richard Parker: In '73 I remember when the movie studio came over and started filming [the movie] "Cooley High." They had a lot of stand-ins but we wasn't old enough to get in. I think that was the last year of the school. Everybody wanted to go to Cooley because Cooley was the school to be in. I went there only once to watch a basketball game, that was my only way of getting into it.

I remember going to school and they'd have different parts of the row houses closed off when they were doing the filming. You could see the camera men, the lights, it was a pretty big set-up....Everybody around here's seen that movie hundreds of times. People thought it was realistic, like how it really was back in the time. In the film itself everybody was out having a good time. There wasn't really much gangs and people doing drugs. And like I said, there were a lot of quarter parties, where you got to pay a quarter to get in. Everybody felt it was pretty much as close as you can get to it...[and] people from outside the community wanted to see what Cabrini was all about, the same was true after "Candy Man." That was filmed here too, which made the flow of traffic through here pretty heavy.

Lillian Davis Swope: One of my sons was killed on the hard top, which is where they're building the new Jenner school now. That was 1974 and he was about 17....At the time of his death, I felt like moving. But, I had to rationalize with myself that this was happening all over the City of Chicago, and it wasn't gonna make any difference where I moved at, whether I moved or not, because the same thing was happening in all communities. Anyway, it was like a drug mix up....There has been a lot of stories about it. They said an individual killed him, then they say a police officer killed him. So, we never did actually find out what had happened. All we know is a young man went to jail for it – he was given time for it. But, that was the type of life my son was living, and you could almost expect something violent was going to happen to him – and, uh, so, it happened.

Anita Walker: Then came the era when children began having children. Children became pregnant for one reason or another – rape or carelessness – but they became parents too soon, and they began to fill up the vacancies.

I came over here with the respect that if I couldn't do it in front of my mother, I couldn't do it around their mother, I couldn't do it on the corner or down the street. A lot of children just wanted to get out of the house, so sometimes pregnancy was the thing to do, to get your own check, and do your own thing. Without them havin' that basic foundation of respect, self-respect and self-determination and uh, self-esteem, a lot of what the outcome was children who made up their own rules, who became parents who allowed their children to do anything and, with people coming over infiltrating money and drugs, things just got worse. You get kids growing up any way they want to, treating people any way they want to and they don't have the compassion to be concerned about how it is for anyone else.

Rosalind Kirkman-Bey: My children have more freedom now than I had growing up. Even though I grew up here, my knowledge is limited because my mother was so strict. She was strict for a reason, she wanted to make sure we didn't follow the wrong crowd, that my four brothers wouldn't get into the gangs....For a while she wouldn't even let us play out on the sidewalk...and the kids would tease us and call us early birds because by seven or eight o'clock we had to go to bed. We were considered early birds.

I remember church services, and dinners my mom would make. She was married and got divorced, so she was a single mom raising six children. I think she did pretty good. She kept the boys away from gangs and drugs, and that was mainly what changed [this neighborhood]. And later I noticed the parents basically stopped caring....You'd see more parents not working or parents who were working stopped working. That was also a major difference.

Richard Parker: I got close to joining a gang. They were going to initiate me. It was right out in front of Holy Family church. They had like six or seven guys lined up, and to get initiated you had to go through there and they hit you in your chest and hit you in your back. And my father must have seen me out the window from the porch and he came downstairs and got me out of there. He said, have you lost your mind? You're not joining no gang. I was in sixth grade. The guys were bigger – like in eighth grade, from Cooley – and that's why we went. They were initiating me into the Deuces.

Our life was based around my father and his saying that you can't move out until you get an education. When you get home from school you do your homework first and then you do your chores. He'd say, without an education you can't be nothing. You don't want to be stuck with nothing.

I got interested in electronics because of my father. He was teaching me how to repair TVs and things around the house so I learned it from fourth grade on how to work with tools, and I've been good with it.

My father was one of the highly respected persons around here. People more like feared him because he was a strong father and he was given a lot of respect. It was like 50-50 on parenthood here. That's really why they call it a project, because most people come from broken homes. But really when they built Cabrini it wasn't supposed to be here this long. It was just to get you started off. You weren't supposed to be here for good – it was just to get people on their feet and give them a chance to move on.

Walter Burnett: I was still just a kid but I remember them filming "Cooley High." A lot of folks from 1156 was in that movie. Rick Stone and a couple of those guys....Oh yeah, it was very exciting.

It was around that time we started hearing about folks getting killed and things like that. Before we got out of grammar school, the gang fights were starting. Then as I got older and went to high school, that's when gangs really got worse.

I went to Wells High School like most folks in my area did, and there were Puerto Rican gangs and on the West Side was Vice Lords and Disciples and all that stuff. So gangs started and you started seeing more drug activity. It became more of an open thing.

Angie Smith: I went to Wells High School, and me and my friend would walk to school all the time so we could save on car fare. It was a fun time for me, but for kids today it's more of a challenge. The problem is more drugs than gangs, I think. But kids today have to watch out for a lot of things.

Gerald
Washington

Gerald Washington: I think I was grumpy, and people knew our family in the neighborhood and knew that none of us would be in to the gang stuff. And, I don't think they would want to deal with my parents because if my parents were to find out, not only would they get on us but they'd go after whoever was trying to get us involved. Everybody in the community knew us in some form or fashion, especially in the row houses...everybody in that little village, if you want to call it that, knew everybody else. I mean everybody knew everybody because everyone was out doing something. Now people stay in the house and you don't know who's moved in next door.

But, ya know, you hear about Cabrini-Green a lot more than anywhere else because Channel Two, Five, Seven and Nine are right in our back yard. They just come on over here when anything goes down.

Lillian Davis Swope: You take an individual that is seeking an apartment, and you're trying to find another apartment. You tell them where you live, Cabrini-Green, and automatically that's not gonna be your apartment. Or credit, if you're trying to get...anything you do, you tell them where you live, and that's thumbs down. The services that you need – say like, Sears, and your big stores – they don't want to service you 'cause of where you live. I'm a dialysis patient, and I have a hard time to get the drivers to pick me up in the morning.

Zora Washington: You'd hear on the news, there were three people shot in Cabrini-Green. A liquor store was robbed in Cabrini-Green. But in the same news, way up north, it doesn't say on the Gold Coast or wherever that something was robbed or there were two men that got shot or whatever. They didn't put the names of the community with those actions, only if it happened in Cabrini-Green.

A lot of people don't really know but some of your biggest prejudices come from other black people who don't live in the area. As a young parent when people found out that I came from Cabrini it was like, oh, dear Lord, you live there, I would never guess. My oldest daughter, where she works she told them she came from Cabrini and they were saying, well, you don't look like you came from Cabrini. So how do you look when you come from Cabrini?

When you get down to it, cut color, cut everything – people are people. You've got the good, the bad and your in-between. It's just as simple as that. You've got parents that want to parent and you've got parents that are not going to parent.

WALTER BURNETT

Walter Burnett: When I was 15 or 16, I worked at a Burger King on State and Chicago Avenue. I mean I'm right in the heart of a lot of different people. I didn't feel any different. I was accepted. You know, people didn't have a problem with me, a young man working, etc. I'd walk around there all the time going to work. It wasn't a big deal, so I never really got into stereotypes like, there's a white person, they don't like us or they won't give us any of that.

Until I got into politics, that's when I started seeing the segregation. When you get into politics, you see it a lot, you know, and you start identifying people as Polish, Greek, Italian, you know them by their last name or you can tell by their accent. I never knew the difference before. You know where the neighborhoods are. You learn more about that in politics.

We have a segregated city. Growing up in Cabrini-Green, I never noticed that...because when you go to Wells High School you're around different people, but they're your friends, you know. Italians, Spanish, Ukrainian, Polish, they're your friends.

Richard Parker: I seen people get killed myself. It's not a good sight. I can remember one girl I went to school with – I was probably about a sophomore in high school so she had to be about 15 – but she was married and she was messing around with some guy while her husband was at work. He must have come home from work and caught the guy in his house...and so...the husband has a .38 and the guy ran out of the house just unaware of him. He shoots him in the back. The guy is still running so he shoots him in the head and blows his brains completely out.

I'm curious, and I want to see where the guy has his brains shot out, so we walk over there and we see brains splattered all over the walk and it's pretty ugly. And then I witnessed my niece's boyfriend get shot in the face by a nine millimeter...and that was ugly. All over another woman, which is stupid. Both are painted pictures in my mind, but I can't say it was really that bad for me here.

My years at Wells was probably one of my best times of life. I was in the band and I had a chance to play in a concert with the band. And I had a teacher, Mr. Mims, who was like a second father to me. So I didn't have fears really.

Our high school years were all about parties, and who is going to throw the best party. And who was the best dressed person or whatever....The greatest fear I had was how I looked.

Walter Burnett: As I got a little older, I started going and hanging out at, well, I had a couple of girlfriends at 1150 and 60 and started hangin' around 1161 and 534, you know. Each building is different. Each area was different. It was like there were cultures in different areas. The row houses, the fellas in row houses were not like the fellas in 1161-1159, you know. The fellas in 1150 and 1160 was not like the people in 1161 and 1159, or like the guys in the row houses. Everybody had their different characters.

I was fortunate because I had the opportunity to travel amongst all of them and befriended all of them, and I didn't have to gangbang. As I got older gangbangin' was really prevalent and if you were in a certain gang or perceived to be in a certain gang, you couldn't come inside the area. I never had that problem thank God. I was able to go all over.

As I said, the guys in 1150 and 1160 were mostly like businessmen, basically big time into drugs and prostitution and all that stuff. The guys in 1161 and 1159 were more gangsters. They were Disciples, they were gangsters, they did their drugs and stuff but they were rough, and the row houses at that time was not seen as really having gangs....Let me put it this way, I didn't know guys from the row houses were in gangs until I got older, because even if they were in gangs, they would hide it so much. Even if they were selling drugs, they would hide it so much. You wouldn't know it. You didn't know it. They were older to me and I never knew it until I got older.

I found out that there were some guys who were this and who were that...and every once in a while you would see a guy that you know who hung out in the projects who lived in the row houses. Anyone that was really gangbangin' hung out in the projects or hung out outside of the neighborhood, out of the row houses. If they hang outside the row houses, that's really where the activity is. None of the activity was really in the row houses. They didn't have that much negative stuff going on, for whatever reason.

Angie Smith: It's closed down now, but before they moved people out of 500-502 there used to be conflicts that would go on between the high-rises and the row houses....Guns were shootin' back and forth and I was living on Oak Street so it was like we was stuck right in the middle of it. We'd have to sit on the floor in case a bullet come through the door. Actually, one did come through my door. My sister was stayin' with me at the time, and that really scared her.

Zora Washington: It took my youngest daughter getting shot for me to make the final decision to move. That was just it for me because I was the one that was always just hanging on. This place is home, this is where we live – basically it was my home because I was the one that had been raised here. But you think about it, 14 years ago we were paying almost $700 for rent – 14 years ago. My mortgage is still not as high as my rent was down in the row houses. I remember one time – we didn't have a checking account or anything like that – and I remember one time I went to the currency

exchange to pay my rent and a couple of my friends walked with me. My friend saw me pull out a roll of bills because I had to deal with cash and our rent was $649, if I'm not mistaken, and that did not include utilities because in the row houses you paid light and gas. And she was saying, Zora, you give that kind of money up to live here?

But this is where I live...and that was something you had to do and I felt insulted when people would get on the news and talk about people paying $50 for rent. I am not one of those people. Not everybody is on welfare that lives here. That's still true.

Anita Walker: Let me say that I have no respect for gangs. But, I had exposure to gangs before we moved over here....What I like was the days when, if you got your butt whipped, you knew not to do whatever you did to 'cause the problem, and that's how it was.

I got here and saw a bunch of little boys trying to imitate, takin' over property that didn't belong to them. But with most of them not having fathers they didn't know how or what to imitate, and a lot of the fathers are locked up, okay, so I feel it's like they're trying to play a piano in the dark. They don't have a clue as to what their places are. And, because of that, I have seen a lot of death over here.

I had a brother who felt that he didn't have to hide behind my skirt-tails or anybody else's and he decided, stupidly, that he was going to come with his own gang. I remember him once telling me, 'Nita, I'm very good with my feet and my hands, and it didn't dawn on me at all, I was like, what is he talking about? And then maybe two weeks later, three guys, with three guns killed him. They told him that he had to drop his fork, ya know, disrespect his gang, because it was their way or no way. One of them, um, I think he spent a year in jail.

My brother had just turned 18. Eighteen's the turning point for a lot of guys, and that year I had a relative killed at 1117, uh, one that was killed at 1340 the next year, and one that was killed in 1015 and it was just, like, constant teenagers that were turning

18 and getting killed, and all these guys that did the killing worked with someone who gave them guns....It's not a speculation or my opinion, it's fact that these guys sold drugs, did drugs, were in a gang and had guns, and these guys are no longer here. The ones that are here are locked up, with no chance of parole.

What it is that I see is more drugs are infiltrated through gang members, so that means someone, whoever it is, can bring in drugs and guns through the gangs without ever being detected. That's the purpose of the gangs that I see now....This is infiltrated trouble, and that's how the gangs exist.

Walter Burnett: You know, I never really saw Cabrini as being bad. I saw some things on the TV and everything....Cabrini used to be on television all the time. And you would hear it when you visited your relatives and stuff, yeh, this is my cousin, he's from Cabrini-Green, ya know, and that kind of crap [*laughing*].

They would be like man, you live over there? Wow, it's bad over there. You'd be like, man, it's not no different than here, it's not that bad. I kind of didn't like that to be quite honest about it, because it was no different than anywhere else. I used to go up north sometimes and you know, the North Side is more of a mixing pot and, to me, in growing up where I grew up at, it used to seem ten times worse than Cabrini.

But the funny thing is when you're a part of it you end up being conformed to whatever changes happen and it just becomes a natural part of how things are. I mean, there were several times where shootings would happen. It was natural for us to get down sometimes, to hide up under the bed. That occurred, you know. When guys first started getting machine guns, they were coming around and you know, stuff like that would happen occasionally.... Sometimes we see things, but we don't see things, until you really think about it.

Angie Smith: People are gonna say what they want, but you actually have to live in the community to judge it....I've gotten a lot of different reactions before. If you go out or something and a guy approaches you and asks where you live, when you say Cabrini they have second thoughts about you. Sometimes they say, how can you live over there? That makes me feel angry toward them 'cause you can't judge it. You only hear what you wanna hear...you have to actually live in the neighborhood to judge it. It doesn't matter where a person lives at, it's based on the person and if you like them or not.

Walter Burnett: Mayor [Jane] Byrne didn't move in there. I remember when she was supposed to move in to Cabrini. I remember how they came and infiltrated the area, gave it a lot of attention. Yeah, I remember that garbage.

The [residents] thought it was BS, yeah. They knew. Everybody knew she wasn't there. It was media stuff. The public didn't know, but we knew.

I don't know why it gets so much attention, because there are a lot of places so much more worse than Cabrini. I saw that when I got older. Henry Horner Homes, it's worse than Cabrini. The conditions were a lot worse than Cabrini.

Zora Washington: It wasn't so much drugs as I would say violence. Drugs I think were still basically under cover in the '80s. You knew they were there, but they were still under cover, but the gangs and stuff that's when they were visible.

As I said, that's one of the things that made me move because when my daughter got shot, she just happened to be sitting over by her boyfriend's house on Oak Street. This young boy wasn't shooting at her, he was shooting at somebody else, but it wasn't dark outside, it was broad daylight. So that was the turning point — for me it was.

If the bullet had moved about an inch — she got shot believe it or not in the rear end and it came up through. If it had moved an inch she would have died and she was very, very afraid. She was very afraid. She was afraid in the hospital. She was afraid to be left alone. Whenever she heard footsteps she would break

down....She was afraid afterwards so I really didn't have too much choice but to move.

Anita Walker: The key word is raising, so that the [kids] can't do down the street what they wouldn't do in front of you. That's raising....My son's going to be pushed out if I have to move, because he's gotta be a man, he's gotta make a difference in the world, and provide — as well as my girls — but my boys have to be motivated to be responsible for your sisters as well as your mother, your girlfriend, your babies, ya know, they're the strong point, the men.

So I tell him a lot, you let those gangs know about me, 'cause I'll be at every meeting, I'll let them know he's not going to be able to come out, he can't. It's all as one...and with the fact that I had a pair of brothers involved, they know me, and I will be at meetings and they don't want me to be there because I might say something or do something, but I don't fear man or beast, I only fear God, and however I must leave here, I must leave one day. So for him I will go tooth and nail.

Walter Burnett: There was always good people there too. There was always more good people there than the bad. The bad stood out. The bad stood out and they made you think that they was like the majority, but they weren't...and they're still not.

Gloria Purifoy is singing. And clapping. And stomping her feet in the front hallway at Friederich von Schiller Elementary School. With a wide smile and bright eyes, she urges a small boy named Marcus to join in. He bashfully resists before softly surrendering the words to "Devotion," an old Earth, Wind and Fire tune. Gloria's been teaching the song to a group of children who are part of the after-school program she leads at the school. "Hey, this was the song when we were coming up," she reminds Marcus.

When Gloria was coming up, her life was filled with the activities and opportunities offered by youth programs in the Cabrini-Green area. Today, she's even busier, having devoted herself to keeping those activities and opportunities alive for the next generation. As program director of YouthNet, one of 25 such programs in Chicago supported by the Mayor's Office and the Near North Development Corporation, Gloria works with students aged eight to eighteen. She's 27. Her childhood experiences, she says, have helped shape the programming at YouthNet.

"My sister and I were pretty much raised in those organizations," she says. "I mean, I went to Sunshine, and I went to CYCLE for tutoring, I went to Fellowship of Friends for club, I went to Lower North Center for Drama Club, and that was pretty much what we did....My tutors or recreational leaders [at Sunshine] were all teens from my community. That was our family, and those were my friends." The organizations she mentions continue to serve young people of the community. "There's a lot of resources in this neighborhood that people just don't realize."

Ironically, Gloria's program serves students of the Green Homes, or white high-rise buildings, while she was born and raised in the red high-rise buildings. Although she counted few friends from the white buildings when she was growing up, she sees Cabrini-Green as one community — and, she recognizes an equal need for organizations that provide support and guidance to the area's youth.

Gloria was not yet born when Chicago policemen Anthony Rizzato and James Severin were killed in a field behind a red high-rise in 1970, and she was too young to remember when Hollywood came to Cabrini to film "Cooley High," or when Chicago Mayor Jane Byrne came to Cabrini to live. She does remember the increase in gang activity and drug use in the community, but she says she never paid much attention. She was too busy.

"I respect my mom for getting us involved in these different agencies," Gloria says, "and for making sure we stuck with it....All of those people played a factor, and an important role in how I turned out, how my sister turned out and how friends of mine turned out." Like Gloria, who now lives just west of Cabrini-Green, many of her childhood friends went on to college and moved into careers that, as Gloria says, give back to the community. "We're educators, social workers and social service providers. Even my friend who is in financing, she deals with helping minorities to understand the process of saving and home buying and things."

Gloria is convinced programs like YouthNet can help mold young people into productive adults, no matter where they come from. "In being active in those agencies when we were young," she says, "we were able to see it was possible to obtain the same goals that anybody else was obtaining in any other neighborhood...because the very people who grew up in it were doing so. They were living, breathing proof that it was possible."

Gary Hall is also proof that young people from the area can exceed the expectations of others. A 32-year-old Chicago attorney, he was awarded a White House Fellowship and is spending a year at work in the United States Treasury Department in Washington, D.C. Having spent the early part of his youth living in the red high-rises, Gary admits he did not openly talk about his Cabrini upbringing until recently.

Cabrini-Green is one subject Jan Morgan has no trouble talking about. In his 41 years in the community, he remembers playing ball, riding bikes and, eventually, dodging bullets. Jan has been married for 20 years and has one child and three grandchildren.

When she was in grade school, Runetta Thompson's family moved from North Carolina to Chicago and took an apartment in the 1159-1161 building on N. Larrabee Street. She says it took some time to adjust, but she soon felt comfortable in school and in the neighborhood. More than 20 years later, with four children and a job that keeps her on the move, she's no longer as content with her surroundings.

When she turned 21, Evelyn Turner felt like it was time to leave Cabrini-Green, so she did. She moved to the North Side and took college courses before completing paralegal studies at Roosevelt University. Now 37, she works in real estate paralegal, keeps in touch with old friends from the neighborhood and looks back on what she describes as a happy childhood.

At 32, Steve Pratt can sound older and wiser than his years when reflecting on life in Cabrini-Green. Back when he ran with the gangs, he says, "[they] didn't hide behind guns." He still lives in the red high-rises and works nearby.

Rochelle Satchell and Marsha Crosby (who we met in Chapter Two) continue to offer a broader perspective on the red high-rises and what's become of them.

In the front hallway of Schiller school Gloria Purifoy is still singing. She's still clapping, and still stomping her feet. And so is Marcus.

gloria purifoy

Gloria Purifoy: I always felt like I was growing up in any other normal neighborhood. I grew up in a time where parents and families cared about their children. They had expectations of their children and so did the extended parents, i.e., the teachers or elders in the community. There were always positive role models that you would come in contact with. As a child growing up, I don't ever recall completely just feeling like I was in this destitute place. I don't know, I just figured I grew up like any normal child.

Jan Morgan: I was five when we moved from the row houses into 1015 Larrabee. I remember it was real sweet. We could sleep outside in the playground behind the building. You could sleep out on the porch, keep your doors unlocked and nobody would bother you. It was real nice.

We played ball from sun up to sun down. We went from baseball to football to basketball. We played hockey in the basement with our roller skates on and we'd have dust flyin' up in the air. It was fun, and we did this everyday. The field between us and the 500-502 building was our playground, right....It was a big 'ol empty field but it was our playground. That was our baseball diamond, our football field, our soccer field, whatever you can think of....I mean we'd have parties out there. This building would have a party out there this week and that building would have a party out there next week...and the older people would be out there watching us play ball. I'm talkin' about some good times...barbecues and everything. The guys here today, I never see them play ball like we did back then.

Evelyn Turner: We moved from Douglas Park to Cabrini when I was in the third grade. We moved to 923 North Sedgwick, on the first floor. We stayed there about two years, and then we moved down to 412 West Chicago Avenue, on the first floor again. I went to Richard E. Byrd School...and when we were there, it was a happy time. The gangs and the drugs and the – just the bad things that happen there now – didn't happen when we lived there.

I think the first day that we moved...it was like, still brand new, and, you know, we were thinking, we're going to an apartment, and it was totally the opposite of what we expected. We all just looked at each other like, wow is this where we're going to live? [*laughing*] But we adapted to that quickly...because everybody there had kids, and that's when people really cared about what their children did. I must have been about eight years old, maybe, in '68. It was easy to make friends, you had people all around you, you know, you met up with these people, you walked to school, you came home, do your homework. You go out for an hour, you come back, you eat your dinner.

There was Lower North Center you could go to and Seward Park. Fourth Presbyterian had a tutoring program, some folks actually got together and walked to the YMCA. It was really a lot different then than it is now....Back then, you actually cared if you made A's or B's [in school].

Back then, they always had people out who, if we needed something fixed they would be there....The janitor, Carl Williams, he lived in 911 Sedgwick on the first floor, and he kept that place spotless. He mopped from the 10th floor down to the first floor, and, you know, he'd mop the elevator also. Throwing paper down, and breaking bottles, dumping the garbage on the side of the incinerator instead of inside of the incinerator, that was like a cardinal sin, that was a no-no. You always had somebody's mother who just so happened to see you when you did this [*laughing*], and so, it was like, I cannot believe, every time I do something, there she is.

Steve Pratt: When I moved into the projects I was about 12, but before that I stayed on the outskirts of Cabrini, over on North Avenue and then on Franklin Street, but I went to Byrd school already. We moved into 929 [North Hudson]. I got three sisters.

Me and some of my buddies, we was like nine or ten, we'd go downtown, go bike riding and just explore downtown. We'd go all down by the movie shows. We'd go to the McVickers like every Sunday because they used to have the Bruce Lee movies every Sunday. We didn't miss one Sunday. Everybody wanted to be Bruce Lee back then [*laughing*].

Jan Morgan: When I was a kid we had a janitor that lived in our building, Mr. McGee. I'll never forget him either. He was a janitor slash reverend...and everything was beautiful then, this was before King was killed. The grass was green and cut, the elevator worked and everything. Then, when King passed, everything just went. Mr. McGee was still the janitor but since everything was tore up and garbage was everywhere, it was like it was just too much, like it just blew over on us or something. I mean everybody just like gave up for a while, and it was like we was all in a depression after that. We didn't have that great leader, and we was mad at everything that wasn't black, ya know. I mean I was ten years old, but I'm listening to the older people. I'm sittin' there, ya know, I can hear it. It was tragic.

Runetta Thompson: I was born in North Carolina and we moved to Chicago when I was 12 years old. When we first got here it was scary. It was very scary. I guess because we had lived in a flat level house and we moved from that to an apartment and, looking at twenty-story buildings, and ten, I had never seen that kind of housing. Where I was from you didn't have stuff like this. We moved into 1159 Larrabee.

I went to Jenner school and graduated from Jenner. The pace of life coming from North Carolina to here was totally different....I mean, people moved a whole lot faster. People act a whole lot different. Don't get me wrong, when we first moved here you had some very friendly people, but people in Chicago are different.

I had to adjust to the people first and get a feel for them before [*laughing*] I actually started mingling.

My mother and my father had separated and my father was up here, and they were deciding about getting back together. So my mother moved up here thinking her and my father was reconciling.

When we first moved here, Cabrini was, like I said, it was different, but it was clean, okay? Our building stayed clean from top to bottom. We had a janitor, a regular janitor that lived within the dwellings of the building. And the playgrounds were attached then, and the little bar fences they used to have around the buildings, they were up.

And, we had a lot of people around...I mean people would go outside and you would see people sitting on the ramps, or what they call these gangways or whatever. You would see people out there, you know, at different hours, playing their music and things. Now you don't get that. You go outside now and all you see is empty and that's it.

It was like the parents had no control. It was like they had come from a dysfunctional neighborhood and they had infected our neighborhood. That's just how I felt, and I've always said that and I know children are not to blame for what their parents have done or who they are, but this group – like I said, everybody had this respect for adults – but this group that they had moved in, it had respect for themselves, so they didn't have any respect for the rules, they didn't have respect for what had existed here....It changed from a neat place, to a hell hole.

Jan Morgan: I didn't know how to ride a bike until I was about 13, and the reason for that was when I was about six years old my mom would say, don't ride in the streets, don't ride in the streets. She drove that into my head. Well, one day all my friends are ridin' their bikes out there in the street. I was on a tricycle...so I get out there with them on Larrabee and almost get hit by a car, so my mom says, now you'll never get a bike...and she never did buy me a bike.

But we used to go to this place. It was on Wells Street and it was like the bike junk yard. We used to make our own bikes. Nobody over here bought a bike, we just went over to the bike junk yard. There were piles and piles of frames, handle bars, uh, seats, wheels...and we'd put 'em together and make our own bikes, and these bikes could outrun some brand new ten speeds.

We'd ride to Lincoln Park and we'd go to what we called Devil's Hill. It was right at Chicago Avenue and Halsted, right after the bridge. To us, it looked like it was the longest, biggest hill in the world, but I look at it today [*laughing*] and, I mean, it's a little shorty, ya know. But, we used to ride down there and you had to make this sharp turn, and if you didn't make the turn you'd end up in the Chicago River...so it was like dangerous.

We're down there in our homemade bikes thinkin' we're doin' about 100 miles per hour and you'd make that turn and – for our brakes, we didn't have the hand brakes, we used to put our foot on the back wheel and your shoe would be your brake, but then we had to get a new pair of gym shoes within two or three weeks.

Rochelle Satchell: The riots, that was Cabrini's nightmare. I mean before that you didn't see paper in the yards. We had garbage cans and benches all around. It was clean lawns. But that all changed, because some thugs moved up in here. You had some girls and guys and all they wanted to do was fight. It was a nightmare. They moved a whole new – I would say a whole 'nother culture of black folks [*laughing*] in. I was like, where did they come from? I'm being honest. There were more fights in the schools, more fights in the buildings. The basements that adults used to open up for the children for activities were bein' shut down, uh, drinking increased among teens, and smokin'. It was just a 180 degree turn.

The process that the Chicago Housing Authority had used for screening families in order to move in here, that was no screening, they was just putting families in. They didn't have time to screen because a lot of families on the West Side had been burned out [during the riots], and the mayor declared emergency housing, so it was not a screening process. They just started letting anybody and everybody in here.

Remember the Converse All-Stars? We couldn't afford them, they were like $12 per pair. We used to get what they called the Pro Wings or Pro Basketball. They costed about three or four dollars. The only guys that had All-Stars were the guys who had paper routes and stuff like that...so that encouraged everybody to get a paper route or something of that nature. You'd go to the white neighborhoods and clean their yard or shovel their snow thinkin', we gonna go get us a pair of All-Stars. You knew who was workin' and who wasn't by what gym shoes they wear.

Steve Pratt: We used to have fun back then, it was a lot more goin' on, like the block parties. But then it was like one minute you're out there having fun and the next minute some guys come down from the other end and start some trouble and then a big fight kicks off and all that. Everybody would be scattering and all kind of stuff. There were more conflicts when I was younger than now.

I remember the swimmin' pool behind 929, it was like three feet deep. We used to go in there a lot, but a lot of people would dive in and it was so shallow that they'd bust their head. It was only three feet deep. They started callin' it the bathtub. Now, kids get down in there and play baseball or kick ball. I don't know what happened, but one summer they just didn't open it anymore.

Gloria Purifoy: There used to be ministers, youth ministers, and they were closely associated with Sunshine. And we would go there for what was like little youth rallies. Our club, is what we called them. We would go and sing songs and do skits, and we would learn about the Bible....And, as we got older, we would become involved in high school rallies, then we would help with the younger kids, doing the same things that they would do with us. Eventually, that meeting of teens grew into a church, which became Fellowship of Friends.

Fellowship of Friends is really where a lot of us got our Christian base, and one of the places that we were able to grow and develop as youths. They sort of just reinforced into us the values that my mom, and my grandparents, and my aunts and uncles instilled in my sister and myself, at the time. I don't know, growing up in the neighborhood was very much different than it is now. It was freer then, it was – you were kind of free to be a kid. And, you were not forced as much as kids are today to raise yourself, or to determine right or wrong for yourself.

Rochelle Satchell: The best thing we had over here was the Black Panthers. They was providing breakfast to the community at St. Dominic's church. The gangs were here, but they weren't in an uproar....Then we got the Black Keystones and some other gangs – there was really three different gangs over here first. It really wasn't a lot of shooting, it was a lot of beating people to death. That was going on. I mean they were actually taking people and beating them to death.

Jan Morgan: After King was killed, it changed dramatically around here. It was like a depression...and that's when the gangs came. I mean there was gangs before that, but it wasn't really nothin'.... The first gangs I really remember was like in '69, the Black Stone Rangers, 'cause the Black Panthers wasn't really a gang. But then another gang formed, and another. They still weren't really that big of a deal, but it was somethin' to think about, ya know.

Then came the Blacks, the Disciples, the Vice Lords and the Deuces and the Players. The Blackstone Rangers turned into the Cobra Stones, and they was over in 1150-60 Sedgwick and the building where I stayed, 1015-1017 Larrabee, was Deuces Wild.

Marsha Crosby: Basically things started changing, I would say, not too long after I got out of high school, which was in 1967. I graduated from Cooley Vocational High School in 1967. All during the time I was in high school there probably were maybe those gangs or something, but it wasn't like we were aware of anything going on....It seemed like the older I got the gangs got much worse [and eventually] you could look out your back window and see people shooting and everything.

One memory that stands out in my mind is that two policemen got killed over there. Wow. They got shot down in back of 1119 Cleveland....I remember hearing gun shots and I just got up and looked out my bedroom window and as I got up looking out the window, I saw the policemen falling onto the ground. That stands out because it was a big field and the grass was so green and pretty and you just saw him fall – I saw him falling down to the ground. I saw him laying out there.

Of course, that caused a big uproar. The [police] came in and they were going door to door searching peoples' apartments. One bad thing about that, some people were not at home, like one family, they were on vacation, and they just tore through and broke their door down. That was something; that was a big thing. That stands out vividly. Of course, after this, the gang warfare got very bad.... They said those policemen got sniped, I think, out of 1150 Sedgwick, one of those buildings. It was like a sniper thing.

Steve Pratt: Okay, at 911 Hudson, they got the basement down there and we used to skate down there and they had a game room down there, pool tables, ping pong. I miss that, and then the Lower North Center would have skating parties over there.... As far as the basement at 911, Mr. Elax Taylor was the one who would run that. He stayed on the first floor, but he moved away and I think that was it.

For a little while there a lot of fights would break out 'cause guys from the other end used to come over there, sometimes they'd come down and it was like peace, but other times somebody would come down and they couldn't control their alcohol or whatever and somethin' would just kick off.

I think the white projects have always had somethin' against the red projects, some personal animosity. They can't seem to stay away from over here 'cause we got more goin' on over here than they got over there.

Rochelle Satchell: The place began to deteriorate, because the services were no longer rendered, and you couldn't keep it up. Like for instance, all the stairways used to have doors to them, and that was pretty good, but they began to take the doors off, doors was hanging and it was horrible. You didn't know what was on the other side of that hanging door. They didn't have light fixtures no more. People were taking the lights. The building wasn't what they used to call policed any more, where the janitors would go from the top to bottom replacing light bulbs. Before, you had that sense of security with the managers, with your janitors being on 24-hour call...and I came in this building so much because I had family and friends here, so I felt at one point, safe coming in and out of here. Then when the transition took place, it wasn't safe. It was scary. It was like going trick or treating every day around here. I mean it was.

Management had a bunch of different programs that they came in with and they were going to try to get things back to the way it was, but even though you said you wanted to give this to your community or you wanted to come in and make a change it was basically all about salaries and it was who you know got you the job. A lot of the people that were on the Local Advisory Council were using their positions as clout and a lot of them had family members that were dealing drugs or involved with gangs. Well, they weren't being penalized for their behavior, but the people that didn't have that clout was, so that did contribute to the increase in change.

Jon Morgan

Jan Morgan: When I was about nine, we used to play on the elevators, not inside the elevators, but on top of it. We used to ride on top of it. We'd sit up on it and we used to shoot spit balls down on whoever was riding it...and people would be like, who did that?

Getting on top of the elevator was easy. If the elevator is on the first floor you just go up to the second floor and use a key to open the doors....Our key would be a hangar bent into a "Z" shape. We'd seen the firemen with some sort of tool that looked like this so we'd make our own "Z," stick it in the opening, turn it one way and the doors start opening up. We just get on top of the elevator and start riding up and down on it.

What I'm gettin' to is that my friend was riding up on one and ya know there are weights on the cables that helps it go up and down...and he was riding up and it just cut him in half. This was in our building. He must have been leaned over too far, and didn't see the weight comin' and it just come down right on him. He must have been seven or eight. After this incident, they shut down the elevator for about three years.

Gary Hall: I was coming up during the years where gang activity had just subsided tremendously in that area....Let me say, I'm a third-generation resident of Cabrini-Green. And initially, we were in this building at 911 Hudson, then we moved to **862** North Sedgwick. I attended Richard E. Byrd up until the fifth grade, then we moved to the South Side of Chicago....During that time, the Chicago Police system had cracked down on gangs, very harshly, a lot of the major leaders were in prison, and there was a major truce between many of the gang leaders. So, I was fortunate that there wasn't a lot of formal gang activity then. We're talking about, primarily from '72 to '76, those are my formative years, I would say, being there. Additionally, we hadn't seen the infusion of crack cocaine and other illegal substances really permeating the community, where you had that being a major supply area, and you had the trafficking to the degree that

you have, at least, in recent times. So, I was pretty fortunate that I missed that. I think that may have made a tremendous difference in my own evolution, who knows?

I would say it was probably 90 to 95 percent occupied at the time, so you didn't have the sort of vacancies you have now, and sources of, you know, destructive activity going on in those areas. I would also say, the continual elevators being broken and all those things, those were a constant source of frustration. You know, every building was assigned some sort of maintenance attendant, but, you know, whether or not he did his job, or she did her job, was still an issue in that particular time. I know my mom had problems with that whole process. So, I would say the living conditions were vastly different than what they are now, to my understanding, because you didn't have the vacancies. But the services were still pretty deplorable.

Evelyn Turner: My mother would let my older brothers and sisters take us downtown. The old McVickers Theater used to be at Madison and State. And then we used to go the Chicago Theater. They just had a bunch of shows, and the main one was the McVickers because it was the cheapest. I believe they were one of the first companies to offer more than one movie at a time....You would get your popcorn from across the street and you took it into the show, even though you knew you were not supposed to bring it. We'd go to Grant Park. We also went to all the museums. Hated it.

We used to walk down to Oak Street Beach, a lot. And while walking to Oak Street Beach, we never thought anything about, you know, being divided, because I guess, you know, what we were headed for was the beach, and you didn't have time to really think about anything serious. But as you grew older, and you started to go past Wells and Division, down toward Dearborn Street, you noticed the difference.

Gary Hall: One of the great sort of dichotomies about that whole area is the proximity it has to the Gold Coast. So, you ride your bike two or three blocks, and you realize what you don't have – which was a constant reminder to us, where we should not be. And so, think of that, you know, we would get in trouble, the police would mess with us in those sort of areas, so we just tried to stay away from them.

As I got older, I would then be a little bit more adventurous in going in those areas, and I was just, really just enamored with that whole lifestyle, of people just walking around, seemingly happy, much different, dressed differently, and looking at me like I was crazy, on Michigan Avenue. I would say to myself, I want to live there.

But, as it relates to the people in Cabrini-Green, there were people who lived there for years and – third and fourth generation people – who also enjoyed some sort of social status. They had lived there so long and people knew them...and so, that provided you with a little armor that you carried, a little badge you carried on your chest, as being somebody who'd been around long enough to see the changes, and it gave you a little elitist feeling. But, it was just like any other community, I mean, you know, obviously you were poor, but so were your friends, and so you didn't know what you were missing.

Marsha Crosby: I didn't see too much of the filming [of "Cooley High"] because I was working, but when I saw the movie, it did bring back a lot of memories from going to high school there and everything. It really did. We must have seen it about 20,000 times. Every now and then they'll put it on TV and some of my friends' parents was in it and stuff like that. Our friend down the street, her father was in it and everything. He played a good little role in it and...then the guys who played the gang bangers was from Cabrini, so seeing them in the movie, it was a little amazing....Ironically, [one of them] got killed in the movie and he got killed in real life.

Jan Morgan: Everybody over here went and saw that movie. I still see it on TV now and then, you can reminisce on the streets and how they look. There was a lot of extras in there from the community...and I remember havin' quarter parties, but most of

'em was free. Somebody would just get their hi-fi, put on some Sly and the Family Stone or something and have a party.

Yeah, the two guys that co-starred in it were from the neighborhood....They had the gift of gab, ya know, and they somehow got in the movie. They played the two tough guys. Ricky Stone was the dark one and ah, Norman – I forgot Norman's last name – but I remember the day Norman got killed right out in front of Countdown liquor store at Larrabee and Hobbie Street. It musta' been a year or two after the movie come out....He got shot on the sidewalk. I knew the guy that did it....He's still in jail and his family still stay in my building.

Ricky and Norman used to mess with [the guy who shot him]. They used to rob him and stuff and harass his girlfriend. When he went to the store they'd take his money, so it wasn't no joke, they was bad guys in real life. I mean it was funny because the way they played it in the movie, that's how they was. It was the real deal.

Anyway, Norman and Ricky used to harass this guy and this went on for a coupla' years. They'd rob him and beat him up...but he got fed up with that and he and his boys came through and stopped the car in front of Countdown and just unloaded on Norman. See Ricky, just like in the movie, was usually with Norman, and if he was with him that night he woulda' been killed too. I think the guys got somethin' like 88 years. I figured they got all them years because the news [media] was sayin', the guy who was in "Cooley High" got killed and stuff.

Ricky lived in 1150-60 Sedgwick, where Mayor Byrne lived for a while after that. That was a Cobra Stones building. That's where them two cops were shot from, and also where little Dantrell Davis got shot from.

Gary Hall: I remember that those students, for whatever reason, who went to Byrd school, were presumed to be smarter and softer than those who went to Jenner. And so you used to always have this confrontation between Jenner and Byrd, you know, they'd throw rocks at us and take the candy and stuff like that, during lunch period. You were always, you know, sort of fearful of the guys who went to Jenner, which speaks to this whole issue of classes, and within a poor society, it's amazing, how we adopted some of those principles.

It's funny, because the white buildings, for whatever reason, were, like, off-limits, you know. My family didn't want you to socialize with anybody from the white buildings. I don't know why, to this day I don't know why. So the only opportunity, I had to interact with kids who I actually went to school with, who were from the white buildings, was during those sort of block parties, in the summer.

Gloria Purifoy: I never felt poor, I never felt unloved, and I never felt like there wasn't any hope for me, or the people around me....But you turn on the television, and the only thing about Cabrini that caught five minutes on the news was something bad that happened. And here you had this large group of us — youth and young adults — who were doing something totally different and you never heard those stories.

Then I would go to Near North High School — at the time it was a magnet school, so we had people from all over — and there was people who lived right up the street from it, or right across the street, and they didn't want to go to Cabrini. And, they'd say things like you're different from other people in the projects, and I always tried to figure that out. How? I mean, how are people in the projects supposed to act? How are they any different from anyone else? Because we weren't.

Marsha Crosby: We never got pizza delivered down at 1015.... Yeah, Chester's Pizza, they delivered to Cabrini. They didn't have no problem. Come down to the car with the money. They were about the only people that did deliver at Cabrini, as far as I know. No cabs either.

And I, for one, got tired of being classified when, okay, what's your name? Where do you live at? Ya know, as soon as they find out I'm living at Cabrini, it's like, I'm a stereotype and I didn't like that. I didn't like that.

But for me it was more people of my own age that I would meet on a social status, that would say, oh, I'm not coming over there and this and that. If we wanted to go out on a date, they wanted me to meet them like at Hudson and Chicago Avenue. My thing was okay, if you can't come in and pick me up, well, really I understood it, but yet I still resented it in a way. Maybe I resented the fact that it had to be like that.

I guess you feel safe in your own little...in what's familiar. I lived in the red projects, so if I went into a white project, I was a little shaky. So I guess you can understand it, but still...that's one thing I never wanted for my child; to be branded because he lived in Cabrini.

Runetta Thompson: I work around some people that have the house and the homes and I tell them I live in Cabrini. They ask me dumb questions like, have you ever, you know, gotten in any trouble? The first one is about my kids. Are my kids in the gangs? The second one is, how do you live over there? They assume a lot about how crime infested it is. They're always like, okay, if something comes on the news about Cabrini, I don't even have to know about it but I can come to work and they'll tell me about it. They'll be like, girl, did you hear about Cabrini? Cabrini is a very big complex. When I get home off of work, I'll be in my house. I don't know what happened....I come in the house and mind my own business.

You know, people do have bad misconceptions. And I have this attitude, if you cannot come to where I live at, I can't come where you live at because you ain't no better than me. I feel like there are some places worse than Cabrini.

I have dated males that are scared to come up here, and I won't talk to them because I can't respect a man like that. How can you be scared of something where you have never been? Sorry. Try something, and then if you have issues with it, then I can say at least you tried. But you've never been over here. You're just making a rash, snap judgment of Cabrini. And if you don't think enough of me to come over here to see me, you don't need to see me.

Evelyn Turner

Evelyn Turner: When people find out that you are, or have lived in Cabrini, they expect you to be violent, rude and untrained — anything associated with the negative. I have actually had an opportunity to sit at a table with ten people, all of different ethnic backgrounds, and we were just there, and we drank together afterwards sometimes on Friday, and so, they showed, on the news, one of the project buildings. And a woman, she said, "Oh, God, you know, aren't those the projects? What's wrong with the bad people there?" She said, "That's all they do is shoot, do drugs, and I mean, just kill people. Every night I look at the news, and I'm thinking, that place is..." she just went on, and said everybody over there was just full of shit, and everybody was untrained, and they were people who would never amount to anything. I said, "Well, do you feel that way because you have firsthand knowledge of it, or do you feel that way because of what you see on TV?" I said, "Until you have actually walked the walk, then you shouldn't say things like that."

She was like, "Why?" I said, "Because I used to live there, and I have gone to different social events with you, and you've left your purse on the table, I've watched your purse when you came back and there was nothing missing, was there? We've ridden in the same taxi cab to the bar, you know, we've done a lot of things together. We've eaten at the same table numerous times." She was apologetic, and I said, "No apologies are necessary, you know. I just want you to know that all types of people come from all types of places. And just like there are some rude people over there, there are some rude people in your neighborhood. There are some rude people in this bar right now."

So, I mean, I used to get that a lot, you know. And then, the time in school where you had to stand up and you had to tell what side of the city you lived on and where you were from. All you had to do was say Cabrini, you wouldn't have problems out of anybody. And, you know, it was just that way. "Oh, she lives in Cabrini, well, we won't bother her."

Gary Hall: My role models were people who lived in the area, people who would help me when I got in trouble. Now, I wasn't around when that potential role model could have been a drug dealer to influence me to have some destructive habits, that didn't take place, fortunately, when I was there. But I, you know, I could tell you, you didn't have a lot of influence outside of the community.

My mom was the last one of our family to move out, so I heard the disparaging remarks that other family members would make to her about still living there. I think that had a lot to do with her moving out, the fact that, you know, it was positive peer pressure to get out of there.

Once people left Cabrini-Green, they never came back....It was like a memory they didn't want to go back to and it wasn't until recently that my family would even talk about their roots at Cabrini-Green....Yeah, I mean, they didn't talk about it, and you would see people on the street who would remember you from those days, and they would be a little bit avoiding the whole issue. I think the more we've evolved, and especially, the more success that we've seen, the easier we are in accepting that part of it, because it speaks more to how far we've come. When I first moved out of there, my mom told me not to tell kids that that's where I had come from. And it took me a long time to get past that.

I mean, there were attributions that I didn't understand at the time, but now I do. It wasn't just the issue of living in Cabrini-Green because let me tell you, the place we moved to wasn't exactly the suburbs. But, I think there were other aspersions people cast on it, and attributed to you. For instance, subsidized housing, in certain cases, at that time, meant that you didn't have a job, or your income was limited. And so it was not only that they'd tell my mom, you should move out of there, but you should be more productive, and you should be a better role model for you kids – all of that was attributed to Cabrini-Green.

When I was at Howard University, initially I didn't bring that up. I had a little chagrin about that whole part of my background. I worried that people would judge me the same way my mother was judged. It is only, and I'm being frank, it's only until I got to my own personal state of inner confidence, and had other credentials and other things that I felt validated me more, that I felt comfortable talking about that. I feel ashamed that I felt that way, but it's true. Early on, I wasn't the person that said, I'm from Cabrini-Green, and saying it with pride. It took me to mature a lot as an individual, and even more so as a professional, to get to the point where I can be confident about that. Now I see, since I made that turn, my family has, you know, there's some sort of badge of honor and they use me as, look how far we've come, we've gone from, you know, living in Cabrini-Green to have somebody working at the White House. But, you know, that was not always the case.

Marsha Crosby: When Mayor Byrne moved over here, everything really got, like totally quiet. It got much, much better. A lot of people felt good about the knowledge that she was there, because it did cut down the shootings. Now, a lot of people had questions about, was she really there? They see her coming in and out, but did she really take up residency in that apartment? Did she really? Was that apartment just there? People were saying that, we never knew. She didn't stay for too long but anyway, whatever it was, it worked.

Jan Morgan: When Jane Byrne moved over here, if I walked across this field I was arrested. See my mother lived in 1150 and my girlfriend lived over here at 1015. I musta got locked up 13 times for disorderlies for just going home. Mayor Byrne stayed at 1160 Sedgwick at that time and the field, or the black top, was right where the new Jenner school is being built.

After a while I started runnin' from the police. They would be like, hey you, come here. I wasn't gonna spend the night in jail...so I'd just wave my hand and say bye-bye. As soon as they get out of the car I'd break and run, and they knew they weren't gonna catch me so they'd just look at me and say, "Ah, can't catch that guy, he gone." I mean that's the truth, every time I was stopped, I got arrested and had to stay overnight. For nothin'. I'm not drunk, I don't have anything on me. I'm goin' home. I'm goin' home. Get in the car? I mean it was rough around here then, real rough. At that time in the early '80s it was rough...and it was dark out here then, you were easy pickin'.

So, in a way it was good that the mayor moved over here because it stopped the shooting, and they were shootin' up a storm back then. I mean, every night and a matter of fact, even in the day time...and people from 500-502, they couldn't even go to the store. See 500-502 was Vice Lords, 1015-17 is Disciples and so the only store that was open was the shops over here on Larrabee. They couldn't go over there 'cause they'd run into Disciple guys...so I guess they'd send their children or somethin' that wasn't affiliated with the gang.

But it didn't matter if you in a gang or not, if you comin' from this way at that time, they think you one of them. You come from the other way, they think you one of them. Even worse, you don't ever go across the baseball diamond, not in those years...there's too much light out there and everybody's shootin' at ya. You don't know which way to run. Every time we went home anytime past night fall, you takin' a chance just gettin' home. We seen it everyday.

Marsha Crosby: I never forget the time this white guy got beat up in Old Town. There was eyewitnesses and stuff, they picked the photograph out of yearbooks, and this guy named Joe Green, I'll never forget, a nice young man, for some reason they picked him out. He was living in 1119 Cleveland and they went to his house and he wasn't there. So when he came home his family told him the police came to question him about a beating or something. He said he was going to go down to the police station because he didn't do anything. He went and they charged him with that murder. He was in jail for almost a year for something he did not do. Now people knew who really did it, but if there is

gang retaliation, they didn't say anything until the person that did it got killed himself. Then someone came forward and Joe Green was released, but this was after a long time in jail.

Runetta Thompson: Being a female...as long as you do what you're supposed to do and you're not doing anything you're not supposed to do, you can go anywhere you want to go in Cabrini. If you want to participate with the so-called gang bangers, that's when you have the issues. I never had those issues because I never mingled with those folks. I went wherever I wanted. I never had a problem. I have lived over here since I was twelve and no one has ever harassed me or tried to, you know, initiate me into a gang. That was a choice thing. It's all about choices.

Steve Pratt: There always have been conflicts....I used to gang bang, but when we did it, didn't nobody hide behind guns or nothin' like today. We were considered men. We'd get out there in the field and we'd fight, a bunch of them and a bunch of us and just fightin'. Now you got guys who call themselves men but they hide behind guns. They ain't tough unless they got a gun.

Gloria Purifoy: I was always aware of the gangs, but never afraid of them. When I was growing up, most of the gang members were older guys...and they had a certain amount of respect for things in their community and for the people....When I was going to school and stuff, these guys would be concerned about my education. Sometimes they'd even take our bags upstairs.

Jan Morgan: There's a lot of guys out there that don't wanna be about [the gangs], they just got caught in that web. They wanna go, but they ain't got no place to go. They didn't finish school or whatever...then they got the luxury of makin' a few dollars. This is narcotics money and it's lookin' good, ya know, they pockets is fat, so when you talk about gettin' a job at Jewel's, that's a joke. I mean, you makin' seven an hour at Jewel and you can make 600 or 700 dollars an hour sellin' narcotics, so now they stuck for real, and the only way outta that is the hooskow.

They start yourn too, ya know, workin' "S." That's security, meanin' they stand out front of the building on the lookout for cops. They get the shorties doin' that at like 14, 15.

But you just can't do all that forever. When that's over with, they gonna be one of the guys on the street, drinkin' they wine, askin' for quarters and can I have a cigarette, blah blah blah.

I done seen it happen to a coupla guys, ya know, he was a big wig sellin' whatever it is and drivin' a big cadillac, and even if he don't get caught and go to jail he got younger guys comin' up eventually gets cut out. Now, he didn't have an education, never really worked in his life, now he's out there with his wine. I seen it happen.

Evelyn Turner: The gangs, they didn't even bother down at 412, for some odd reason. I guess 'cause the older ladies in that building just would not even think about tolerating the gang activity that went on in other places. Or, because our building was right on Chicago Avenue, but it was just unheard of, you know, "you will have to take that some place else. Don't even come through here with that, you go back in the other direction."

So they stayed down toward the big ball field....I guess when you grow up around people and you are the older person, you learn to respect your elders, I don't care who you are, you know. Could be one of the toughest gang members, if he grew up around there and he knew my mother, he was going to show my mother the utmost respect. That was that, you know.

Steve Pratt: Back then, basically the gang was just like a club.... It's a lot of following and what your friends are doin' and you just come up with names for your friends. Fights was like, basically, don't cross this line, and they'd cross that line and it was on, so it was like kids just fightin'. Or you just bored and say, c'mon let's go call them out. We was doin' it for fun ya know.

It started out fist fighting, then bats, throwin' bricks and stuff, then somebody would start fakin' like they had a gun to make the other side run, ya know. Then from there they actually did

come out with a gun, and come out and start shootin'. So the other gang's like, oh, you wanna play with guns? So they get guns and so on and so on.

I just decided I ain't fittin' to do this anymore. I got two kids now, especially since my son, I don't want him lookin' at me like, oh, that's what my father does so I'm gonna follow in his foot steps. I tell him to this day, no, you ain't gonna be like me, you're gonna be better than me.

Jan Morgan: There was a time when I was walking with my older brother, he had just got out of job corps after bein' in there six months, and he had come home for either Thanksgiving or Christmas and I was tellin' him how they had been shooting real bad around here. So there was like five young guys, they couldn't have been no more than 12 or 13 years old, and I'm smokin' a cigarette and we're walkin' across the field and the two young guys say, excuse me, do you have a light?

Now, I had just lit a cigarette and I was like lookin' at 'em and thinkin' this don't look right. I'm thinkin' there's five of you guys and don't none of you have a light? So I just dump the whole cig and say, "Oh, my bad, that was the only light I had." So me and my brother walk past and I start tellin' him, "See, little brothers like that, I don't trust them." Then I happen to turn around and look back at them and out from one of their jackets comes a little rifle and right then I hit my brother on the arm and yell, "Split!" So he goes one way and I go the other, that's so they don't know who to shoot at, and if they do then only one of us is gonna get hit, maybe none of us. That was the reason for the split. I'm runnin' and I hear whack, whack, whack, whack, whack, but which one they were shootin' at I don't know, but we could hear it hittin' the ground in the middle of us. This had to be 1977 or so.

Everybody who grew up here knows when you say split, that means you go that way and I'll go that way 'cause somebody back here's fittin' to start shootin at us and if we runnin' together one of us gonna get burned up, and maybe both of us. So when you say split and you on the left side, you go left. If you on the right side, you go right. Everybody around here know that.

Steve Pratt: It got to the point where you got guys with high-powered rifles who start snipin' and you gotta watch out when you come out of the buildings. You had to think about what side of the street you walk on. The Vice Lords, they had the tallest buildings, 500-502, so they could go up on the top and see everything. Then 1150-1160, they was Cobras, so they was able to see on the field, and both of them had rifles. They was both going against the GD's, so it was a real danger during that time just comin' in and out the building. A lot of innocent people got shot. One lady got shot in the leg, another guy was sittin' in his apartment and he got shot in the neck, it just came in the window.

Runetta THOMPSON

Runetta Thompson: I think Cabrini really started changing in, say, like maybe in the '80s to the mid '80s....But people think everything about Cabrini is bad. There are misconceptions about Cabrini. I mean a lot of people think everybody in Cabrini is ignorant. Everybody is poor. Everybody is jobless. Everybody wants money. That's a misconception, because I know when I go to work I'm not the only person going to work in the morning. I see lots of people coming out of their houses over here going to work.

And, I have been in some peoples' houses over here that are so nice that people wouldn't believe it's supposed to be a project.... But, still, the conditions are enough to make you want to move....I don't consider Cabrini my home. I just consider it a place where I sleep [*laughing*]. Home shouldn't be like this.

I mean we have problems with the mail, with maintenance and people just have too much access to our building....Nobody's got control over what the [gangs] do over here. They allow them to do whatever they want.

And then, as an example, you got kids over here that go to school, and don't do no wrong. They're just trying to have a normal childhood, and you got police harassing them. They'll harass a teenage boy going to school and then going to his after school job, but then the guys can sit right downstairs there sellin' drugs all day without a problem. And then there's people coming here from all over and I got to go past them in the hallways while they're smoking pipes and snorting coke and all that. I don't have much respect for that.

Evelyn Turner: When I still lived there I saw the lack of participation from the Housing Authority to come out and fix things that they should. I noticed that there were less repairmen around. The buildings that I used to go into that were always clean were not so clean because they had one person for three buildings.

Then I noticed the gang activity picked up. Then they started to have, well, young girls in their teens started to have babies. That became the thing to do, I think, in the early '80s, young girls having babies. They started to rent the apartments to the young girls, and that's when the big change came. Because they could then move the younger men into these apartments, and they could, you know, sell their drugs and do whatever.

And I think, when you lack that stability, you'll do anything...and at that age, I don't think you can make a sound decision anyway. You haven't even begun to live yet, you know.

And then, you know, when the times started to change and a lot of younger women had babies, some of the older folks moved away. Because back then, a lot of the families worked. It was more of a working community than it was one that was on assistance. I think, had some of the working people stayed, the community would be totally the opposite, because when you don't have a leg to stand on that just makes it even worse.

Gary Hall: I remember walking to Water Tower mall on Michigan Avenue. and thinking, wow, I want to be able to shop here one day. It was so pervasive in my mind that the first place I looked to live when I got my job with the Mayor's Office was a place I could not afford [*laughing*]. I think it was like 1113 North Dearborn, because I wanted to live on the Gold Coast. I wanted to live in that area that I could not live in or go in when I was a kid, where I could not feel comfortable in. I remember when I moved in and looking out my window, on one side was Cabrini-Green, on the other was the John Hancock tower, and you couldn't tell me anything. I thought I made it right then and there. I was 22 or 23 years old, so, I mean, it's just to tell you how your self-definition is affected by the proximity of weatlh and poverty. I definitely think it's pervasive.

Runetta Thompson: What people don't know is some of the [drug dealers'] best customers come from the Lincoln Park area.... There's a lot of white people who come here for that. You see them walking, you see them driving. I mean they pull up, they stop right here, then they walk right into the building. You know what's going on. You've been around here long enough that you know.... I'm not judging nobody. But I'm saying you know when people are coming to visit and when people are coming to buy drugs [*laughing*].

Marsha Crosby: In the back of our building was 500, and that was rival gangs. Our building, 1015, was Disciples and 500-502 was Vice Lords, so they shooting constantly back and forth at each other. In the meantime, our living room window was facing 500, so we had like three or four bullets come through our window. One time somebody had just came in before a bullet zoomed in and it was horrible. Just like on New Year's Eve, I mean it was just like a war zone....I thought, thank God, our bedroom windows was on the front, but it's just like a nightmare on New Year's Eve. You just hear bullets popping and bullets popping and you prayin'....It's just the idea of the bullets comin' through your bedroom window. I think that New Year's Eve, I think two did come through my living room window, but those other times, it wasn't New Year's Eve, they just came. Then one time the police came because I always call the police afterwards and they were saying, well can't you just stay out of your living room?

Well, how can you stay out your living room? My kitchen is right there. You've got to come through there to come in and out. Sometime I be sitting down on the couch talking and they get to shooting and you just hit the floor. It became to be almost a routine thing. You talking on the phone, they get to shooting, you just duck down on the floor and just keep on talking on the phone. And that's terrible, that's a terrible way to live.

Steve Pratt: The understanding I always got was the cops over here never really cared. They put on a front, but all the time it seemed like it was just, let 'em kill each other, like that's the attitude they had. Let's say a minor incident goes off, you got like the whole police force swarmin' in, but if you got some real shootin', you don't see the police until it's over. It's like, let 'em kill each other.

chapterSIX
The Rap on the WHITES

His name is Demetrius Cantrell, **but everyone in Cabrini seems to know him as** Sugar Ray Dinky. **Follow him along Division Street and you hear shouts of "Dinky" raining down from high-rise buildings. Walk through Schiller or Truth school and you notice pint-sized students saluting him as, "Mr. Dinky." Stand on the ramp outside his fourth floor apartment at 630 Evergreen and you see a group of teenagers attempting to impersonate the man.**

Sugar Ray Dinky's been a sort of hero around here for years, since writing a rap called, simply, "Cabrini-Green." Based on all things Cabrini — from disabled elevators to police brutality — and inspired by the murder of a friend, "Cabrini-Green" was first featured on local television in 1982. "I was with the Jesse White Tumblers and Channel Seven came out to do a story on Mr. White," Dinky explains. "Then Mr. White says to me, do your rap for them, ya know, for the television. So I start doing it and the next thing you know I'm with more news people and I'm walking through the projects doin' the 'Cabrini-Green' rap."

Other media outlets, including the Oprah Winfrey Show, featured Dinky and his rap, which led to it being recorded and distributed internationally. Dinky went on to win three amateur contests at the Apollo Theatre and performed everywhere from half time at Chicago Bulls games to the show, "Rock On, Chicago."

Although this breakthrough did not make Dinky a household name beyond Cabrini, he continues to write and perform as a rapper. He's created music for commercials and public service announcements and regularly performs at local events and school assemblies. But, as the leader of the drum and bugle corps at Truth school, Dinky focuses most of his attention these days on young people in the community.

"I could have probably made it out of here," he says, "but I was really concerned about these kids. Ya gotta keep them busy to keep them from thinkin' of the negative stuff. We try to have fun. And the ones that I talk to, the ones that are involved in the drum and bugle corps, they show me respect and listen. And it seems like a lot of the negative stuff has died down for them."

Richard Blackmon **spent most of his youth trying to avoid the negative stuff in Cabrini. As a star athlete and solid student, he worked his way through Lane Tech High School and gained a football scholarship to Southern Illinois University. Later, he earned a law degree from Notre Dame University. Despite losing his mother and a brother while living in Cabrini-Green, he claims his memories of the neighborhood are more good than bad. At 37, he is a practicing attorney and works for Options for People, one of the oldest welfare to work programs in the country. He often returns to the community in support of its schools and youth organizations.**

"*Dinky!*" shouts the security guard at Schiller school, a wide smile on his face. Sugar Ray Dinky enters the building rapping. The security guard cups his hands around his lips and with rapid-fire blowing serves as Dinky's one-man rhythm section.

"*Yo, you're ballin', and makin' stacks fast,*" Dinky sputters, "*dropped out of school 'cause ya think it's gonna last...you just bought a car and your wardrobe's tight...from servin' those geekers and hypes all night...you probably doin' "S" in the morning or afternoon...either way you got grown too soon...14-15-16, damn, 5-0's at the door with a battering ram...*"

They both break into laughter.

Debra Wilson **and her family moved from a red building to a white building when she entered high school in 1967. She currently lives in the white high-rise at 1230 N. Burling. Today, she says the community seems like a different place than the one she grew up in. "I saw Cabrini-Green in its first beauty," she says, "and I know what it could've been..." While she remembers a happy childhood, the last several years have proved disappointing. She says it's been painful watching the gradual deterioration of a community that could have thrived here.**

Like Dinky, Tyrone Randolph's **interests revolve around music and kids. His job with DePaul University's Urban Systems of Care involves assisting residents of Cabrini-Green with domestic or social problems, and includes referring troubled children to more specialized care. He too lives at 1230 N. Burling, with his wife and two children. His own childhood was spent learning and performing music but part of growing up here, he says, included learning how to avoid the gangs as well. At 30, he's unsure how much longer he'll live in the community.**

Ms. Wanda Hopkins (**who we met in Chapter Three) continues to offer a broader perspective on the white high-rises and what's become of them.**

Sugar Ray dinky

Sugar Ray Dinky: My sister had a piano she got when she was seven, eight years old. She never played with it. I liked it, you know, so I got to messing around with it and I started making my own stuff on it. One day this guy, Junior Miller – his dad was Reverend Miller, who had a church on Sedgwick – Junior had a bass guitar and we started talking about who was a better musician. He brought out his bass guitar and he really wiped the floor with me, so that made me wanna really get into it, ya know. I went to my mom, even though I knew she couldn't afford it, she gave me like fifteen bucks to buy a guitar. And I was like, naw, I need like a hundred and some bucks, but we gotta family and have to eat, so I went out there hustling. I got me a paper route and went to doin' peoples windows, sweeping some sidewalks...and finally got my guitar.

Richard Blackmon: We moved into Cabrini in 1967, it was the fall of '67. We had been living on the West Side and at that time Cabrini was emergency housing. We had a fire in our apartment on the West Side so we moved into Cabrini as emergency housing. I remember it real clear. It was different. First of all, there were quite a few Hispanic families....But it seems like almost overnight it went from a Hispanic and African-American population to 100 percent African-American.

We moved into 714 West Division. Right at the corner of Division and around Halsted. It was nice, it was clean. People were friendly. You know, I remember having very few bad experiences at Cabrini.

Mostly what I remember was just growing up, you know, it was the only place we knew.

I do remember the riots, though....It was just a depression [after Dr. King was killed]. It was just...everybody was down, you know, not knowing what was going to happen next. I mean it was the not knowing of it that was tough. And then one day it was just like nothing happened. Everything was back to normal.

Debra Wilson: I moved here when I was three years old. First, we stayed in 1117-1119, the red building that they tore down. Being the fifth family to move in, it was an exciting time. It was still new, and it was mixed....My father became the janitor for the building. I went to Jenner school, and I loved school. I had loved school so much that one day I got up and went to school real early....The newspaper man was coming in and the milk man was coming in, and I was just sitting there [at school] waiting for everybody else to show up.

We had moved into the white projects when I started high school in 1967. My father's job, they had moved him. He had an option, he could move to Florida or get another building in the white project. My mom didn't want to move because she would lose her friends and family, so we stayed here. We should've moved. We should have moved.

Sugar Ray Dinky: They just used to call me Dinky around here, I can't remember why. But Sugar Ray comes from...well, kids was always coming over to 1230 Burling and beating up everybody so my uncle, an ex-marine, he bought some boxing gloves. He set up like a ring downstairs and he like put the guys in the ring. It was back when they had the iron fences around the buildings and they'd put the guys in the fences and the whole community would come around and watch. I would start kickin' butt like I was Sugar Ray Dinky, man, and the crowd start sayin', "Sugar Ray, Sugar Ray." I had to be about 13. I was boxing all the time, and I went to the Golden Gloves tournament at Seward Park. Now my sons are tryin' it.

Richard Blackmon: My mother had six kids. There was me and my three brothers and two sisters. But my sisters didn't grow up in Cabrini. They were younger. My mom actually gave custody of them over to my aunt so they didn't have to grow up in public housing.

Like I said, almost overnight it went like from a mixed population, to pretty much 100 percent African-American. I mean there was still like maybe one or two Hispanic families even when I was in eighth grade, but not a lot.

For me, Stanton Park was the place to go, and Isham YMCA. At that time, New City YMCA was called Isham, and we would hang out there, play pool there, play ping pong. Jesse White was the gymnastics instructor there. They also had a Boy Scout and a Cub Scout troop that were formed out of Isham YMCA. At the park district you could swim, do gymnastics, play basketball, so there was a lot to do.

I met Mr. White at school. He was the gym teacher at Schiller school and he was the physical education instructor at the Y. He worked at the school during the day and then at the Y after hours. He was also the disciplinarian at school [*laughing*]. I mean, any time you got in trouble, they'd send you to see him. And at that time you could still spank. I think he spanked me once in the entire time that I've known him. He doesn't spank me anymore [*laughing*].

But the main thing for me was swimming and Cub Scouts. We really got into Cub Scouts. Later, I joined the Jesse White Tumblers. The other thing we did, which I thought was kind of neat, on the black tops, the areas right in the middle of the buildings, they used to have big circles painted in the middle of the black top. And on the weekends the DJ's would bring like all of their music and they'd play music. The people would roller skate on the black top and that was one of the things that I really, really remember being a lot of fun.

We actually had the guys with the turntables and the records, and they'd spin records all night. People would just dance. They'd come out and dance and roller skate.

And when we got older they used to have the basement parties, and then there was quarter parties or waist line parties. That's where you pay so much for every inch of your waist. It was a penny an inch or something like that.

Wanda Hopkins: Early on it was almost, you know, we were just all together. It didn't start dividing, I don't think, until the '70s. That's what happened because the [the red buildings] were the strongest gang force, I thought. I don't know if it's true, they may say the same thing about us, but in the red buildings I can remember the two main guys who ran the buildings. People were afraid to death of them. You couldn't even walk in front of them, you know.

My brothers used to tell us, please don't go around those guys 'cause they have the power to do whatever they want to you, you know. So the reds and the whites had began to separate then.

Debra Wilson: The only thing that I think brought things down was when those two policemen got killed behind 1117-1119, and the police went through all the buildings breaking down doors, getting people out of bed and everything, trying to figure out what happened. We had already moved out of that building, but my father had a drum and bugle corps that he had started in 1117 and we rehearsed in the basement. In the summertime there was too much noise so they moved it to St. Joseph's church.

One of the guys who is in prison for killing the police used to harass my brother and his friends and everybody in the drum and bugle corps. Now, I didn't know him prior to the police getting killed. After the police got killed then I started learning about who it was that was harassing my brother.

Across from us when we lived in 1117 was a really nice man. He taught karate and he had three children and one of his sons was also sent to jail for that same murder. The father was well known in the projects, too. He and his wife were very active and it was a shock to me that his son would be involved with that. So things started getting bad, I believe, after that. That put a damper on everyone's spirit.

Wanda Hopkins: Because of that, police harassed every young black man in the immediate area. It was just terrible. I don't remember anything happening to my personal family, but I can recall people saying they were harassing them, throwing them over the cars, you know, taking them to jail, doing all kinds of things....That's why we always tell young people, you know, when I'm in workshops, you just don't shoot police. It's just out, you're going to jail for life. I know some people who went to school with that boy who's in jail for life for that. I mean, it was a bad scene.

Oh, we knew we were doomed then. At that point we knew that there was nothing else going to happen in Cabrini that would make us want to stay there, because everything was, I think, they gave up on us. I still believe that the city, with the old Mayor Daley, had said that those people are not civilized, that's the only way that they would allow us to live in trash. It was some days that trash was so high in those buildings that I wouldn't stay in my own house, 'cause I lived right at the garbage chute and it was just horrible.

I think the maintenance people were told that they just didn't have to do it anymore. That's what I think.

Tyrone Randolph: I've been livin' here all my life. That's 30 years. We started off livin' in 714 West Division Street. That was with my grandmother, she had nine kids of her own, and then my mom and me and my sister. I have three siblings, an older sister who is 31, and a younger brother who's 22. We were all in a five-bedroom apartment. My grandmother stayed on the fourth floor.

I remember when I was about five, Christmas was the big thing. My sister and I were the only young kids, so we had a lot of toys. My mom was workin' at the time.

Later we moved to 630 West Evergreen and stayed there 'til I was 11 or 12. It was a pretty cool building. That's where the majority of my friends are now. But it was real fun, we'd play hide and seek and stuff like that. We would go to Stanton Park, too. I was into music so I would do a lot of talent shows or apartment shows as a kid. I had a group of friends and we would imitate the Jackson Five [*laughing*]. We would do these quarter shows in his apartment, and invite our friends. My best friend, we still work on music together.

But we would also play shows outside the community. My dad would drive us to our different shows. It was funny, we would play all over the city for different parties and talent shows. At the age of 14 and 15 I'm out at one in the morning 'cause I'm doin' a show, but my dad would be there. One of our biggest shows was at the Field Museum.

Debra Wilson: After the police were killed, I wouldn't even go back in the red projects. And all of my friends lived in the reds. But once I went to Waller I got new friends that stayed in the white projects, so I kind of kept myself with them.

There was some strong gangs that was forming. My brother was said to be in the gangs, too, but he always denied it. It was the Deuces Wild or something. He always denied it, but he was wild.

But, for my brother, when he was getting harassed by that guy who went to jail, by being in a group of guys already from the drum and bugle corps, I guess they formed their own little thing from that....I think they were forced to unite as a group of guys for protection.

Tyrone Randolph: Most of the kids I knew, their dads were there, and then later they weren't there. But, we were just kids and we just didn't worry about that. Our parents knew who our friends were, and that's who they expected you to be playin' with. If they went lookin' for you they expected you to be in one of those homes, and once you heard that call, "Hey Tyrone," no matter where you were that call would just ring in your head. Oh, they're callin' me and you get back to the house.

We'd do a lot of stuff like jumping on and off of train cars. We'd play hide and go seek on the trains that was over near Halsted.... There was two box cars that was there all the time, and we were playin' in the trains once and a police car came and they got us in the car and took us to the station and my dad had to come and pick us up. It was crazy. We didn't really think about how dangerous it was at the time.

RICHARD BLACKMON

Richard Blackmon: Just like in the movie "Cooley High," we'd have those kinds of quarter parties. And Martha's, which was in the movie, that was right over there at Elm and Larrabee....When they were filming, I remember it was big stuff. Everybody was trying to get in it. There were a couple of people from the neighborhood in it. Those guys who played the two thugs. They were neighborhood guys. There were people like fighting to get roles in that movie. Just to be stand-ins and stuff like that.

When they shot the scene for the school, that was actually the YMCA. That wasn't actually Cooley, that was the Isham Y. Isham was a big part of this community. That's why people really kind of hated it when New City took over. They felt like they were kind of being abandoned because, of course, New City came in with a new fee structure. There was a formalized relationship, where at Isham it was kind of informal. If you couldn't afford to go to the Y they would let you in. On Larrabee, right before you get to North Avenue, right by the railroad tracks. That's where Isham YMCA was.

Debra Wilson: My brother was in that movie, "Cooley High." He was an extra. He was in the restaurant scene. He ran to the bathroom trying to get away from the bad guys.

Tyrone Randolph: I went to Schiller and I was part of the Jesse White drum corps. He was there up 'til my fourth grade year. He was my gym teacher, he was a tough gym teacher, he was real fun but he was tough. There was the Boy Scouts, and the drum corps and the flipping team.

I assisted with the tumblers, we would perform together a lot and some of them would do that and drum corps. It was just the way Jesse tried to keep us focused. He's not as able to do it as much these days, but he's passed it on to other former tumblers.

Sugar Ray Dinky: When I first moved to Cabrini-Green it was in June, 1973. Me and my four sisters and my mom and my step-dad moved up to 1230 North Burling. When we first moved over there was a lot of crazy stuff going on so my mom was kind of scared to let us go outside, you know, with all the shooting.

Before that, we lived over by Sedgwick and Mohawk, so I moved from one rival gang area to this side. There was another gang over there, the Vice Lords, and over here it was like the Disciples or whatever, so I remember that walking my sisters back and forth through here was like kind of hectic for me because I was getting all this pressure from all the guys, you know, from the gangs over here.

But, really I hung out at the New City YMCA with Mr. White. Mr. White used to be at the New City YMCA and I ended up there, and I joined his tumbling team. So by me being a tumbler, it kept a lot of pressure off of me. Still, I lost a lot of friends because besides tumbling, I used to hang out with the guys that were gang bangers. I wasn't with the gang, I was just with 'em, and by me being with them it made me like affiliated.

I was losing friends at two a month, you know, two guys a month being killed. The war that was going on was like building against building, 714 would be fighting 660. Those buildings are right next door to each other and they shooting nonstop at each other, you know. And innocent bystanders were getting shot and, man it was wild over here in the projects.

Reverend Miller, Junior Miller's dad, he had a church on Sedgwick, and one day they found him dead on the elevator at 1230 North Burling, someone shot him up in the head, just shot him up on the elevator at 1230 Burling.

From ten to fifteen, I had a lot of problems over here. They were beating up my sisters and stuff, you know, catching us, calling us Mohawk boys....At one point, they tried to recruit me into a gang and everything, and I knew my mother wouldn't have that, you know, so I didn't join the gang. Instead I hung out with a local band they had over here called the Electric Force Band.

Larry Potts was the lead singer vocalist, and then there was Ronnie Williams, Jenny Williams and myself. We played blues and, you know, we played in front of buildings and stuff like that in the summertime. People would hear us and just come on out. We had a lot of crowds gather around. It was great to have something to do besides the wild stuff.

Tyrone Randolph: There a lot of nicknames around here. They call me lots of names; T-bone, Macaroni T, T, Ty. Everybody gets them from your friends, from what you're like and stuff.

We did a lot of bike riding when we were kids. We'd ride all the way up north, ride to the beach, ride downtown. At that time they had Rubics game room, which was located on Division and State. That was one of the hot spots...everybody from school would go and hang out there. It was a cool place to meet girls and that's where I got a lot of my eccentric friends, punk rockers with the wild hairdos and stuff, and we'd go and have a beach party at the beach every Friday or Saturday.

I had a lot of friends that stayed up north. A lot of times I didn't hang out in the neighborhood, I don't really know why. Maybe

because I just wanted something different because around here it was just cluttered, and I'm more of an adventurer. I like to find out new things, see different things, meet new people and over here it's more like everybody's the same and wants to do the same things. I wanted to do other stuff.

Debra Wilson: After they killed those cops, it really wrecked everything. The CHA had began to stop screening people...and people from all over the City of Chicago was moving in 'cause they were low income people and they would bring their ways and habits with them. That's what tore down the working class people who were beginning to move out. And the fear of gangs.

Young people were beginning to get apartments and they had their gang banger friends living in that apartment, and then the girls start having babies and the welfare went up and everything. The whole purpose of the projects was to get you to save and to move out. It wasn't no permanent thing. If my father hadn't been a janitor, we wouldn't have been here that long.

Sugar Ray Dinky: So one day our band was rehearsing, it was March 9, 1981, and some guy walked around to the side of the 1230 Burling building where we was practicing in a room, and shot through the window, you know, three times shot through the window with a .357 magnum, shooting Larry Potts in the back and killing him instantly. The bullets skinned two girls in the leg. I couldn't believe it. I was standing right there.

After that, I was inspired to write the song called the "Cabrini-Green Rap." I wrote the "Cabrini-Green Rap" back in 1982-83, and I was performing it around all the local clubs and people seemed to like it.

Channel Seven came out again and then the Oprah Winfrey Show picked me up. I.M. records saw the program and immediately called over and got me from my mom's crib, and took me and recorded the record. It went world wide, and that kinda opened doors for me.

Richard Blackmon: If you lived in the white projects you couldn't go into the red projects. The other thing that happened was the gangs separated. Of course, the Black Stones, you know, that whole organization, it's color is red. So the red buildings fit them perfectly. Whereas, the white buildings were more like the Disciples, and you might have one or two buildings in the white buildings that consider themselves Stones or something like that. But the majority of them were Disciples. And so, it was a big rift, and you couldn't cross Division.

Now, the row houses was just a whole separate thing. I mean, you might have anything going on down there. Still, we'd come over and play baseball games at Seward Park, but we'd have to run off right after the game.

Tyrone Randolph: There was like four different gangs over here, even when I was young. They were much more organized. The boundaries were basically the whites were Disciples, the reds had Disciples, Vice Lords, Cobra Stones. And I think the row houses also had Disciples and I'm not sure about others, but those were the boundaries. We really couldn't go past like Division and Clybourn because of the building that was sittin' there, 1160.

That was a hard time because even workin' a summer job I got jumped on by the gang bangers. I was going to see about my check because at that time with the summer jobs program you didn't get your check on time. This parent of one of my friends decided she would take us down to see why we weren't gettin' our check...and I had this sweater on, and it had rhinestones on it. The guys said it resembled the pitchfork, ya know, which stood for Disciples, and so they started in on me. I was about 13, 14, a freshman in high school, and the guys chased me almost all the way home.

I knew after a certain point they didn't want to chase me into the whites, and that's what happened. It was weird 'cause when I got older I worked with one of the guys who tried to jump me. He remembered and he was like, oh man, ya know, a big apology. So me and him are pretty cool but that was my first time havin' any interaction with the gangs.

Sugar Ray Dinky: My friend, Andre, he got killed right here in this building, 630. He got killed downstairs in the lobby....He wasn't a gang member but he was kind of wild. It's like if you shoot at somebody, it's going to happen to you, you know. You live by the sword, you die by it...over here anyway. That's the rules.

When there was a lot of shooting going on, it was like you tie your shoes in the morning and you don't know who is going to untie them at night. That's how it was, you go outside and they be shooting, boom, boom, boom, boom. Once the shooting stops you get back off the ground and life goes on like normal. You get kind of used to that, you know. You get used to it. When the shooting stops, you get up like nothing happened. I mean not only me, other little children, too. When the shooting stops, we go back to normal, like it's no big deal.

Now, I can tell a shot from a firecracker, ya know. You can tell what building it's comin' from and everything. It's like a marine havin' that thousand yard stare. That's what it's like with me after 27 years here.

Wanda Hopkins: We moved out in '73. My sister had witnessed the plan to bomb a place, and the district attorney moved us out in the night. I'll never forget, we were moved out of the building quietly, I mean, it was like, we didn't have to do anything. People came and got our stuff together, boxed it up, put it on a truck, and moved us to the West Side of Chicago. They got us away in the middle of the night...in one day, we were gone!

What happened was these gang members had, you know, asked for protection money or something like that from a lounge in the neighborhood....My sister shouldn't have been in there, she wasn't of legal age at that point, but she was in there and saw the whole thing. The gangs had said, well, we're going to blow this place up. She saw the guys.

So later the police officer brought some guy right to our house and said, is this the person who threatened to do the bombing?

Totally illegal, totally not supposed to happen, 'cause he sees us and sees where we live. So, they moved us out, but I was crazy and I went back in 1976. I'm not afraid of them. I've never been afraid of the gangs.

Richard Blackmon: The other thing that's not always considered part of the equation but really should be looked at is this whole area right where the Oscar Meyer plant used to be. That Sedgwick Street area was another area that you didn't go into. Now everybody had to go over there to go to Farmer Browns restaurant. But it was like a neighborhood on to itself. So you got these four little sections, and then on the back side of Cabrini off of Halsted near North Avenue there used to be houses there. That was a whole 'nother area. So you were kind of boxed in, particularly if you lived in the white buildings.

I used to have to come to the store right here [at Larrabee and Hobbie]....We used to get robbed, you know, coming right up this street to go to that store. And so my mom had to sew like pockets on our underwear to keep the guys from robbing us, because they'd pat you down and everything. It was pretty bad.

I mean you always heard about it, and people sayin', "Man, you can't go in the red projects from the white projects, what's wrong with you?" I actually had relatives that lived in the red projects that I couldn't visit...unless I got escorted by one of them over. So that was kind of weird you know.

And whoever the genius was that came up with painting the buildings, or having different bricks and names for the buildings, I mean nothing separates us more then color. You have a set of white buildings and a set of red buildings, and they call them all Cabrini-Green, right? Then the other thing is, all of us went to Schiller, and right over there in the reds they went to Jenner school, so it was just more separation. Anything you could look to separate you, that's what you kind of gravitated toward.

Sugar Ray Dinky: If you go in the red projects back in the days and you have on a blue hat or they'd recognize you from down here, you could get shot. If you go down Milwaukee Avenue where the Puerto Rican or Spanish guys are you can get shot coming from Cabrini, you know. You can't go on North Avenue, 'cause the same thing.

You know, we get surrounded by violence. Different people want us out of the community and because you from the projects assume that you automatically bad, so I had a hard time going to high school, Lincoln Park High School, coming out of Cabrini. People think you a project guy so, you know, they wanna fight and eventually...they end up kicking me out of school for fighting all the time. So I had to take the GED and go to Washburne, Washburne Trade School, and pick up where I left off there. So my high school days was really just marked by gang stuff.

I had trouble every day. I mean because if I'm caught walking by myself, I got in trouble from some guys who don't even go to school there but are affiliated with those who do.

So, you know, I've been shot at about [*laughing*], I have to say about 15, 16 times. I mean actually shot at, you know, when the bullet hit the poles and the fences and you're running.

One day I was with my mom and we was walking down the blacktop. We were on our way to Mohawk, and someone shot and hit the school and we got up and we carried on. Went on about our business. Used to it, man. Checked to see was each other shot and walked on. Cabrini-Green, man, it's somethin' else.

Wanda Hopkins: I came back in '76 and at that point I had my own family. When I moved back, I moved into a different building. It was 624 West Division, and it was different....I witnessed a lot of things that as a young mother I was trying to shelter my children away from. Over 25 years I have witnessed a lot of things, you know, walking out of the buildings with my babies in strollers and people shooting over our heads, and walking up the stairs with 17 bags of groceries, you know, with two babies.

It was really strange because I didn't have to be there, that's what was so crazy about it. I just felt that Cabrini was my calling, even in my downtown job now [with a parent organization], I still let my boss know that I'm going to do certain things for the schools in Cabrini. I still come in this community all the time because I still have work with the schools. That's my calling. I love this community, and always have.

I stayed until '86 or '87. For me, the rent got so high. Ya know, it's like 30 percent of your income. I can't live here and have to walk upstairs and then pay eight or nine hundred dollars a month in rent. I wouldn't do it, so I moved out.

My children, once they graduate out of college, have to give back to Cabrini. My daughter, I made her teach a year at a Cabrini school. My son, who will receive his engineering degree this year, I don't know what he can do at Cabrini but I've asked him to do at least one year of service in Cabrini. That's just our dedication to it. I think that Cabrini made me who I am and because of who I am is what made my children who they are, so I asked them to give one year of service in the community after graduating from college.

Sugar Ray Dinky: As kids, we'd make our own trampoline so we could be like the Tumblers. We'd get an old mattress and take all the cotton off of it and the fabric, then you take the bare frame and you tie them up together and you got a homemade tramp.

I joined the Tumblers when I got older and Mr. White always been a role model to me. He was like a father figure to a lot of people over here....He always reminded us don't mess with the drugs, take advantage of the books, ya know, not look out, book out.

Back in '73 or something like that, I remember we'd all cram into his black Chrysler, or was it an Olds? But all the Tumblers would pile in and he'd drive to the shows. Sometimes he'd have to go back and get the equipment.

Without him a lot of guys over here wouldn't have survived. He helped a lot of guys out by taking them to see the world, taking them out of this square mile, out of this box.

You keep kids busy and they don't think about all the stuff that can get them in trouble. I try to be like Mr. White. I've been teaching them how to play drums and how to read music over at Truth school. I work with them from two to five everyday. I've been doing that for ten years.

Richard Blackmon: One of the things that I do remember real clearly is that when we first moved in, the gang situation was not as bad. It got progressively worse as we got closer to the '80s. I think the early '80s to mid-80s was the peak of it. One of the justifications that I came up with for it was that the first floor apartments are two story apartments, with more rooms, more bedrooms. So on your first floor apartments you have your larger families.

You might have a family with 10, 11, 12, 13 kids. Whereas, up above that as you went higher the apartments got smaller. So you'd have less number of kids. Some of the apartments above the seventh floor only had one or two bedrooms. The theory I kind of think of was one of the reasons the gangs got so bad was because on those lower floors, if you got into a rift say with one larger family, there's only four of us and there's 13 of them, they could keep us from going upstairs. They could keep us from going home.

They put one brother by one hallway, the other by the other hallway, and two by the elevator. And they'd wait for you and you couldn't get upstairs. So one of the ways that the kids in the smaller families combated those larger families was to form gangs....You know, there's no way you should have a family with 13 kids in the same building with a family with three kids. I mean, you're going to have disagreements. With 13 kids they could beat you pretty bad you know. And there was always older brothers or sisters that would take up for the younger ones. So if I got into it with a kid that was my age, he might have a brother or sister that was three, four years older than us that would, you know, beat me up and then I'd go get some of mine and they'd beat them up and that's how you started getting the gangs.

Sugar Ray Dinky: After all that stuff with the rap music, I got older and eventually had eight children. I have eight children now. And I took up a job in construction, and also at the school. My two sons were at Truth and my daughter was there when I started. They was about six, seven years old so I volunteered to be a parent to keep an eye on them. Then, I started the drum and bugle corps.

I have a lot of negative memories, and that's why I try to focus on the kids....Back in the days, we used to play baseball and football and other sports. I don't see no one out in the field and I haven't in years. We'd have basketball tournaments all the time at Stanton Park. Sometimes the all-stars at Stanton would play the all-stars at Seward Park. I blame the park district on that because we used to have baseball tournaments, softball tournaments, you know what I mean? Every year we had something to keep the kids busy.

But the money, sellin' the heroin and the drugs, the money is too big for the kids, you know. They get those sixty, seventy dollars and they're not thinking about the baseball game. They can make a hundred dollars every two days, they not thinking about no sports.

Tyrone Randolph: I knew the boundaries, but I wasn't in a gang so I wasn't scared of not going. That's how I am now, if I'm not a part of it why should I be afraid of going somewhere?

I really didn't have too many friends in the red buildings except the friends I had in high school with me, and I really didn't know where they lived, except for one.

One time he came to visit me and when he was leaving he got shot, shot in the back. I found out the next day at school and that led me to the second time I was involved in gangs as far as defending myself because the guys approached me about the situation. These are guys I went to school with and I let 'em know he's not a gang banger. One of the guys figured he knew who the guy was so he decided to swing on me.

Debra Wilson: You can't tell the gang members [that this is not the way]. Even though they might think that what you're saying is right, the peer pressure is too much, the money is too much.... McDonald's is over here, but nobody will work there. I shouldn't say nobody, maybe a few whose parents are holding tight and making their children see other values in the long run....But that quick money looks good. It looks good but it's so short term, and you can't explain that to them. You can't explain to them, you're

in fear. You can't enjoy your life because you're always watching your back, worried about who is going to pay you because they already got theirs. There's a lot of stress, a great amount of stress. And they're young people.

They're so organized and they all have potential, they could be business corporate managers if they put their minds to it. It's like they do the drugs, some go to prison, they get back out and do the same thing. So until they clean up their act they're not in the mind to do it. They haven't had enough instruction in their lives.

Sugar Ray Dinky: You know, a lot of kids over here have no parents. They're scared, you know, and they look to the gangs as a family. A lot of the times most of the moms don't have the money. They're on welfare and all of a sudden their kid is bringing home three hundred, four hundred dollars in a night...and they look the other way. I hate that, because some of these mothers are really proud of these boys, ya know, that's my baby this, and that's my baby that. Man, at the funeral home, that's my baby too.

Richard Blackmon: You know, it's funny, I never saw cocaine physically until I got to college. I mean I saw marijuana, I mean everybody pretty much smoked marijuana. But you know, not cocaine. Certainly not heroin, but people don't believe that. They think of public housing, they just assume.

I can remember being in a classroom and telling people I'm from Cabrini and they grab their purses like I was going to snatch them. That was kind of a shock for me. Or, I'd go to places on the West Side that were like 10,000 times worse than Cabrini. I'd be scared, you know, and they found out I'm from Cabrini and they start getting afraid of me. But I'm the one that's terrified. People have different perspectives. I mean, we had three bedrooms, a living room, a dining room, kitchen, a bath, and it was in pretty good shape. We didn't live like, you know, like these pictures you see of how people live, but we had a pretty decent place to live. I'd go to other peoples houses and I'd be like, maybe the projects aren't that bad. I can't wait to get home. It's all perspective.

Tyrone Randolph: When it comes to the differences between now and then, then it was more like unity and nowadays they don't really care. It's like the same gang fightin' within the same gang, everybody has their own cliques.

First it was about community and now it's like building based. If you're not in this building or not a part of that building it can become a problem for other people and their relatives that wanna come over and visit. The way they do their security these days they want to pat people down because of their insecurities of the police. It makes it difficult because you think, well, if my family or friends come over will they get patted down?

But, now I stay at 1230 Burling and it's more of a rehab building with tenant management so people are trying to keep the problems down.

Debra Wilson: I separate myself from what's on television [about the community]. It's usually the news that gives it to me first, and it's usually negative. I guess I just have high expectations of myself and separate myself from it. Because I saw Cabrini-Green in its first beauty and I know what it could've been and I know why it's not there.

Wanda Hopkins: When Jane Byrne moved here in 1981...well, first of all, it's not the real world for Jane Byrne coming to Cabrini, because she had security. They had cleaned up the hall-ways, they had special lighting in the hallways, all around her apartment, I mean, it was not Cabrini, it was not the same.

But, I must say that the parents of Cabrini were very happy when she moved here. For Christmas, she gave out Christmas trees and dolls for their children. I think she gave trucks for the young boys, so she really won over some parents at Cabrini around Christmas time. There was turkeys and hams and all kinds of things that she gave away, right here in the community.

No, it didn't stop some of the negative activity, it just moved it. Nothing was going on where she was, it was so secure that you could have, in that building you could have left your door open, but everybody just kept their mess over on the other side.

She was there during the day, but I don't think she stayed one night. I think her intentions were good, but she didn't see the real Cabrini. You coming to live in Cabrini, you've got to come in like I did, you know, just come in, and she didn't do that. But, she did do some positive things.

Richard Blackmon: I don't think it ever came to a point when I wasn't proud and happy about where I lived....'Cause you got to remember when you're in a place and that's all you know, no matter what happens that's still home. I mean I always compare where I live to where other people live, and I was like well, where you live ain't that great either, you know. So I mean I live in the projects, so what? I know a lot of places worse then the projects. I could be outside, I could be in a shelter. So for me it was never a matter of better or worse. It was home.

A lot of who I am is because of this place, so it's kind of hard to turn your back on that—good, bad, indifferent. I can remember after my mom died when I was 17, I quit school for a while. I can remember days where I didn't have money to go to school, and I'd come up here and wait for the Clybourn bus right on Larrabee and Division. There would be like bums who were getting money for me to go to school. I was too proud to beg for it, but they would beg people for money and then come and give me the money so I could get on the bus to go to school. You know, that's how much they wanted to see me go.

I can remember the first time I was in the newspaper for football. I played football at Lane Tech High School. One Sunday we woke up and there I was in the paper full as life. I mean I had little articles in the paper before...but this was like a full spread. Well, everybody went out and bought all the newspapers and cut them out and gave them to my mom. Seemed like the whole neighborhood was coming over to our house to say, hey, did you see Richard in the paper this morning? The pride other people took in what I was doing, you know, it was almost like they did it too....I mean you could never feel bad about a place that cares that much about what happens to you.

When we played in the city championship, I can remember everybody being glued to the television watching. You know, watching the game – being proud.

Sugar Ray Dinky: When Larry was killed, I mean, I needed some help on that one. I didn't have no counseling or nothin'. I couldn't believe that because I was a young guy, you know. I saw my friend get killed right in front of my face. I seen people shot at and laying out on the street and all that, but I didn't think it would actually happen. I couldn't take it. It happened over 20 years ago and I still feel the pain of it, I still talk about it and still dedicate all the stuff I do to him because he was, he rapped first. He was a great rapper and a great singer too. I didn't do nothin' but play the guitar back then. When he died I just tried to carry on what he'd want. And we had promise. We played at the Park West. We was getting ready. We was the next Impressions over here [*laughing*].

Thinkin' about Larry makes me keep going. I'm 37 and I'm still rappin', still doin' my thing.

Richard Blackmon: There was another time when I was on TV with Jimmy Walker. Jimmy "J.J." Walker was the one in "Good Times," the TV series which was sort of based on Cabrini, I guess. He had come into Chicago and they invited a couple of us down to WLS-TV, so we gave J.J. the key to Cabrini-Green. Everybody watched that. Oh, we saw you on television last night. So, I don't care what happens, I don't care what tragedies you have to experience, or anything like that. You still have that feeling of home.

Tyrone Randolph

Tyrone Randolph: I knew things weren't too kosher in Cabrini by the way the media portrayed it and talked about it. I think it was overly done, because you'd turn on the news and you'd see the same things were happening in other neighborhoods...but with Cabrini they'd make it seem like it was more like an every day thing. They'd make it seem like it's just like Beirut.

It's definitely not perfect. I have an uncle who was injured from someone throwin' a bottle out the window. Now he has a metal plate in his head, so people do a lot of crazy stuff...and when it comes to laziness, you can find it in a lot of people here.

Still, I love Cabrini. It's my home. I have a lot of friends here. With my job I have a connection with a lot of the kids and my job, basically, is to educate the kids on the negativity and how they can overcome it. I can tell them my story, and maybe somebody can catch something from it that helps them to overcome.

Richard Blackmon: One thing that bothered me later was this whole concept of project and that word. I came to really understand as I got older that there were people that were keeping track of who was dying, how many kids were being born out of wedlock, who was graduating, who got hooked on drugs, who went to jail. There was actually somebody keeping track of that stuff.

They could predict certain things about your life. Now to me that was scary, but when you think about it, it really is a human experiment. So it is a project.

I studied urban sociology in college and the professor walked up to me once and asked me where I was from, and how old I was. Then he just started telling me all the stuff that had happened in my life up to now. And I'm like, well, how did you know this? He said, based upon how old you are and where you grew up, I can tell certain things that are going to happen in your life. So I said to him, well, you got to come up with solutions to stop it. He said, well, I'm a sociologist, I just study problems. I don't come up with solutions.

That kind of, you know, teed me off. That's when I stopped using that term, project. 'Cause it really is an experiment, you know, there really are people that watch what happens to you and how it happens. And the next question you have to ask is, why would someone do that?

part III THE LATEST GENERATION
(1984-2000)

Standing outside of the row house apartment he shares with his mother and sisters, Erick Moore can't help but carry on about a new job that should help him pursue admission into an arts college in the fall. At age 20, he says he's eager to dive into life after high school.

It's obvious Erick tends to look at the positive side of things. He's made a habit of passionately promoting the virtues of Cabrini-Green and all that this area has meant to him. But even Erick admits he, and his community, have been profoundly impacted by the more negative incidents that have occurred here.

When considering the most powerful contribution to the tragic legend of Cabrini-Green, it's not surprising Erick points to the day, in 1992, when nine-year-old Dantrell Davis was shot and killed by a sniper's bullet on his way to Jenner school. Not just the police, but hordes of media types descended on the area in the days and weeks following the incident. The national exposure once again painted Cabrini-Green as a dangerous place to live.

Erick, a sixth grader at the time of the killing, was standing on one side of Jenner school that morning when he and his friends heard three shots ring out. "So everybody ducked," Erick recalls, "and we were thinking it was just regular gang bangers fighting so we ducked and ran into the school. And then when we got into our classrooms they announced over the intercom that a little child by the name of Dantrell Davis just got shot."

It wasn't the first time Erick heard shots, nor the first time he learned of a child being killed in the neighborhood. Still, Erick says the death of Dantrell Davis changed Cabrini-Green in a way that no other event had. "It made a lot of things quiet," he says.

On the positive side, gang members forged peace treaties and violence in the area quickly declined. At the same time, however, Erick says residents became more withdrawn from each other. There was less interaction among neighbors and more fear. "From then on," he says, "I never felt like things were back to normal."

Noreen Rhodes **agrees that for a variety of reasons Cabrini-Green is not as close of a community as it once was. She has lived in the area all her life and, at 25, longs for the days when the neighborhood felt like one big family.**

When Dwayne Ford **went away to college, he never realized he'd have to convince people that he was indeed from Cabrini-Green. "They wouldn't think somebody from Cabrini is in college." At 24, he is now convincing young people from the area that they too can go to college. Having recently moved just west of the community, Dwayne returns to the row houses each week day, where he works for a youth organization called Project Education Plus (PREP).**

Jermaine Savage, **23, also felt the weight of Cabrini's national reputation when he went away to college. He describes Cabrini as "a world within itself," and after graduating from the University of Iowa he returned to his family's row house apartment.**

As Alderman of the 27th Ward, Walter Burnett **(who we met in Chapter Four) continues to offer a broader perspective on the row houses and what's become of them.**

In front of his apartment, Erick Moore continues to talk about how well his job interview went. "I start next week," he says excitedly. "I gotta go through an orientation, but this should work out great for me."

Erick Moore: I've been born and raised in Cabrini, born and raised in Mother Cabrini. Born in 1980.

When I was younger, about four or five years old, the best thing for me was block parties. I loved block parties. It was just a block party for the family of Cabrini. The family was still tight. You had more violence in the '80s than you had in any decade, but we still had more love in the '80s. Cabrini was more alive in the '80s.

Anybody was invited but it would just be certain blocks. Like Cambridge Street would have a block party, then Cleveland would have one. It happened like five or six times during the summer because it would be on different blocks. They'd have families on that block who would barbecue and make sure that there was free food for everybody. Families would get together, go grocery shopping and then there'd be barbecue chicken, ribs and all that and they would barbecue right on the street.

Everybody was welcome and everything was happening on the street. You get the Jesse White Tumblers, and they would perform a show for us. There would be games, like I remember this one game where we used to go inside this big balloon and we'd be flipping and jumping around. Block parties was a treat for me.

Another thing that was fun was when we flipped on dirty mattresses, like mattresses they throw out. We would be doing it behind our mothers' back because they didn't want us flipping on these dirty mattresses. We had about ten friends and we all get dirty mattresses from the garbage and we'd flip on it. We'd all go to the back of Chestnut Street, and that's how the Jesse White Tumbling Team actually started. We'd be practicing to join the Jesse White Tumbling Team. Every child wanted to be a Jesse White Tumbler....That was one of my biggest dreams.

Dwayne Ford: When I was young Chicago Avenue was the basketball court, and they had city tournaments. I was too young to play. I remember a few players, like their street names. They had basketball nicknames like Dr. Pepper and Shake and Bake. And William and Curtis Gates would play, this was way before "Hoop Dreams" came out.

Then they had the block parties. It seems like they don't have those as much anymore, but you would come out and dance, play basketball. Jesse White used to come out and tumble. Everybody liked to see the girls and the guys flippin', and the music guy used to sit on the side....That was one of those good times where we'd hang out and just eat chips and drink pop without worrying about no cars coming by.

Jermaine Savage: When I was young I was involved in different programs in the neighborhood, like the Montgomery Ward tutoring program and Sunshine. They used to take us on different field trips and stuff outside the neighborhood and for me that's when I started to see how different Cabrini-Green was from everything else.

For me Cabrini-Green is like a world within itself, so when you start venturing outside you start to see there's a lot more to the world than just what I'm seein' here in my neighborhood....Just drivin' through certain neighborhoods you could see things were different.

You got crime and violence everywhere, but in some neighborhoods a shooting is very rare. But if a shootin' went off right here, right now it wouldn't really be a surprise to me....I mean I might even hear some shots and not even jump.

Noreen Rhodes: I've been livin' here 25 years, my whole life. My fondest memory was when I was about six years old, we stayed at 862 North Sedgwick in the reds and moved down to the row houses. I remember the trees were beautiful. The flowers were blooming. It was summertime, and everything was beautiful.

I was used to being in a big building, so when we moved to the row houses there was more space. I had four sisters, no brothers. We had a front and back yard, so we had more room to play. We had a little sliding board in the back. We had fun. We made our fun.

I was in the same neighborhood, but I just didn't go back to the [red] building. My friends, we met up in the playground and we played together there. They went home and I came back to the row houses. To me it felt different. As our group got older, it just felt different.

Dwayne Ford: I was born in Cabrini, been here all my life, 24 years. I went to Jenner school from kindergarten through third, and then I went back to Jenner for seventh and eighth. In between I went to West Side Prep, where Marva Collins teaches. It was with some program where Mr. T. would give kids scholarships. But then when Mr. T. lost his funding, I went back to Jenner.

I grew up at 907 Cambridge. My aunt stays there now. My aunt has been there for maybe ten years, and before that my grandmother was in that same apartment forever.

At a young age I became a ward of the state, and I stayed with my aunt. At that time she just lived a couple houses down from my grandmother, on Cambridge.

Like I said, I was into the Cabrini-Green Tutoring Program and also at the CYCLE program. At CYCLE a lot of students from Wheaton College would come down and volunteer. I just remember Wheaton because to the kids everybody wanted a Wheaton tutor. I lucked up on one. Actually, my friend had one so I kind of clinged on to his. And this tutor, her dad used to play for the Cubs a long time ago. And her brother was with the Mets, but he got traded to L.A. So she was very nice. She used to take us out to her house on weekends in Palatine. We just hung out, she would teach us how to drive in the parking lot.

Noreen Rhodes: I went to Jenner up until first grade. After first grade, I transferred to Oscar Meyer, over on Sheffield Avenue. My aunt transferred my cousins there and she felt we should be out of the neighborhood to get a different experience of different cultures so she transferred us as well.

I don't know if it's the best thing that happened to me, but I felt it was good for me because it gave me a chance to be around a mixed crowd. It enabled me to adapt better, you know? So I was glad that I did go to the school.

I was young, but I felt that there was a togetherness in the community. We had block parties, I mean everybody came

together and it wasn't about where you stayed. Everybody was welcome. If you was homeless and you came and you wanted to have something to eat, you weren't turned away. It was come on in, get something to eat.

My mom used to organize it for Cleveland Street. She would bring all the stuff to our house. We had a freezer and we kept all the ice cream and sandwiches and boxes of chips there. We kept everything in the house until it was time. When the day come, we all moved the cars and everybody would come out and get the brooms and sweep up all the glass everything, so we would have room for the kids to come and play. We used to bring all the stuff down and set it up and we would just get it started.

Jermaine Savage: The most vivid memories of Cabrini to me is probably the shootin' that goes on, 'cause to me that's the thing that Cabrini-Green is known for and labeled for.

A lot of people you mention Cabrini and that's the first thing that comes to mind, the violence that goes on. But despite all that, I'm glad I grew up in Cabrini-Green 'cause I think it gives you an inner drive and a determination to do things a little bit harder, ya know, than somebody who didn't grow up here because you see how hard it is. You see what people are going through. You come outside and it's just an everyday struggle for people. When you constantly see that, it makes you wanna have somethin' better. It'd be different if you came outside and everything was bright and positive 'cause you'd think what else is there to ask for? But when you constantly see bad stuff happening and people strugglin', I know for me I think of, well, how can I keep from goin' through this stuff? Or, what can I do to help other people get through this stuff?

Walter Burnett: When I was in school they gave me a nickname and not one I'm proud of, but it humbled me. We didn't have a lot of money. We used to get new clothing once a year. We would get our clothes when my dad got his income tax check. Him and my mom had separated, but they were still married....He would come out at income tax time and he'd take us and buy us a whole wardrobe.

This was around April, spring time and he'd buy me a whole wardrobe of knits and flower shirts, you know, summer shoes and stuff like that. By the winter time, since I was a kid and I was growing, they all would be tight on me, and in the winter time I got on flower shirts and knit pants.

My pants would be so tight that they would call me britches. That was my nickname [*laughing*]. They used to laugh at me, man...tight old pants. I guess tight pants wasn't in. They called me that in my fifth grade class and that was my name throughout school. What's up, britches? I didn't like it, but it stuck for a while. They still call me that. That humbled me, because that let me know where I come from you know.

Dwayne Ford: My father started calling me Scooby. As far as I can remember, when I was little he gave it to me. Why, I don't know. I don't know if I liked the cartoon a lot, or if I looked like the dog or what. But now I got the tattoo on my arm, the Scooby tattoo. I got it on my spring break when I was in college. It kind of stuck with me.

Around here you pretty much have a nickname, because of the secret identity type thing. I don't know where everybody gets it from, but the people who know they're doing wrong usually have an alias name just so if they get caught doing something nobody will know their real name. That's not why I got it...but around here everybody's real name is pretty much a secret.

Erick Moore: I like to tell more of the sweet than the bitter about Cabrini but I do got to slide towards the bitter because of the death. Sometimes when we were just in the middle of us having fun, something terrible could happen. But as fast as it happens, it leaves your mind just as fast because you had so much fun before. So, it's like, oh man, somebody else got shot. Oh well, you know.

When you're kids you just don't think about it. In the row houses there wasn't too many shootings that occurred in the '80s. It was more in the projects, but there were some shooting in the row houses, just not as much as in the projects. So, in the row houses everybody got pretty yards, you walk out you can hear birds chirping, but walk outside the row houses and, like, there goes the war right there.

I mainly stayed in the row houses but I had family in the red zone, like 1150 building, and I would go there occasionally with my family. Other than that I rarely would leave the row houses.

Dwayne Ford: I was into playing basketball on weekends at the Y, on Saturdays. Every Saturday we would play. I didn't really go to Lower North Center until I was in high school and when I would come back from college.

My basketball team that played at the Y, our coach used to take us downtown to a video game place. We would go there and spend all our quarters. Sometimes my tutor from CYCLE would have tickets for the Cubs game and we would do that. We used to walk to the beach, too. I wasn't too much of a water person, so I would go just to be going.

When I was younger it seemed like more people were more into having fun around here and hanging out, doing a lot more things. Everybody kind of strayed away. When I was young it was like happening, it was kind of cool to be outside, you weren't worried about too many gun shots. It's not like it can't happen anytime, but it was more like everybody hung out.

Jermaine Savage: Of course, Cabrini is not all bad. There's a lot of good people and I've learned a lot from older people around here. There are a lot of people who are willing to take you in and look after you and let you know the right way, ya know what I'm sayin', like Mother Vassar. She's a close friend of my grandmother. As a child I remember going by her house and she'd always give us candy and talk to us about stayin' out of trouble. Of course as

a kid you love the candy but I always listened to what she'd say because it would echo what my grandma was tellin' me.

When you hear all the time from two people to stay out of trouble you think there must be a lot of trouble to look out for, then you start seein' stuff and findin' out about people going to jail and gettin' shot and stuff and you really realize what they were saying all that for.

Noreen Rhodes: My mom and Marion Stamps were very good friends as I was growing up. They were both community activists and I would see them marching and they had on their Afro-centric clothing. I really didn't know at the time what it was all about. As I got older, Ms. Stamps would come down and I'd hear them talk about the marches and they'd talk about their opinions about Cabrini.

My mother's level of intensity was fight for the community, the same as Marion's, but they had different opinions on certain things. They would go at it with each other, but they still remained friends, they just had two different personalities.

It had to be around the mid-80s when they were marching for housing, for jobs, for rights of the residents in Cabrini. Marion was from up on Sedgwick and my mother was from down here, so it was like they came together as one for things to better the community. I was looking at both of them as inspiration.

Dwayne Ford

Dwayne Ford: Shootings would happen more at night than in the day. Back then you would hear gun shots, but when I was younger it was kind of rare. Still, it wasn't a surprise when it happened. It would be more at night, and when you're young your parents already had you inside. You didn't know who's doing what, you just can hear it. Sometimes it would be close, sometimes it wouldn't.

Walter Burnett: You know what, it seemed to me I got to live in both worlds because my dad lived on LaSalle Street. I got to go up there, you know, and people up there most of them were white and middle class, but they were just like some of my mother's friends in Cabrini. Some of them drank, they did everything. Some of the couples would get in fights and all that stuff. They were just like regular people there. They had challenges too. Some of them got kicked out because they didn't pay their rent. Even on LaSalle Street. It was quieter, it was nicer, there wasn't a lot of kids, but it wasn't a lot different. It was boring actually.

So I didn't pay too much attention to those boundaries. The only time that I paid attention to those boundaries is when I was limited as a kid, where you couldn't go across Chicago Avenue, that's a big street. Don't go across there and don't go past Halsted over there. When you go past there, it becomes ghost town. We used to call that area ghost town. You got the train tracks over there, and rabbits that we'd try to catch. That's the ghost town. You'd hear stories about ghosts coming over there and all kinds of stories.

Erick Moore: If we were riding bikes we may go to all them places in one day; Lincoln Park, the beach, downtown. We might go to the beach early because it's hot when it's early and everybody's on the beach. We would go to the beach and we would do like something stupid, like steal some pops or whatever, steal a couple of pops and chips, and then we'd have a nice time at the beach with pop, chips, looking at the girls and chasing the girls up in the water. It was fun. We would take our bicycles downtown. One thing we used to do downtown was rap.

We would go right down Michigan, right there across the street from Water Tower. We would do our raps and we would generate a nice crowd, people would be giving up donations, like quarters, pennies, dollars, dimes and then [*laughing*] food stamps, too. That was fun.

We would go to ghost town, which was right beyond Montgomery Wards. It was called ghost town because it's like people didn't know too much about it so we would go there, you know what I'm saying, to have fun.

There was a Milk Dud factory that was over there. We would go there and the Milk Dud factory would give us free Milk Duds.

Noreen Rhodes: My step-father is also an activist in the community, mainly on police brutality and homelessness. He was basically the disciplinarian growing up, so I was in the house doin' my work and I rarely came outside, ya know, to hang out until I was about 14 years old.

When I came out, that was the life. I really didn't have the street knowledge. When I would come out at 14 it was like a whole new world to me because I never seen anything like that. There was stuff I wanted to do, I wanted to hang out more. I don't say I didn't listen, but maybe I wanted to start doing what I wanted to do, you know? I still kept the line....I could only do this and so I had to uphold their trust before anything else. If I misused that trust, I was out.

Erick Moore: I went to Jenner school. It was great but the only thing you had to worry about at Jenner school was, you know what I'm saying, was getting teased. You teasing somebody and a shooting may occur. I ain't saying that just to make it seem like shootings occurred all the time because it didn't, but you still had to worry about that.

Like teachers and the principal were always ready and we would do practice for shooting. They would sound a horn and it was the horn signaling gun shots, so you know what I'm saying, we would practice. They'd have us all drop to the ground and crawl to the front door and get in the doorway.

But Jenner was the best. I had so much fun in Jenner, and most times for me you didn't worry because as a child you've seen what's going on as far as the negative. The child is already in his own world so it was kind of hard for me to look at shootings that way. If somebody's shooting it would be like, okay they're just going to shoot somewhere else.

But the most horrible thing that I seen that made me wake up to it was when I was 11, when I saw a man literally get his brains blown out of his head. And for me, as an 11-year-old child, that wasn't nice to see. I wouldn't say it's like a horror or anything but I was kind of scared to come out for a couple of days. Because as a child you think you might get shot.

That kind of gave me a slap in the face at an early age. I knew what reality was. I knew that this was the world, before then it was just fantasy. I didn't think nothing. I could hear shots but I didn't see no one actually getting shot. I didn't think nothing of it. I'd hear it on the news and be like okay. So it was like, man, things could happen.

Noreen Rhodes: My mom would take us out. We would go out to eat downtown, up north. The first place I remember was to Gino's East on Superior. We went out for pizza and that I can remember. That was like our family night. We all went out and had dinner and just talked.

We'd also have Sunday night dinners. My mom would barbecue all the time, so I would come home from school and if I see that gate open I knew that my mom was barbecuing. And so I would jet down real fast, and even though it wasn't a special occasion she would get the barbecue out. If I came around with friends, they'd get something to eat. It was togetherness.

My mom would take pictures of all of the kids, different families with kids. We have pictures of all the kids together, she'd say c'mon let's take pictures.

Erick Moore: One of the best programs when I was young was the Sunshine Ministry. We had activities to do, they'd teach us about God. After they finished with the Bible teaching we would play basketball and other activities. We would go on trips, camp trips, that was so fun.

Like me seeing Cabrini all the time, it was fun to be outside Cabrini and go to camp like to Missouri and Wisconsin. It was so fun going up there because it was away from Cabrini and you really felt how people truly feel about each other.

Noreen Rhodes: You know, the saddest time was when it seemed like it just started going away...the togetherness, the love that the community had, you know, you could tell the feeling was not there.

The block parties are still going on, but not like we used to have back then. It's not as much activity as we used to or different types of food to give the children different experiences. They don't have it now. It's not like that any more.

Dwayne Ford: When I was in about eighth grade, I used to have to walk over to a place called Olivet, it was like a daycare. It's torn down now and they got houses back there. But I used to have to walk over there, and here is one gang, and over there is another gang. And at that time I didn't know too many people. I didn't know anybody, I think, in the white buildings. I had friends in the red buildings. I also had friends on the other end who was in a different gang. So because of everybody over here knowing me — I was maybe a little popular — but they just knew me as Scooby and they know I play basketball, so they wasn't pressuring me to try and put me in gang. And the same thing at the other end, they got to know me and they knew me as Scooby, just a basketball player, so they never really tried to distinguish me from one gang to another or bother me just for that reason, ya know, he's Scooby he plays basketball, let's not mess with him. So I was fine walking from here to over there and back.

Erick Moore: With gangs in Cabrini there's no pressure. The only thing that would turn you on to the gangs is what they draw. How much money they got in their hand, what they doing. But there ain't no gang coming up to you, saying, "You gonna be one of us or we're going to kick your ass," or whatever.

People get in the gang because, it's totally up to them to get in the gang. You be that because you're turned on to that lifestyle. You're turned on to that lifestyle and you like hearing the stories about being in gangs.

Once when I was seriously thinking about joining the gangs I was like, no, because I started looking at it different. I guess it was lucky for me that I looked at it on the negative points, but man, most of them are friends and cousins and a lot of them are dead. That's what I looked at.

I'm not in a hurry to die...so that's why I never joined. You got people joining for other reasons. Some people join for protection because they got a big crowd that can protect them, but little do they know that you're taking the protection away from yourself. If you're neutral you're able to walk in any neighborhood, but you still gotta worry because they probably still jump on you. But, by you saying you're neutral you've got less of a chance of getting shot or beat down than being in a certain gang.

Noreen Rhodes: Once I remember, it was after Thanksgiving, we were in the house and somebody knocked on our door. I can't remember the guy's name. He was working for the CHA and he got shot. He got shot down here off work and he got shot in the head and that was really the first time that they was so bold to do that. You know, that was a bold thing. I had to be about 12 or 13 then. And I would ask my mama, why would they do that? Why would they do that? And she would say, I don't know what is going on.

Erick Moore: When I got older I went to Cabrini Connections. I heard about it from a friend. He said it was a tutoring program for high school students....When we first went to Cabrini Connections, man, it was so much happening. It was so loud. There was so many girls to meet, so many tutors.

All of us got together, like we was real tight. I ain't saying this just to make it up, but the things that the students are doing now is because of what we did. And that's the truth. We helped start a magazine and a film group and, man, it was a lot of fun.

Walter Burnett: You get to see a lot more negative things as you get older, but in the child's eye, you really don't see negative things. It was always nice to hang out with my friends in the different buildings and stuff. As a teenager, it was the most I thought about. That was the real thing that was on your mind as you got older, because teenagers were just bein' teenagers, you know. It's like that's your whole concentration for the whole day is boys and girls.

As I said, when I became a teenager, then things got a little rougher. Gangs started to get more prevalent in the neighborhood. But back then they used to have respect. It was Ms. Jones, Ms. Burnett, Mr. So and So. There was a lot more fathers around, and a lot of grandparents were around too. It was a lot of respect, and then it started changing.

Noreen Rhodes: Maybe about 1989 the shooting got real bad over here. You couldn't really sleep....I thought I was dreaming that I was hearing a lot of shooting, but there was so much it woke me up. I ran to the back room to where I could see up more towards Hudson Street and I was seeing the people shooting, and the lights or fire coming out of the gun and I was just looking out the window in amazement 'cause I never seen it or heard that much shooting.

It was right close, right in front of me. I'm in the back and Hudson Street is right there. So they're on Hudson, like on Hudson playground, and I can see them from where my room is at.

It was scary because I was dreading when New Year's came, thinking about all the people that might get hurt when they all shoot off their guns at New Year's. I was dreading when certain holidays came around because I knew they'd be doin' certain things and it made me real scared.

On New Year's I try to be in the house. I don't try to go nowhere because of fear like man, I have to hurry up and get home before they start shooting. I can't even go out and enjoy myself, because I'm thinking about the shooting. I can get shot, my friend could get shot going home. These people might be walking down the street. I was isolated in my house and I didn't like that.

I would pray, ask to protect everybody. And protect those who are shooting, because they need protection too. They need help themselves because something is wrong for them to be out here doing it. So I would just pray about it and because I would be thinking, oh I hope my mom she don't come home yet. Or you know, I hope my sister won't get caught in it. I had to get my mind off it, the worry. So I would just pray. Just pray.

Erick Moore: Everything was so fun in Cabrini in the '80s and early '90s. After the death of Dantrell Davis it made a lot of things quiet in Cabrini. I don't know why because — I'm not trying to be bogus 'cause that's not fair — but there was a lot of children who died before Dantrell Davis. But the death of Dantrell Davis was a big thing. It changed the whole look of Cabrini. People started to slow down. You got gang members startin' to slow down. They started calling peace treaties. They ain't never called a peace treaty before in Cabrini, they started making peace treaties. The death of Dantrell Davis changed a lot of things.

I remember that day. I was in school and we were playing football outside and just before we walked into school, I was in sixth or seventh grade, but just before we walked into school we heard three gun shots. So everybody ducked, and we were thinking it was just regular gang bangers fighting so we ducked and ran into the school. And then when we got into our classrooms they announced over the intercom that a little child by the name of Dantrell Davis just got shot.

They announced that. About five minutes after they announced that over the intercom...beep, beep...parents are there comin' to get their kids 'cause it was on the news just that quick. Parents come to get their kids real quick.

I was one of the kids that stayed at school. Parents were so frightened, so scared they got their children immediately. Like, it was some classes had only three students in there. In my class there was about ten students left, and while we were in class every teacher looked like zombies, like our teachers was cryin'. It hurt them that bad. The death of Dantrell Davis shook a lot of people.

Jermaine Savage: When we were in grammar school, there were times when they'd have to cut the day short because the gangs were outside warring, shooting and people were coming to get their kids out of the school, so after a while you just become numb to it, ya know....When that happened I realized that, yeh, growing up here really must affect you. But whether you are part of the negative things goin' on or not, it's going to have a certain effect on you and it's hard to explain, but everyday you're seein' people getting beat up or drugs bein' sold and things that you shouldn't normally be seein' but when you do see it it becomes a norm....It's hard to be separate from the negative part of Cabrini-Green. You might say I'm not gonna kill anybody or sell any drugs or anything but seein' that everyday, to me it has to have some type of effect on you, 'cause most kids don't grow up with that.

Noreen Rhodes: I would say things to certain people that I knew were involved in gang activity. Why did you all do that? Why? Give me an explanation. And they'd give me an explanation and I tell them I don't think that's a good explanation about why you're doing it. I try to tell them everybody is here together, we are all living around each other and we should be able to get along. It's just us in this area anyway, so why put yourself in jeopardy? Why put your family in jeopardy? Why jeopardize everybody when we can all just be together?

There's a lot of people around here that's real cool. They love it here, they care, but the mentality is not like it should be and you know it's hard to believe that they don't know, but they don't know about that. They weren't brought up like that....A lot of them don't know what love is or how to love somebody...because they wasn't brought up like that.

Jermaine Savage: When I was at school at the University of Iowa and I tell people I'm from Cabrini-Green, most of the time the only thing they've heard about in Cabrini-Green is like gang violence and stuff, so they expect you to be this outright, crazy person who may shoot you or rob you and they're not real eager to hang with you and stuff. They have this expected image of you because the television makes it seem like it's all violence. You rarely hear about kids in Cabrini doin' positive things 'cause most of the time they only talk about it when there's shootin going on, other than that Cabrini's not really in the news, and that kinda causes people outside the neighborhood to get this thought in their head that everybody in Cabrini is negative.

The thing I like about Cabrini is the people here. Even though there's a lot of bad things happenin', I have a comfort level here. I mean I feel more comfortable here where there's shootin' and all that goin' on than I did when I was at school. I mean, this was in Iowa City, and I didn't have to worry about people shootin' at me or something, and you'd think I'd be more comfortable there but I wasn't. I'm more comfortable here because people know me, people aren't lookin' at me like he's from Cabrini and he might be this dangerous person. They're lookin' at me like I know him, we grew up together and all that, but you'd think it would be the opposite.

At the University of Iowa, when I came home here I always felt better, even though it's a risk and stuff can happen. And that's what I don't like about Cabrini because things can happen in the blink of an eye. I mean everything can be goin' along good and there's months between any incidents, and then in a blink of an eye it can change.

Walter Burnett: I didn't like gang bangers, I never did, so I don't care for them. I think they're misguided. That's how I look at them....I remember when they started beating up on people, innocent people. When we grew up and it was like we were going to fight, we were going to fight with our hands up and everybody got around the circle and watched you, best man wins....We never used a whole bunch of people to jump on one person. These guys intimidate people. Not only do they intimidate innocent people, they intimidate their own. They beat up on their own. They shoot their own, they beat them down and then everybody in the neighborhood knows about it.

People talk about gangs providing a need for belonging, but that's a cop out. There are opportunities, and resources in and around Cabrini. There's more resources than any other neighborhood.

One thing about the reputation of Cabrini, the reputation of Cabrini has attracted more people. People say why don't we do it in Cabrini. I know where we can do it in, let's do it in Cabrini. Let's help those poor people in Cabrini. They get so much over there and there's so many resources, scholarship programs. It's just a lot going on that people don't take advantage of. Maybe part of it is it's not marketed right. Maybe part of it is that people just don't have faith in the system.

Cabrini is so close to downtown and job opportunities right at their fingertips that they don't look for them. I've been working since I was a little boy. My first job was passing out flyers for restaurants. Emptying garbage. I always had money in my pocket as a kid. There's job opportunities if folks want them. I worked at Burger King. I never had a problem getting a job, never. I went and looked for it. I didn't wait on somebody to come and give it to me. I wasn't no highly educated kid, you know. If I waited for somebody to come and give it to me, I wouldn't have anything, and my mom and dad didn't give me anything. I had to go out and get it on my own. A lot of folks that I grew up with, same thing, they worked. They worked.

Noreen Rhodes: Our generation is not doing it. The generation before us did it. They had their sit-ins, and they marched and protested for what they believed in. For us the focus is not there because I don't think the reality is with them, the reality around them is not there.

They are into this drug thing, and selling drugs. It's always like money, money, money. You got to have this, you got to have that. It's not about that. You can work and get you money. You don't have to be on drugs or sell drugs. No, you don't have to do that, you can go to school and get an education. Get out there, meet different people. Don't be isolated to where you're scared to come out and talk to different races. You have to come out of isolation and try. If you don't try it's not gonna work.

Erick Moore: With the death of Dantrell Davis everybody was just like, we're tired of all this back and forth shooting. Tired of all this gunfire and things going on. We're tired of it. It's fittin' to end now.

And that's what happened. The shooting rate in Cabrini dropped tremendously after Dantrell died. Shooting still goes on to this day but not, I mean, they used to shoot every day all day, there was not a day that went by without a shooting going on. Now, it's like every month, every other month a shooting may occur and it won't be severe. Somebody run over here and shoot and run back and that will be that.

I feel bitter and sweet about the situation because it took a child to die to shut down a lot of shootings going on, but I'm glad a lot of shooting stopped goin' on and I'm glad it slowed down a bit.

From then on I never felt like things were back to normal because it never got back to normal. Cabrini stopped being, everything just stopped.

That's when Cabrini was dyin'. People didn't seem as close. Seemed like, ya know, I've been here for many years and I don't know you and you live right across the street from me.

Dwayne Ford: For high school, I went to Providence-St. Mel for my first two years. Then I went to Wells High School, where I graduated from. St. Mel was real strict. I mean, you can't be late for classes, no chewing gum in the hall or in classes....You step on the grass you get fined. Detention is like an hour after school or something, or in school suspension for the whole day.

Wells was much different. When I switched, at the time I felt I'm free, because I was young and I didn't understand. I would just think, man I'm glad I'm here. It seemed like a burden off your shoulders, but the reality is worse. It was bad because it was easy to get D's and F's at Wells, where at St. Mel's if you know that you had so many D's and F's you would get kicked out, or you couldn't play sports if your grades were bad, and I really wanted to. So just out of sheer embarrassment I wanted to get good grades at St. Mel, where at Wells ya know you fit in with D's. You don't even want to get A's and B's there, people will talk about you [*laughing*].

Noreen Rhodes: Wells High School, to me it was...I'm not racist or anything but it was more Latinos than African-Americans. At Wells we had to run home from school because they would fight African-Americans. We had to all be in a group, even though you wasn't with this group, they counted you as one, so we were all in danger. We had to run to the bus stop and pray and hope that they don't corner us today.

It was like, you know, wild. We are all together, why do we have to go to that process? Four years, we had to run to the bus stop. They would fight. One day I was in class and I'm looking out the window and I seen a Latino guy was running with a two by four,

chasing a black boy. Next thing I know this black guy done took the two by four from him and he's chasin' him with it...and I said, uh oh, there's gonna be some mess now, now they gonna be fighting.

We all have to run and take different streets home, go down different streets, because we were in danger....That's the only thing I didn't like.

Erick Moore: Wells high school was a different experience for me. It was fun, but it was a different experience. It showed me how Mexican and Puerto Rican gangs act, how they different from black gangs. And it is a difference. Like with Mexicans and Puerto Ricans, you never catch them alone. And if they look like they're alone, [*laughing*] they're not!

Hey, bro, what you is? A GD? You're like, no. Throw down the GD fork. We're like what's with this man, we fittin' to beat him down. So we put our fist up and you see about 15 Puerto Ricans right around the corner, peaking around the corner, waiting for you to swing.

With black gangs, they real calm with it. They sneaky with it. Black gangs are real sneaky. Like with Puerto Rican or a Mexican gang, you know they're fittin' to jump on you because they make it obvious. But with the black gang it's, like, they put their arm around you, hey homey, where you from, Joe? Well, I'm from wherever. Oh yeah, well where you goin'? And you're like, I'm going to go to my girlfriend's house. No, not today man. You ain't going to go to your girlfriend's house, you're going to chill with us. You know, they real sneaky.

Dwayne Ford: Going to Wells, the majority of the time we took the bus, unless my cousin had a boyfriend that drove. Sometime I would get a ride if they was on time, but taking the bus was kind of dangerous. Not necessarily the bus, but when we got off the bus, because it was with the gang thing.

It was Puerto Ricans or Mexicans, but it was in a Hispanic area, so they had their gang, other people had their gang, and the blacks were in a gang. It wasn't distinguished by races, but if you was black then they look at you as you in one gang. I couldn't distinguish them, and I just knew a few names of the gangs. I didn't know who was in what, so by me coming to school, they would say okay, he's in the Disciple gang, let's get him or whatever.

For a while there I had to go to school with the gang bangers, just for protection. If somethin' did happen there would be more than one person. So after a while we started taking the Division buses.

We start walking over to Division because they expecting us to come from Chicago Avenue because that's the route everybody took that came from this way. So we started taking the Division bus, and just come back that way. At first it was cool, and one time, I don't know if I came to school late, but I went by myself and I got kind of close to the school and like two or three of them came at me.

And they was like, GD, which they thought all the black people was GD's, and I'm like I ain't in a gang. They was like, well, throw down the forks — which was, the GD's throw the forks up, so they made me like disrespect the fork by throwing it down. So I'm like okay, I threw it down. I didn't care. Ya know, it was just to save a beat down, ass whooping' or whatever [*laughing*]. Even if I was in a gang at that time I think I would have done it anyway. And I wasn't, so it made me that much prouder to do it, so I really didn't care. So when I did that they let me go, and I just went on in the building.

After school, even if you did have a ninth period, everybody, all the blacks would wait for each other and go down to the bus stop, and there was a lot of us, girls, guys, young, old, it was a lot. And we walk down to the bus stop and pretty much nothing would happen. But come to school in the morning by yourself...

Erick Moore: There'd be times where I was like don't pay attention to it and then there were times that I had to pay attention to it because even if you're not in Gangster Disciples but from Cabrini-Green you still in it — because the Puerto Rican and Mexican gangs, they ain't tryin' to hear it.

They know you're from Cabrini-Green. They know you're GD, although you ain't, they know you is 'cause that's what they figure, so you still have to fight along side the Gangster Disciples.

You couldn't walk home from school, you had to take the bus. And then when you take that bus and you walk from Augusta Street to Ashland you gotta be in a group. If you're walking by yourself down a Viking neighborhood, a Mexican oriented gang, walking in the neighborhood down Augusta if you by yourself chances are you're going to get jumped. But if you're in a crowd, see with Mexican gangs if they see a lot of black kids in a crowd — I ain't saying this just because we're black, either — they see a lot of black kids in a crowd they don't do nothing. Even if they got a crowd, nothing. They'll stand across the street and throw bricks, but they'd be scared about it. But if they catch you by yourself, it's over.

Some people dropped out because of that reason, because they got tired of having to worry about gangs....Me, personally, I wasn't going to let them drop me out of school....Don't get me wrong, I had plenty of Mexican and Puerto Rican friends. They were cool guys, but you got the gangs, too, that whoops people.

Dwayne Ford: One time it was like six or seven of us, it was senior year. We seen a couple Puerto Rican guys, and by me bein' paranoid I'm lookin' around tryin' to observe the scene. One guy is standing across the street with his hands behind his back, and we're across the street and we walkin'. So as we passed him, he came up behind us and a couple of guys jumped out in front of us with like bats and sticks and whatever. So, we was close to a corner, so I ran back and ran around the corner, and so much happened so fast I don't know the people that was with me what they did, but I know as I ran past like one of the stores, a glass shot out from a bullet, ya know, from a gun shot.

So I ran down the back street, and ran back to Chicago Avenue. I was just waiting on the bus to come back home, and they came up that way, so I ran a little further down but there was another gang down that way....So the bus finally came, and I came back home.

Once you got in the school, I felt pretty safe. Once you got in. It was just getting there and getting out, and going back home that was the problem. For that reason I was happy to be out of that school.

Erick Moore: One time we were standing on the corner, me and my guys, we just talking. We're standing on the corner, police roll by, they stopped the car. One cop says, "Hey, do any you niggers have any government cheese?" I'm thinkin', what? Then I said, hell no, but if you looking for some donuts you can go right down the street.

Two white cops. They got out of the car and we sprinted off. They didn't catch us. It was about 10:30 at night and that made me so angry. And another thing is when they flash the lights dead in your face. They say, you seen such and such? You fit the description of such and such....They harass people a lot.

There's been plenty of times I could've been in jail because of just hanging with certain friends. It makes you angry, makes you uncomfortable....You can't talk to nobody when the police arrive asking you stupid questions like, what are you doing here?

But you got some good cops out there like the Slick Boys and Eddie Murphy. They call him Eddie Murphy 'cause he looks like Eddie Murphy. So there's some cool cops.

Walter Burnett: In Cabrini, I never really thought about the police, to be quite honest. Any time I got in trouble, it was outside the neighborhood. In the neighborhood, I never had the police bother me, harass me, check me, any of those things. Maybe it was because I looked like a good, decent kid but I never had that problem when I was in the neighborhood.

When I started hanging with guys outside the neighborhood, then that's when I got in trouble, when I started hanging with people that didn't live in the neighborhoods, older people.

Dwayne Ford: As I got older I started to see a lot of people on the drugs, and to get the drugs people were stealing and then selling things, coming to your house and trying to sell you something. One time, [*laughing*] somebody knocked on my aunt's door, and the guy tried to sell us the sink. Really, like the kitchen sink.

People used to sell Pampers, people would sell anything they could get their hands on to get drugs. In Cabrini, you got your boosters, the people who go around and sell stuff. It's like a daily market. People were stealing clothes out of stores and come around to sell them. If he was real good you could tell him what you want, like I want a pair of Levi's, size 34, two pair, blue and gray. You would like put in an order, and they would go get it and come back to you....They would come with the price tag on it, and even with the little beeper thing that supposed to make the [store] alarm go off. So you wonder how did you get that out of the store?

Erick Moore: What happened recently was — this was like October, 1999 — and when I seen the guy laid out, he was stretched out and I knew this guy and this was my friend's cousin, on the ground laid out. He was shot, and nothing else was moving but nerves. And that kind of brought me back to, well, this still is Cabrini. It's great and it's been calm for a while but it's Cabrini.

Walter Burnett: Let me tell you about the challenges the gangs create in public housing. Folks always mind their own business. Nobody will call the police about anything, they would be afraid. They wouldn't call unless something really bad happened.

In my ward, I get more calls in my office about things that's wrong....They don't do that in public housing. People keep their mouths shut, they're afraid of retaliation. Back in the old days in Cabrini, if a fella was aware of who was shooting, they wouldn't say anything because what would happen is that person would find out who told or come to your house and bust your windows and stuff....Everybody in the neighborhood would know who did what, but the police wouldn't.

Noreen Rhodes: People don't care now. You can tell because there are children out here at midnight and one o'clock in the morning. Children are out on State Street and some are seven and eight years old, hustlin' to get them something to eat...washin' windows, playin' drums, tryin' to keep surviving. Seven and eight years old some of them will sell dope in that situation, trying to take care of themselves while the parents are all getting high.

That's the change that you can see because you got the children doin' what the adults should be doing. That's where you can see the change. It doesn't make any sense because they too young, they babies. They shouldn't have to go through that. I didn't have to, why should they?

It hurts me to see the kids. They just babies, they only know what they see and what you teach them.

Jermaine Savage: Not long ago my friend, Jamar Barnes, got shot by Jenner school. Things transpired so fast, in like ten minutes he was gone and like four other guys were shot and two other guys I know went to jail. I mean this is like in a ten-minute span, and for some people this don't happen in their whole lifetime, and that's what scares me the most about Cabrini, you never know what's gonna happen.

In life you never know what's gonna happen but it seems like when you live in Cabrini it's just a notch higher....Even when there's peace, your mind is stuck on what might be about to happen. But I'm conditioned to it, I'm used to it, I've been around it all my life.

As a child there was less worry, but when you get to be my age it seems like you start to become a target yourself even if you're not a part of the gangs...it's almost inevitable that people will try to tie you in to certain things, ya see what I'm sayin', like you could be standing out on the block with the same friends you grew up with, and some of 'em might be in a gang and some may not, but these are your friends and you're not looking at it like that, he's in a gang, you're lookin' at it like this is my brother, I grew up with him. Shouldn't I be able to stand right here and talk to 'em? But you might be standin' there with your buddies like you always did as a child, and a car could come past, a rival gang or whatever and they want these guys, they gonna get those guys and 'cause you're out there with 'em, they're not gonna say, well this guy is in the gang but not that guy, there's no time, they're not gonna separate you from him. Just you bein' out there involves you so it's just about association when you get older.

People automatically expect you to be the same way as your buddies, so you get associated and the danger level kinda goes up.

But, it's up to you to protect yourself and you have to make certain decisions about everything, even about hanging on the corner. There's really little margin for error.

Dwayne Ford: It is really not as bad as they say on TV, but people only could go by what they hear....They going to say it's a reflection of Cabrini.

When I got to college a lot of people would ask me where I'm from. I would say Chicago, and they say what part? I would say Cabrini-Green, and they would look at me funny. They wouldn't believe it because of the way I was. They wouldn't think somebody from Cabrini is in college.

Then, when I would tell them I don't drink or smoke, they wouldn't believe that....They would ask me, is it really that bad as people say on TV?

I wouldn't get frustrated. I would just try to ask them specific questions, you know, what do you want to know? And I would tell them the truth of what happens....I would tell them we do have our knuckleheads, we do have our bad people, and that's all that sticks out. It's the bad things that people hear about.

But, also, I'd say we do have a lot of good people here. Maybe we don't have people who make a lot of money, but people here still are good people. But we do have our idiots that want to drink or deal drugs or sell drugs...and that sticks out on the news so much when something bad happens....I would try to tell them as best I could that it's not that bad. It's kind of hard to say that when you see stuff on the news. It's kind of hard to tell somebody that this really isn't that bad.

Erick Moore

Erick Moore: I look at it this way now, ain't no place a safe place. Things happen in Columbine High School and all the rest of those places, so there's no safe place. For you to say that Cabrini is a horror flick would be wrong because the world is horror, you know what I'm saying, the world got horror in it. No matter where you're at.

Rachella Thompson **is only half kidding when she says the redevelopment of Cabrini-Green was her idea. What she means is,** "they stole my ideas."

Standing on a new play lot that's part of the freshly designed landscape in front of the Seward Park fieldhouse at Division and Orleans streets, Rachella points over at the handsome clock tower that recently went up in the northwest corner of the park. "That clock right there, and the tower, we put that in our project," she insists.

As part of an art contest sponsored by the *Chicago Tribune*, Rachella and a friend conceived of an architectural redevelopment of Cabrini-Green. "It was right before they were gonna remodel Cabrini," she says, "and we didn't even know that."

Rachella and her friend entered their design in the contest and received an honorable mention for their effort. The *Tribune* later ran a feature story on the two of them. "They did a nice article on us because we lived in the neighborhood and got honorable mention," Rachella recalls. "This was back in '93, when we were in grammar school."

In the last few years, however, while watching the gradual progress of the now infamous redevelopment, Rachella says she noticed something peculiar. "All of the designs that we put into our project, they are putting into Cabrini, even the clock tower....Where they put the new Jenner school," Rachella points out, "we said put something right there like an activity center. We took all of the buildings they took down. We took down the 1117 building....If they are stealing my design, I want to be paid for it."

As a freshman at North Park College on Chicago's North Side, Rachella has had little time to redesign any other cityscapes.

Like several young people from Cabrini, part of her college experience has included fielding curious questions about her neighborhood. "Even people from California," she says, "they're shocked I live in Cabrini. But I'm shocked they have never seen snow."

At 21, Tobias Holmes admits he too has found himself wrestling with his community's reputation. Born and raised in the red buildings, he says you tend to grow up fast in Cabrini-Green. Ironically, it's his father's troubled past that he says has kept him focused on a bright future. Living with his girlfriend and his baby daughter, Tobias is working part-time and making plans to enter the armed forces.

Anita Gunartt, 19, has lived in the Cabrini community since she was three. "I love Cabrini," she says, but admits that this love comes with some fears, concerns and frustrations. After spending her freshman year at Western Illinois University, she is currently working part-time at Cabrini Connections, a tutor/mentor organization in the neighborhood. She plans to continue her college education in the fall.

At a young age Kiki Coleman took on a prominent role in raising her younger brother in Cabrini. Now, she's raising a baby daughter of her own in the neighborhood. She's also making great strides in recovering from a bullet wound to the leg, which she suffered while walking to a nearby store to buy milk for her baby. She is back on her feet and has returned to work.

Anthony Edwards and his family have dealt with their share of tragedy in the Cabrini-Green neighborhood. Born and raised here, Anthony remembers the day his older brother was shot in 1986. Six years later, Anthony held his sister in his arms after she was hit by a sniper's bullet. Upon his sister's death, Anthony's mother, LueElla Edwards, founded Take Our Daughters to Work, Inc., an after-school club dedicated to serving adolescent girls in the community.

She was honored for her work at the White House in 1994. Anthony's mother died of a heart attack more than a year ago, and, at 27, he hopes to carry on her legacy by starting a program for adolescent boys.

Marsha Crosby (who we met in Chapter Two) and Jan Morgan (who we met in Chapter Four) continue to offer a broader perspective on the red buildings and what's become of them.

Rachella Thompson is shaking her head as she peers out over the sloping green grass of Seward Park. "Yep, this was all part of our redesign....I do think it's nice, but I'm not sure what the rest of their plan is for these people over here. Our plan didn't have everyone movin' out."

RAchella Thompson

Rachella Thompson: As I think back, I remember I couldn't go outside for a long time because my mom was real strict on us going out. We couldn't go out without her. I can remember all the way back to Head Start at Truth school, I went to Sojourner Truth. That's over in the white buildings, but my mom volunteered there so they let us go. It only goes to fourth grade. We all transferred over to Jenner.

I hated Truth school. I was always getting picked on 'cause I was different. I didn't live on that side of the neighborhood, so nobody knew me. And for me to come all the way over from the red projects was different.

Then it was even horrible at Jenner because I had never been to Jenner and everybody else knew each other. So again, I was the one to get picked on. I was the new kid. But even though they tortured me, I got to know everybody.

Anthony Edwards: Growing up I learned what side of the gangs I needed to get on, as far as me being protected. That happened early on in life because in our surroundings we had to go about that, otherwise it's like he's not on our side, and that way I just get beat up. So I had to represent some body to be protected. We're talkin' 13 years old, I had to get on some type of side so I could be protected in school.

Up until then, it was really just a normal childhood for me. All the good stuff, going to Lower North Center, Sunshine Gospel Ministries, coming to Holy Family church, havin' choir rehearsal, going camping in Wisconsin with Holy Family and Sunshine. Bein' bad, ya know, throwin' rocks, just normal stuff.

But at 14 it was kinda rough. My brothers, I have six brothers and one sister, but they pretty much knew the gang life and I had to join it to be protected. So things changed and then tragedy just struck. That changed the whole picture, the whole book just flipped over.

Tobias Holmes: I was born in the 1158 building, which was up near Division, but that's torn down now. Back then there was like two ends to Cabrini, and there wasn't a lot of coming over to the other end because of the gangs. Over there, it was like the families were more tight than they are now. Everybody's mama knew who you were, and if you did something your mama would here about it. I don't see that as much anymore.

Over here, like near Oak and Hudson, this was called the Wild End. It's still the Wild End. If I came over here when I was little, and people knew I wasn't from over here, I'd get into fights and stuff. All through my childhood, I'd get into fights 'cause of the conflicts of the different ends.

I didn't go to school at Jenner or Byrd, I went to St. Joseph's over on Orleans Street. The majority of kids went to the public schools, so that made it even harder to fit in with some of the kids here.... But when you're little you always find a way to have fun.

I played football and baseball for a while through the Lower North Center...and as I got older I played basketball at Hudson Street playground.

Anita Gunartt: We moved in with my grandma when I was about three. We came from the West Side to 1150-1160 North Sedgwick....It was like the whole building carried itself as a family. Someone's mother was always sittin' out downstairs while we was playin' and then they'd bring us up.

Everbody knew my grandmother 'cause she used to do hair, she used to do curls, so everybody would come to the house for that. And she'd throw big barbecues. My family was like known for dancin' and stuff because my grandmother's cousin, when he get drunk he'd just dance and dance and everybody would just be laughin', and they play music and make him dance some more.

I remember at 1150 I won my first dance contest, it was break-dancing and I was about six years old. It was against a lot of guys, too. It wasn't a real dance contest but there was a barbecue on one of the floors and everybody was dancin' and it just turned into a competition and I won.

Anthony Edwards: It was 1986, 1121 North Larrabee, like one o'clock in the morning. It was the most tragic thing I ever experienced at a young age, seein' my brother and his friend...his friend was shot to death and my brother had six rifle gun wounds in his body, bleeding to death. This wasn't no TV thing, I'm talking real experience.

They was in the hallway by the elevator, boxing around, ya know, just playin' and somebody come out the corner with a big 'ol rifle and just start pumpin' it. Over 20 shots went off on that ramp.

I was home, at 1015 Larrabee, so just next door really, and I'm hearin' it from my room, just boom, like a big 'ol trailer tractor dropped a big heavy piece of metal from the Sears tower. Boom, boom, at least 20 seconds. I'm a little boy, 13 or 14, and I'm hoppin' around hearin' this. You heard the rifle then you heard the gun switch to a .45. Whap, whap, whap, whap....So 20 minutes later somebody ran up to the house and knock on the door.

I just felt it. I'm nervous already. I know it. I know it. It's gotta be one of mine. I knew they was on the streets, so my friend knocked on the door and said, oh man, he said, Lue, that's my mom. Her name is LueElla Edwards but they called her Lue. He said, both of them was dead, my brother and his friend.

But there for the grace of God and the Lord. My brother had stayed in the hospital four months. They stitched him everywhere.

He'd been hit six times, but he was gonna make it. It was just a sorrowful moment in Cabrini-Green, everybody knew what happened. It was like they can't believe it happened...and I know these people who shot him. How could this happen, ya know? And I don't know what's happened to them but I'm sure the Lord has taken care of them.

My brother survived, no wheelchair, no brain damage, no nothin'. He can walk, he can run. He stays in Minnesota now. He moved on.

Anita Gunartt: We went to the beach a lot, and Seward Park was like a second home for us. Everyone from 1150-1160 went to Seward Park. It was just like a center, recreational stuff and tutoring. Just when you ain't got nothin' to do you go down there and find somethin' to do.

We moved to 939 North Hudson when I was in third grade. My mom got her own apartment and it was the same number, 907, as my grandma's. We could look right across the field and wave at my grandma.

I didn't know too many people over here, but I still went to Byrd [school] so I had the same friends at school and then I met new people in our building.

I loved all my teachers at Byrd, especially Ms. Heard. She motivated you to get things through your head [*laughing*]. I was so shy, she used to open my mouth for me, say, "Talk young lady, talk!" Everybody knew Ms. Heard, but really all my teachers did somethin' for me.

Kiki Coleman: I remember there was an older man who stayed in our building, and he took care of the garden behind the building. We used to have block parties all the time in the community, and I haven't seen that in a long time....When we went to Lower North Center, we'd go swimming in the pool behind 929 [building]....I remember people started throwing glass in the pool, and my friend cut his foot. It's been closed ever since, and I wish they could have repaired the pool because that was fun for us when we were little.

Anita Gunartt: I can barely remember when the pool [was open] behind our building. I only rememeber being in there one time. I also remember seeing a tennis court behind our building, but I was still young.

But the flowers and stuff they had out there I do remember. There was a man named Joe who lived on our porch. My mom played cards with his wife, but Joe was real old, like 80s, and this man actually went downstairs and every year planted a garden...and when the garden was finished whatever was in there he took out and made baskets of vegetables for people. He always gave my mom a basket so I'm quite sure he gave other people food, too. He used to send us tomatoes and stuff....Nobody would mess with the garden because everybody knew how hard Joe worked on it and they respected that. Oh, he was a real friendly man. Anything he had he would give it to you.

We had flowers out in front of the building also. We used to come down and plant flowers together, clean up the building together. It used to be like that. I don't know what happened.

Anthony Edwards: After my brother was shot, I stepped out, ya know. I'm nothin', you can whoop me, I'm out [of the gang]. Ain't no side for me, forget it....I think I was the quickest one to get out of the gang [*laughing*].

By me being so little I could just step out with no problem. I had to go to my gang leader, and I just said, hey, and they understood it. They said, you're right, just step out. We don't want anything to happen to you. I still love my side, I still got my group, my friends, but as far as gettin' down, naw. 'Cause still, the worst had yet to happen.

Rachella Thompson: I never saw anything, or had any fear in walking over to school, but everybody did have the fear about being in the middle of the field. That's what they would call the area where the new Jenner is being built 'cause that was not a good place to be. But when you're young you just trying to get to school.

Sometimes at school, you know, they say, oh, it's a war outside. They're shooting, so don't walk through the field. But in the morning we still walk through the field, you know, it's too early in the morning. We ain't thinking anybody be shooting that early in the morning. Nobody needs to be awake that early in the morning, only the kids going to school. Now in the afternoon, maybe we'll walk around it. We'll walk down Larrabee, take Larrabee around and just take the long route. It was no biggee, just more time to hang out with your friends.

Anita Gunartt: There was a couple times while I was walking home from [Byrd] school that shootings would break out, usually in the field. I would, like, walk along the side of the field, or we used to sneak around the other way and go all the way to Orleans Street to go home sometimes, or sneak out the back doors of the school. When they say run we run and we'd go straight through 364, and then run out and go home. That's how bad they used to shoot.

I would say the worst time was in seventh grade to my sophomore year, that's when I realized a lot of killing and stuff. You just have to know where to be at the right time.

With me it started in seventh grade because that was the first time I got into it with the rival gang. I was behind the [Lower North] Center, it was like a summerfest for us, the Jesse White Tumblers was out there and it was like a carnival. Me and my family and a couple friends, it was all females, and we were behind the Center and these guys from 500 came across the field by the sprinkler, and they just started messin' with us. Me bein' a tom boy at the time, I stood up to them but I got beat with a belt. I took the belt from them, though. It was like 17 of them and I didn't come out bloody or anything. I got whacked a coupla times on my legs, but that was my first time really noticing how bad it was. That's what woke me up that like this is crazy, we can't even come together and celebrate 'cause somebody ignorant.

Tobias Holmes: I did have people trying to get me to join a gang and everything when I was coming up. I know a lot of people over here and growing up everybody started going their own way as far as gangs. I didn't go that route, but that's kind of the pressure of living over here and a major thing for people of my age group.

Anthony Edwards: July 23, 1992, at 11:57 a.m. We all sittin' outside at 1017 [Larrabee]. It was a hot summer day and we just out there sittin' and talkin'. A fight broke out, so my sister, Laquanda Edwards, she goes over there to see who is fighting, right at the corner of Hobbie and Larrabee in front of Holy Family church.

As the crowd grows four shots ring out. Pow. Pow. Pow. Pow. Everybody runnin', somebody drops. I run in the building. I know it's none of mine, but I'm still concerned. Somebody's shot.

Someone says, Tony, that's your sister. I say no it's not, I don't want to hear it. I'm tryin' to deny it, but they sayin' it.

I go over there myself, kneel down to the ground where she's at, I say, Quanda. No movement. I'm shakin' her, and right in the center of her forehead, I'm lookin' at the bump swellin' up. She's not movin'.

My mother had been cookin' upstairs. I went up and I said mama come down stairs....As soon as she gets down to the lobby there's about 50 people in the lobby and it seemed like they all bum rushed my mama and said, Quanda dead. My mother sat right there where the mail boxes are in the lobby, she grabbed her knees and balled up, just started rockin' back and forth. That was her only daughter.

So the ambulance come. Once they don't turn the siren on, you know what that means....What a terrible scene at the hospital. I can picture it right now like I just left it. I can see her in the hospital, just layin' there. She was just 15.

Rachella Thompson: The only time I ever remember, like everybody being scared was when everybody made it seem as if they were out to kill all of us. That was when Dantrell Davis died. They made it seem like they're out to kill us, you know. We all goin' to school and I'm like, oh, wait a minute now. Then we find out, it was like an accident. He was shooting at somebody else and he shot him by accident.

You know kids run in and out the building so fast. Now I can understand that. We went to class, but you know, didn't anything really happen for like an hour or two after we were in school 'cause everybody was like Dantrell just got shot. Oh, and the ambulance came, and Dantrell's teacher was out there....My teacher was out there. We were hangin' out the window just looking.

Anita Gunartt: When Dantrell Davis was killed, it didn't scare me as much because he wasn't in my world. When I say my world, where that happened wasn't in my world 'cause he was from 500. Yeah, it was pretty close to my house but it wasn't in my world 'cause I never went that way, I never cut through between Jenner school and 500 [building]. It was really right out my window but I just never went that way so I wasn't that shook up by it.

Jan Morgan: I knew the guy who killed Dantrell. He was just one of the regular guys out there, ya know. He gotta be what, 38 or 39 by now. He grew up over here, left and went to the army, then came back and just got caught up in it, ya know....It's really too bad.

Anthony Edwards: Everybody heard about Laquanda, and not much later, in October of '92, was when Dantrell Davis was shot and killed in front of 500-502.

After the Dantrell Davis shooting the community was kind of puzzled. What's next? How can we stop this shootin' and get these guns out of Cabrini-Green, because at that time the gang members had started shootin' at eight o'clock in the mornin', and that's when kids go to school.

They wasn't even hittin' each other no more. My sister, a gang killed her. She is dead 'cause of a gang. She gone.

So what the community tried to do is get some help from the city, publicize this stuff and see what can we do? Because another thing, these were not grown ups being killed, these are kids being killed. These are our kids being killed. These are not the people they are targeting, these are kids going to school. So the city had to bring in security, tear down some buildings, that's what mainly had to come about.

Marsha Crosby: Oh, when Dantrell got killed it was horrible because I lived on the second floor and my son had just went to school and I heard these shots. I thought, someone just got shot. I immediately ran to the door, and everybody was flying down the stairs and going toward the school looking for their children.

I heard a little boy had got shot...and then I got more details who it was, and how it happened — a little boy going to school with his mother, holding his mother's hand, got shot down dead. I felt relieved that it wasn't my child, but it was terrible. Parents were standing down there with tears in their eyes, it was just so terrible. It was so terrible.

Rachella Thompson: Most of the eighth graders that were in my class were like the high-powered gang members over in the buildings. Even in eighth grade. Even the teachers knew who was [in a gang] 'cause they were driving cars to school. This one boy had a car, everybody remembers him because everybody was trying to be like him....He was the biggest gang member, drug dealer at the time in our school. When we get to eighth grade, we had all the little soldiers in our grade 'cause everybody was so cocky and big and strong in our grade. They were like the little soldiers, they all had all the money and the cars.

Well, now [this guy] is the most known hype in the neighborhood. Oh yeah, he's really strung out on drugs. And it's bad. Everybody looks to him, like man, we remember when everybody wanted to be him. He was in seventh grade drivin' cars and then, just one day he just fell off his square, and he's only two years older than me. He been hooked on drugs ever since he was in high school. He looks real old.

Anita Gunartt: With Dantrell, a lot changed but it shoulda happened a long time ago. Before he got killed they had put all those bars up around the buildings and tied us down. That only makes the problem worse. I think they shoulda been more about the community, ya know, and came out and helped people, talked to people. Instead of just takin' our money for rent, I wanted them to see who actually lives here, who runs the office, who does things in the community and what kind of help they might need.

Some of that started when Dantrell happened, but they came on too strict that time too. When the national guards came in the boys already knew they was comin', they had a plan. Before the national guards come to the building the boys got all of the drugs and the guns out of the building. So, after they left it was just more drugs and more guns comin' in, more than before....It was just like crazy, people was like they wanna treat us like we in jail, we gonna act that way. That's how people started actin'.

Anthony Edwards

Anthony Edwards: The gangs came to a truce, it was on TV and everything....They came to each other and said, that's it. Let's stop. Stop the violence and keep peace. "Gangs come to a truce at Cabrini-Green." That was the headline in the paper. I'll never forget it.

You see how powerful the gangs are? They more powerful than the police. The shootin' stopped. We could walk around. It was safer for the kids. The main guys came together...they sat down and said, let's stop it. Enough is enough.

Anita Gunartt: In seventh grade I joined Cabrini Connections 'cause I felt like this was my way out, not my way out of the community like it was bad, but out of my shyness. I was real shy and this was a performance art club. It was before they added tutoring, so that was my way out.

Then, when it went to one-on-one tutoring I think it brought a lot more kids out from the neighborhood 'cause they thought, I can tell this person my problems and this person can help me and I don't have to worry about them tellin' nobody else because they don't live here.

Kiki Coleman: I have my own limits, my own boundaries. I don't go over there to that end of the projects. I go over there to visit my father, but as far as the whites and Larrabee Street, you would only catch me on Larrabee unless I'm going over there to visit Cabrini Connections or if I'm going to that little mall to grab something. I don't feel comfortable, that's like a whole 'nother project....When I go over there I feel sort of uncomfortable and I be nervous, looking around like, let me hurry up and get my stuff and get back to my side of town.

Rachella Thompson: It is sort of separated, 'cause the reds and row houses communicate because they're right there next to each other. The whites are so far away from everything. You know, they got their own little field. They got their own little schools. They're a whole other neighborhood. I mean I'm not a white project person, so I don't go visit. I don't know anything about the white project. I'm a red project and row house person.

Marsha Crosby: You know, when you think back you do think that maybe the police say, okay, let's just let the gangs go and do what they got to do to each other. But that gives them all the more reason to do it, and it gives us more reason to not trust the police.

Like when Dantrell got killed, what did they do? They put security in the buildings, ya know, when they had the guards at the doorways. But they didn't do nothin' or say nothin' to the gang bangers. They were scared of them, but they would bother people that really wasn't doing anything.

Anita Gunartt: I defended my community all the way up until I went to college, sayin', you don't know nothin' about Cabrini 'cause you never lived there. You don't understand it, you'll never know. But when I went away to college that's when I really realized I don't want to be there. I was scared to go home. I didn't even want to go home for vacation because I was scared.

That's when I found out about the killing near Jenner school of a guy I knew. That scared me 'cause he was close to me, and I'm thinkin', man, they might hurt me. I was scared, and I could see what people mean about Cabrini.

When I came home last summer, I wasn't sure I wanted to be here. It's not that it's that bad, I just saw both points of view, from being in Cabrini and then being outside.

I mean, I lived in Cabrini most of my life, I know about Cabrini and I love Cabrini, but I went away to school for not even a year and realized it's a whole new world when you outside. I saw it both ways.

Anthony Edwards: After all that happened, my mother, LueElla Edwards, she started a girls club in memory of my sister. At first it was a little program where the kids do painting and stuff...but later on she developed and founded Take Our Daughters to Work Club. It was the summer of '93. They got a space in our building where the kids would come, and she went on the radio and people started donating funds and computers so she could actually keep the program going, and then President [Clinton] found out that this was going on and he invited them to the White House with ten girls from the program. This was in 1994, and they was on Good Morning America....She had three goals; to keep the girls safe and then, basically for them to not get pregnant and to stay in school. My mother passed just last year but the program is still going.

Workin' with kids was her way of mournin', by giving to others. That was her way of feeling her daughter's presence, by feeling the presence of other girls.

Rachella Thompson: My mom wanted me to go to Montgomery Ward tutoring all the time. That was on Wednesdays, and I went there 'til I became a Junior Assistant. I was there from like fifth grade 'til I became a JA. Before that, I went to the program at Holy Family church forever. Thelma Hicks and Mildred Wright, they were there forever. They know all of my family 'cause we all went there. They had all kinds of activities and games.

I also got into the Big Brother, Big Sister program. My big sister, I see her a lot, and I've known her ever since fifth grade. She has taken us everywhere; opera, plays, Great America. I spent New Year's with her....She's just an angel sent to help us out, I guess.

Jan Morgan: I mean the police know every building in here that's selling narcotics. They know who got it and where it's at....I think they could come in here and just hit a building. You just can't go door by door anymore...but they can just pinpoint guys 'cause of their record and 'cause they affiliate with such and such a gang. Some of the gang guys, though, they want to be known by the cops [*laughing*]. They're tryin' to be big and they're like, hey I'm so and so and I'm head of the blah blah skippy, and then the cops know where to knock on his door when somethin' happens.

There's a lot of them guys have went to school, even went to college, but still they get caught up and then they want to get out. I know some guys who did this thing and then left town, sometimes that's the only way you can get out. If you get a job and be working and you can kinda ease your way out...but there's some guys that'll beat you to death for leavin'.

This one guy, who just happens to be college educated, he's in the gang now but I think he's started back working. He's still with the gang but you startin' to see less and less of him. I say to him I say, I see what you doin', all right.

Kiki Coleman: These policemen here, I don't think they care.... There's kids right here, they can look out the back of their building and see these guys out back here selling drugs. They see somebody getting beat up, and they do nothing.

And when they had the security in the buildings, it was hard for me to get in. We couldn't even get a call upstairs. They say you have to have your I.D. or you can't come in the building, and then you see them smoking weed in the booth, talking to the little girls.

Marsha Crosby: What thoroughly amazes me is the power that the gangs have, because like the truce after Dantrell's death, or every time it's low shooting and everything, it's because they decided not to, not because the police did anything to stop them.

Then, when they decide that something has been violated, then the truce is broken and we are back at where we at. It's not the police department or the mayor's office....I think something could have been done. If they really wanted to, if they really wanted to, something could have been done. They did it when the police got killed back [in 1970]. They did it, so something could have been done. Something could have been done.

Anthony Edwards: The city came in with a new system of security like in '91, and then they tore down "the Castle," that's what they called 1117-1119. See, the gangs had a hole in the wall so you could go from 1119 to 1117. That's where they was shootin' that rifle and the police would come in that building but they gone already. One day the police came in there really late and they found a .22 rifle, shell cases already used, and already loaded, sittin' in the corner. They say a lot of shootings came from that rifle.

They say the shots that killed my sister came from "the Castle." I don't think they ever got those guys....She was just gettin' ready to go to high school. She wasn't but a month and a half away form goin' to high school. Cause of someone's ignorance, it cost a child her life.

I'm not even worried about who killed my sister, 'cause whoever did it is going through hell right now. If he ain't in jail he's dead. There's only two options for him in life right now, jail or death. She's well taken care of now.

Tobias Holmes: Just last night, I was sittin' up reading and I heard two shots. I didn't know if they was gun shots or not. They kept goin' so I'm like, yeah, that's gun shots. I look out the window and I see these fools running into the building and stuff. I don't remember the police coming over as fast as they came over last night. They were quick, and it was like 20 squads and three paddy wagons.

I mean, they doin' a lot of things around the community now that they never did when I was little, so with more things comin' around here the cops probably don't want things out of hand. But to me, all of this needed to be cleaned up when I was little, ya know, the new schools, the new playgrounds and stuff.

Rachella Thompson: I heard about the basement parties, but they was before my time. That was when my mom was a teenager.

By the time it was our time to have basement parties, they changed it to a laundry room. And our basement has been locked off since I remember.

But there were still a lot of parties, like house parties....You see the parties nowadays when you pay to get in, you payin' five dollars and you payin' for drinks, food or whatever else. They have all kinds of parties here, there's no age limit sometimes. When I threw my party it had an age limit. It's just a lot of dancin'. If they food and drinks that means their havin' an all-nighter...so the neighbors are probably there.

In this neighborhood, people are so used to the noise. It's not like this is a quiet neighborhood. That's one thing I can say for sure. The only time it's not noisy is school days, but on the weekend it is so loud. Summer time is the wildest time in this neighborhood. People sit outside all day, just hanging out.

Marsha Crosby: New Year's was always the worst with the shooting. It was all blocked off. It gave me the chills. They probably had their reasons for blocking it off, but it gave me the chills. Okay, we going to block off everything and the heck with the people that's in there. Let them kill up each other. Let them shoot up each other. That's the feeling that I got. Block it off, the heck with us, let them kill up each other....The last New Year's Eve, me and my son huddled up in a bed and it was just horrible.

Anita Gunartt: I think nowadays is the worst years ever over here, because it start off with young girls and these babies and all these young kids think they know too much. If you look at the percent, none of them are in school. With the guys, they never work or finish school...and I wonder, what they fightin' for now? Neither one of them getting anything.

It starts with parents. If your mother lets you do this, you gonna do it, and you gonna go to school and do it...and they can't control you. When you come outside, the law can't control you. That's how I figure it. It starts with your parent. I think most of these kids out here that are sellin' drugs and gang bangin' and stuff, I think most of their parents are on drugs. You can tell whose parent work with a child and who didn't.

Most of the people who are makin' this community look the way it is, just look at their parents. And when you look at their parents, you''ll know why.

Jan Morgan: Since the gangs kinda merged over here, they don't have no one to fight so they fight each other. A lot of times it's just about, aw, you makin' more money than I am...and then you got one building against another building, even though they the same gang.

Anthony Edwards: When people said negative things about Cabrini-Green, it was true. Back in the days the gangs was all about gangs. It was serious.

I would have to agree with people who thought that. I mean at that time, Cabrini-Green was a place where there was nothing but violence and tragedy. In the late '80s we had different gang members comin' in to another building of gangs but on different sides, and shoot up anybody standing out in the lobby. So in the late '80s and early '90s, we had to be careful....We had to watch the back of the building to make sure the rival gang won't try

comin' in there and start shootin', 'cause it has happened. It was like that back then.

It's different now though, and I think people can't judge a book by it's cover. You got to read the whole book, ya know. We got cab drivers comin' way over into the buildings now. You got different races jogging through here, and comin' home from work through here, parkin' they cars on the side of Cabrini buildings and walkin' all the way downtown. You can't judge Cabrini no more. Cabrini-Green's a nice place to live.

Kiki Coleman

Kiki Coleman: I'm glad this community is coming up, but I know we gonna be outta here. I was raised here the majority of my life and by me doing a history fair project on Cabrini-Green, I learned a lot about the past and the present.

It's not the first time they reconstructed this area and started all over. Before us blacks came in it was Italian because this place was known as "Little Italy." And this corner right out there, they say someone was shot out there every night back then.

Then they fixed it up, and then after the [King] riots the people from the West Side came over here. Now they're putting us out again, and only certain families will stay.

Tobias Holmes: My mama told me when I was little, and I didn't understand it at the time, but she said this is prime real estate. But people didn't take care of it.

I mean, if you want to live somewhere, as far as living in Chicago, this is prime. You can get to the train, you can walk right downtown....We're like right here in the middle.

Even though it really didn't effect me personally, 'cause I got out a lot, I do feel that there's like a boundary for people who live in this community. It's not like the suburbs, or even like on the West Side or something. There's other communities where people live where it's high crime, but it's not the same as living in the projects. Sometimes you come in your building and you smell pee....You might come in and someone's coming down the stairs drunk or something. The people are just more concentrated, more on top of you, you know what I'm saying?

Like if you're living on the West Side, where there's houses, you could be more in your house. People can stay out of your yard at least. But here it's like we share the same space.

Anthony Edwards: The police over here are jerks....They treat us like, it's time for you all to get outta here, and they thinkin' everybody the bad seed. Everybody not the bad seed. We respect these cops, you gotta respect the job, but everybody has rights. You just can't go and hit everybody in their faces, shoot at everybody and be thrashin' on everybody.

Man, the police have hit me in my eye, hit me in my jaw, hit me in the back of my head, sayin', get your black ass outta here. We got some cool ones, but man, they label all of us.

Rachella Thompson: In some ways Cabrini has its own way of life....Like we normally shop in our own neighborhood. We get our hair done, nails done in our buildings. A normal woman would be, like, I have to go to a nail shop, then a beautician. We can get all of this within' the buildings. We have boosters, which are basically thieves, who go to the store and steal things and come to the neighborhood and sell it at a discount. So we shop in our neighborhood, and we have boosters that have specialties, We have a Victoria Secret booster, a Gap booster, a Guess booster. Half of these peoples' wardrobe, they got it from a booster, off the streets.

It's like a whole underground thing and other people don't know about it. Getting your hair done, you don't have to go to a shop and pay fifty and seventy dollars, you can get it done in our neighborhood for twenty-five to thirty bucks. It's like almost every building has their own hair stylist, it's right in their house.

They do one person's hair, then she tells the next person. We have another person that just does braids, African braids. I mean to go to the African braid shop and get it done for $200, you go to her house and get it done for $50, big difference. We have the African braid lady. We have the regular person that just does hair. Then we have somebody that does nails, but she doesn't live here anymore. She works at a nail shop.

And we got a lot of candy stores. Everywhere is a candy store. It's really a candy house, because the store is so far away. They go to like a main franchise and they buy boxes of candy, and they bring it back to their apartment and they sell it. It's easier than walking all the way to the store. It's good to have candy houses, because your kids can just go next door.

Jan Morgan: There's some guys around here that just afraid to leave. I know one guy who's got a vehicle and I can stand right in front of my building and count the times he come around, like six times in an hour, goin' nowhere fast. I mean, take the car and go somewhere, but they'd get lost so they just drivin' around in a circle. There's a bunch of them that do that.

Kiki Coleman: I didn't even get out of the projects 'til I was about twelve. My first experience going downtown was on a field trip with Cabrini Connections tutoring program....Now, since I'm living on my own and I didn't have that when I was younger, I don't know how to travel in Chicago.

There was a lot of things I could have been doin' that I wasn't doin' because my mother was doing drugs...so places like Cabrini Connections and Lower North Center help me to go places I ain't never seen before, like Great America or something....I was raising my brother at the time, so I didn't do a lot of the things other kids were doing. In grammar school, I missed like three semesters in fourth grade, and they thought I transferred. I came back and they were like, oh well. I took my tests and passed, but there's a lot of things I missed.

Marsha Crosby: I feel sorry for little kids coming up that have very young parents, where a lot of their fathers are gang members or something. You see little kids four or five, sometimes three or four years old doing whatever gang handshake, that's what they learn. So as they come up, what are they going to be? This is what they know. So if a child turn out bad or gets into gangs and drugs, sometimes you can't look at that child and say, oh he's so terrible. That's all the child knows.

My heart breaks for the little kids that's coming up, because they don't know anything different and it's just going to be a cycle repeating itself, repeating itself and repeating itself.

Jan Morgan: This place really would be all right without these guys selling drugs. It would be a whole different place. I remember one gang guy who used to give back to the community. He'd have little parties for the kids and stuff. He dead now, they killed him... but there's some of 'em who are good guys. They don't really bother me, I know all of 'em and there's some that just flat-out stupid. I mean they have someone beat up for no apparent reason.

One of the guys, he was a one of the big guys back then, he used to drink, steal, beat up people and all that. Today he don't drink or affiliate with them and you see him everyday. He's a family man, goes to work everyday. That's a prime example of a guy who just flat-out left everything alone. I mean he used to do narcotics and everything you can think of, he done it. Right now today, strongest thing he gonna drink is 7-Up. He don't even smoke cigarettes....

He's had about 20 kids from different women, about seven or eight by his wife and the rest are just out there...but that was him.

Rachella Thompson: I remember in high school, up at Lincoln Park, these guys in the gang, it all just throws me off with the gang thing. I'm like, okay, you all still fighting? Didn't we get enough of this in eighth grade. It's like, grow out of this.

You just get tired. It's like games, you know, like how nobody plays Nintendo anymore, its SuperNintendo. It's like move on, it's about real things.

The other thing is, you don't make as much money as everybody think you make. These gang bangers over here, for some of the things they have, they been selling drugs for years. I mean you been selling drugs since grammar school. These fancy cars they drive, they didn't just make this money over night.

Let's say you're a newcomer, that just gets $300, $500 a week. That's just like a regular job, you could just work at McDonald's. You just wouldn't have to stand out in the cold.

I just look at them like, all of you standing out here, you coulda' had a job. It's not like I feel bad for them, no need for me to be feeling bad for them. Some people I can understand....If you have like a horrible background, horrible family life and you had problems. But, it's a whole problem for them to have to sell drugs anyway.

Anita Gunartt: I wouldn't always say it's a bad thing sellin' drugs, 'cause everybody got to make a livin'. The only thing bad about sellin' drugs is, I think, it hurt the people that buy the drugs.

I don't really focus on, well, this boy's sellin drugs. Yeh, he's sellin' drugs but you gotta look at where the money goin' too. You didn't look at that he's not out there pullin' a gun on nobody. He's not startin' a commotion, he's not gang bangin', he's just gettin' money to handle his business.

Cause I know many people like that. This one guy, he's still in school but he's puttin' food on the table because he know his mom

don't be home 'til after seven. He feed his sisters, he clean up the house. He do all that. The only time you see him is when he's downstairs makin' money. Other than that he's bein' the big brother he's supposed to be, so I can't really judge anybody on that.

It's unfortunate, but a lot of people are like, my mama can't give us stuff 'cause she got rent and bills and she's not gettin' paid enough with this many kids...so I'm gonna be a man. My daddy ain't here so I'm gonna be a man and take over the house and bring money in. That's the way it is now.

Tobias Holmes: Drugs affect everybody. My father was a drug dealer....That was one of the things, we did have things when we was little, more than the average kid had. I didn't really think we had any more than anyone else, but people would try to take my stuff. I didn't understand 'til I got older and people would say we was rich. I never understood why they said that until I got older and found out my father was a drug dealer.

That really changed my perspective more than anything else, because that's what made me don't like drugs and don't like gang bangers.

I still try to have love for all people, but playin' that game, the drugs affect everybody. I mean everybody. It affects you in some kinda way if someone in your family is pushin' the drugs or using. In my family it's both ways. I've got people in my family who use drugs and who sell them. And that affected us a lot.

I love my dad, he was a smarter man than that, and by him coming up in the '60s, he had no choice but to kind of get into it. I think back then, when the gangs first got started, it was because they had no choice, they didn't have other opportunities....They was tryin' to make a living. And, they wasn't goin' around beating people up.

Jan Morgan: Some guys, they just got to leave here 'cause it gets so bad for them. There's four or five of them I know that's done that. One guy, he was with the gang thing, right, and he was selling narcotics for the guys. Ya know, the deal is you get so much of that and the gang gets the rest of the money. Well, he had the cops knock on his door one day and he had to flush it down the toilet, ya know. Now he don't have the money and he don't have the drugs. And now they wanna do something to him.

He's like, you want me to get caught with this and get x amount of years, you gotta be outta your mind? They wanna beat him down, so he takes a violation, that's where you get a big 'ol pumpkin head, they beat on you.

There's one that they do that's funny to me. It's the one finger cover up. You put one finger on your nose and you got three, four, I don't know there could be ten of 'em guys and each gets to punchin' on ya. You did something they don't like and now you gotta take this whoopin', fifty punches each, right. That's the violation. So you got one finger on your nose and that finger got stay on your nose or you get another beating. Right, it's impossible. That finger falls off and you get fifty more.

Tobias Holmes

Tobias Holmes: Now it's like, if you ain't in no gang, you ain't cool. And, if you don't want to go to school no more, then just come and sell some drugs then. But see, when you're doing that, now you're affecting somebody's mama, somebody's uncle.

My father, he's very influential in my life....He made me who I am. He's incarcerated now, but he always made his presence felt. He still does. By being who he was and what he had to go through in his lifetime, he made sure I went to good schools. He stressed education. I got my butt whooped for getting bad grades, that's one thing he did stress on us and told us to keep in the books. He still had to live that life, but he wanted something better for me than what he had. If it wasn't for him, things would be totally different for me.

My cousins and uncles too, they always tell me, you're doing it right. Don't do what I did, because I was stupid. I'm proud of you, don't do what I do....I think these boys now in this community, they don't have nobody to come up and tell them, no, don't do this. I want them to know they should feel as if they can get out of the gang. They don't have to be part of that....I try to say that but it's hard. They don't know about respecting your elders and stuff like that.

Rachella Thompson: By your junior year at Lincoln Park, you know who's gonna stick around and who's not. So, mostly the people from Cabrini by the time your junior or senior year comes, they're all female that are there. Males are like scarce.

I can remember like five guys from Cabrini that graduated in my year, not even that probably. Cause, you know, they sort of tend to drop out freshman and sophomore year. Junior year it's more females, they tend to drop out because of pregnancy. Senior year if anybody drops out it must be something really major 'cause you dropped out your senior year.

If you make it through senior year, you can make it through anything. Junior year for a lot of people, especially people in my neighborhood 'cause you got one year to go, that's when everybody starts realizing, ya know, after this what am I gonna do? You know you can't stay with your mom forever. Reality starts hitting a lot of people, like what you gonna do after this? Everybody got a plan on how they wanna go to college. But it's not like that, you say it, but you always ain't got the funds. You gotta face reality, there's a lot of stuff you can't do.

Your so used to going to school all your life, now you gotta get a job. And Kmart don't even want to hire you.

Marsha Crosby: One thing that always frustrated me about the media is seeing that they always picked out the worse looking, drug addicted people to interview...and seeing that they always in the worst looking houses. Seem like they always picked out the worst when they want to interview, or do anything on Cabrini. You never had the camera on a nice looking apartment.

Just like when me and my sister brought people home, they were like, wow, your apartment look so nice. I'm so surprised because you didn't see that on TV. You didn't see that on TV? People was totally shocked, thinkin' just because we lived in Cabrini mean we lived in filth or something.

Tobias Holmes: Everybody reacts to Cabrini-Green, that's just how it is. I try to let people feel comfortable with me. I try to let them know, yeah, it's rough, but we're still normal people. Just because I'm from Cabrini-Green, I'm not gonna act crazy. I try to let people feel comfortable with that.

Rachella Thompson: Since I've grown up, I always get bad reactions from Cabrini-Green. Everybody does. Everywhere I go it's like, you from Cabrini? I say, yeah, it's like any other neighborhood.

At college, now they really are like, Whoa, you from Cabrini? Everybody's from different places, but Cabrini just sticks out. I try to tell people, you can live over here without dealing with the violence.

There's somebody at college from Kentucky. He's from the projects in Kentucky. And even he's like, you live there? I'm like, you from the projects in Kentucky, it's the same way.

People from Robert Taylor project, they live in my school and they say, you from Cabrini? I'm like, yeah, you from Robert Taylor's, that's not any better. So, that's like my whole reputation. They say don't mess with her, she from Cabrini....It's just funny 'cause Cabrini got a reputation wherever I go.

So now I tell everybody I'm in the Gold Cost, so close to downtown, I walk to the beach. I mean the people may not consider us part of the Gold Coast, but I consider us part of it. We're so close we have to be. I mean, all the way to Halsted Street is the Gold Coast to me.

Kiki Coleman: Even when I was in high school, my teachers used to try to treat me differently because I stayed in Cabrini. Like my math teacher, one day I told him I didn't have my homework, that I forgot it at home. He say, well, was it because they were shooting? Did you lose it while you was running through a gang fight?

Tobias Holmes: I think all the people in my generation around here just grew up too fast. I don't know when it started, but when you live in a community like this, you do see things before your age. You see stuff that you ain't supposed to see, you see people getting shot, people drinking and using, people having sex and all that kind of thing.

Marsha Crosby: We came through and my brothers was never in any gangs and nothing. So you can come through, if you have desire to want to do so. I'm not saying it's going to be easy, especially with the children now, it has to be hard.

I used to wonder why my mother was so strict on me as a child, because she was very strict....I couldn't understand then, but I understand now. You have to, you understand, you worry. You worry and you just want what's best for your kids.

Anthony Edwards: I've kept things positive by staying close to the church and the Bible. The people that was there for me has been my parents and the strength of my brothers. Brother Bill too, he's been a real inspiration.

Brother Bill I first met when my brother got shot in 1986. He started comin' around and prayin' with the family, coming to the hospital and prayin' with us.

Brother Bill knows everybody in the community. He's a white man and he wears a long robe and he walks around by himself, late at night, when there ain't nothin' out there but gunshots. He walks right into buildings where bullets are comin' from. Bill, he helps you out, he tells you just pray with the Lord and you be okay....I remember one night, it was like 11:30 at night back when they were shootin'. He walked right into the building where they were shootin' at and he told them, no, no, stop, stop, stop. He hold his right hand out, right in the middle he told them to stop shootin', walked right up to them and they stopped shootin'.

He goes to other projects in Chicago too, and he gained his respect by being fearless, and he has respect for everyone. He's been on all the TV shows, like 20/20.

We just had the Easter march with him at Holy Family. Everybody met up at the church. We had ten different churches and what we did is...everybody reads a scripture in front of each building and then we go to another building. We went to every building in Cabrini-Green.

We try to bless the whole community for what we've been through throughout the days, and years. We do that every Easter. That keeps it spiritual around here.

So Brother Bill, he's still out there....Like I say, his presence is just phenomenal. He can do some things and say some things that can keep you focused for life. I'd say he's one of the most powerful people that I've ever met.

Kiki Coleman: By us just going to school and stuff like that, I think some people in the community be looking at us like we think we're too good for ourselves....That's been my experience because I've had people say, ya know, "your boyfriend a lame" and "you a lame," because we tryin' to get out of the projects. We're not trying to be here the rest of our lives. But they hang outside all day long, 24-7, doing nothing.

Rachella Thompson: Growing up in Cabrini, I just describe it as, um, let me see, a great learning experience, I'll put it like that. Because if it wasn't for a lot of things that I learned here, I wouldn't be doing so good everywhere else. It's like Cabrini showed me the ropes.

But when I think about places to grow up, I couldn't see like people raising their kids in such an environment. Cause it's like, it's too hard on them. It's like kids shouldn't know some things that they know. It don't give you a chance to be a kid, 'cause you grow up so fast, you grow up knowing things that normal kids don't know. There's a lot of things that I've experienced that I would say adults haven't even experienced.

Tobias Holmes: There are two different types of people that live here. People who, like, they can't get their mind out of the projects. And then you've got people who are striving to do better. And that's the conflict over here.

Anita Gunartt

Anita Gunartt: I love Cabrini. Really, I don't see it as bein' bad, I just feel it's bad that it had to go so far that they have to tear it down. If they tear it down I'll love Cabrini the way I used to love it before.

I think all housing projects have a closer bond than a lot of communties that are just one or two blocks, 'cause you get to know people, you see different views of other people and experience different things. The only thing that bothers me is the people who was not caring about it.

Some of the residents didn't care about it and now they see other people startin' to care about makin' it look good and just makin' Chicago look good period, and now the residents say, they takin' away our neighborhood. Well, you let them take it away. You the one set back and played around when they told you to make a change, to do this or do that, pick up the water in front of your door...have your kids in at a decent hour...don't let your kids spray paint my wall. You the one that broke all the rules, so you just getting what you asked for.

chapterNINE
WHITES of a Different Color

Shvonda Young **has heard it before, that there's something different about the whites, something that separates this part of Cabrini-Green from the red high-rises and row houses. Standing in front of the white high-rise building she lived in for eight years, she shakes her head and smiles. "It's just different colored buildings," she says. "That's all."**

From second grade to eighth, Shvonda lived at 939 **N. Hudson Street, which is a red high-rise building that towers over the row houses. She attended Jenner school, and loved it. "Jenner was fun," Shvonda says. "We went on a lot of field trips, like to Great America, and the water park. The teachers taught us well, especially Ms. Bynum."**

After graduating from Jenner in 1992**, Shvonda's family moved to Atlanta for nine months before returning to Cabrini-Green. "When we came back," she explains, "we moved into the whites, at** 534 **W. Division. I was happy to come back 'cause I missed everybody but it was kinda hard at first in the whites because I had to meet a whole bunch of new people."**

Shvonda admits as a young girl she was aware of the ironies of Division Street. She knew gangs considered it the boundary between the reds and the whites. She knew that Schiller and Truth were schools for the whites and Jenner and Byrd were schools for the reds and the rows. She knew there were few community programs or events that brought all these residents together. "When we was younger," she says, "we didn't used to come down here because we used to be scared of the whites. We used to stay on our side in the reds. So when we moved here we were thinkin' it's gonna be different in the whites, but after living over here I know it's all the same. It's all one big community."

Richard Blackmon, Sugar Ray Dinky **and** Tyrone Randolph (**who we met in Chapter Six**) **have all expressed similar feelings, but have also experienced the divisions of Cabrini firsthand.**

In this chapter, they continue to offer a broader perspective on the white high-rises and what's become of them.

Shvonda, who is the oldest of four and at 21 is now raising a son of her own, hopes that despite talk of dramatic changes the community can remain as one. "I just hope they don't tear this place down. I think there's a lot of life left here."

Shvonda Young: When I was in the reds we'd go to Lower North Center and play in the sprinkler behind the Center. I still went when I moved to the whites, and there was camping and field trips and things....I used to go and watch them dance at Seward Park. They had like different dance groups, like when I was in eighth grade. All the girls would be in a dance group and they'd have competitions. They had boxing there and basketball games and everything, and they still do.

In the whites, though, we all went to Stanton Park and would swim in the pool there. I used to play on the softball team in Al Carter's league, and on Carson Field. I played for like three years. I think you can go to age 16, and then you can't play any more. They closed Carson Field and they're building houses there, I think.

Richard Blackmon: Nobody messed with you when you were Mr. White's boy. I remember the tumbling team going over in the red projects and doing a show. We used to have these red caps that we used to wear, these red berets or tams, and I pleaded with Mr. White. I said, Mr. White, look we can't go in the red projects wearing these red caps. That's their color, the gang colors. Come on, you're going to get us killed.

Mr. White said, put them on, we're going in there. We ain't a part of that. So we was getting ready to perform and everybody put their red tams on, and the leader of the gang comes over and says, look, you all got to come out of those tams in my neighborhood. You can't wear 'em.

So Mr. White came over and says, what's this all about, man, you know? Mr. White takes the guy off to the side and talks to him, right. He comes back and he says, well, he's going to let you all wear them for the performance, but as soon as we finish performing we got to take them off. So that's what we did.

He had to make some compromises, but we got a certain degree of respect as tumblers, you know. Mr. White had to be smart too because he wasn't always going to be there and he knew that. And that guy in the gang may say something to him while he's there, and as soon as he leave it's a different story. So he had to learn to protect us even when he wasn't around. It was crazy, something you had to do, just to live, just to perform.

Sugar Ray Dinky: Things really eased up because basically the rival gangs aren't over there in the reds now. The guys that used to shoot at each other were in certain buildings, and now those buildings closed. Now, these guys throw parties together. It just looks like they're rich.

Richard Blackmon: I never understood until I got older why Mr. White always worked two places. The one job was to take care of his family, and the other job was to get equipment and pay for stuff for us. He'd get it all out of his pocket. I remember going to his house and he would wash the uniforms and stuff in his basement. He would take all that stuff home, put it in the bag, wash it and bring it back. And back in those days you had to iron everything, so he would iron the uniforms and all that.

So I take my hat off to him, because I was there you know, nobody is telling me what happened. I know. As long as I can remember he did it that way. He did it all, and never missed a beat.

You got to remember there's 1,500 kids and sometimes he would have 200 or 300 kids at camp...so you have to maintain a certain level of discipline in order to work with that. If you don't, man, it could be chaos....I still look back sometimes and wonder how he did it.

Sugar Ray Dinky: Cabrini-Green is like home to me, but to other people, I guess, the ideal home is not Cabrini-Green....But, you know, it's like the money and the drugs come and go. I think the police have a lot to do with that. But the money pulls 'em in.

And, ya know, you got guys lookin' for role models, so you get the guy's attention and you start hanging around him and, you know, he protects you. He'll put you out in the front, ya know, workin' "S." That's a lookout. Once you get your twenty, forty dollars, you think you're a big shot. So after three, four years of that, you're stuck. You know what I mean?

You got nothin' to fall back on, and you ain't gettin' any younger. I've seen a lot of guys get out but they get beat up. I never joined. I never found no reason to, you know. I didn't want to disrespect, I had a mom and pop, you know. They were separated, but, you know, I have a mom and I had a stepfather. So they was my role models.

Richard Blackmon: Some kids joined the gangs because they got tired of getting beat up. You know, they got tired of getting threatened. Like I said, we had a fight everyday and as we got older it got worse. Expectations grew.

I didn't get so much of it because I was an athlete. One thing the guys respected was athletics, so as long as I stayed in the newspaper and I carried my football equipment home, and I kind of stayed to myself, I didn't get bothered. But my brothers didn't have that outlet. The other thing is by going to school outside of the neighborhood, I didn't have to see neighborhood kids every day. I didn't go to Waller, I didn't go to Cooley, so I was given the chance to get out of the neighborhood. That kind of kept me distant from them.

But my brothers went to Waller, and they had to deal with the gangs, they had to deal with the drugs you know. I remember having a conversation with my brother once about not selling drugs, and going back to school. This was when I was probably a sophomore or junior in college. And he said to me, look at my feet. And I'm like, what are you talking about? So I look at his shoes, right, and he says, what you don't understand is that you got to do what you got to do to wear shoes, and I got to do what I got to do to wear shoes. I'm not proud of what I do, he said, I'm not happy about it. But I still need shoes. He says, I'm not you, I can't do what you do, but what I do is try and keep shoes on my feet and food in my stomach.

I couldn't say anything. And now that same brother today is like turned his life 360 degrees. He's turning totally around. Unfortunately the other one was killed in the same building we lived in.

Shvonda Young: I didn't feel any boundaries in Cabrini. We had family all over the city so we always would go outside the community. I went to high school out west at George W. Collins school, and people will react to Cabrini. A lot of people are scared of Cabrini, they say, oh, they shoot too much and all that, but once you been up here you know everybody and you know it ain't nothin' different from the West Side, the South Side, the North Side. It's all the same.

We'd have cookouts on the Fourth of July, Memorial day, right out on the ramp. We'd go to North Avenue beach, to Water Tower for shopping downtown, and we'd go the shows down there too.

Sugar Ray Dinky: I have one brother. He was in a gang so he was really making it hard to live over here. I had to really, you know, get on his case. It took him to go to jail and when he got out of jail, I guess he got his stuff together, you know, because he was doing a lot of the wild stuff.

I worked hard and I got my mom out of here. I worked real hard for construction companies because she was having real bad times over here. It was like it was closing in on her, so I got out and got her a nice place, her and my two sisters.

But that doesn't mean I don't have good times here, or think about the fun times, too. When you think about the block parties that go on and you see the togetherness. The blacktop is right across the street from Schiller school there. We'd have the whole community come out and just have fun. It's important to have fun sometimes.

Richard Blackmon: My brother was 19 years old when he was killed. I had to come home from football camp to bury him. Shot six times, the original story that I was given was that he was trying to find my other brother, and went into this apartment. I found out years later that he was trying to rob the people in the apartment and they killed him. It was a drug house and he was planning on going in and robbing the drug house. He opened the door and the guy just let him have it. So that's another memory. Not a good memory.

Tyrone Randolph: Going to Schiller school was pretty cool. I had one teacher, Ms. Morgan, she was very tough. That's one teacher who I really respect now. If you didn't come in with your homework, it was punishment time. She had this paddle, like a fraternity paddle....She was so short her legs would swing over her desk, and she would have the paddle sittin' right on her lap. You don't have that homework, ya know, hold your hand out right away, and you'd get two little whacks.

She really kept me straight all these years....My mom and dad were pretty strict, but in knowing how important education was, it was Ms. Morgan. And no one liked that paddle.

Richard Blackmon: I grew up believing in scouting, in the Cub Scouts. I've served in a couple of different capacities in Cub Scouts.

But growin' up we went to camp two or three times a summer.... One of the first lawyers that I ever met actually went to camp with us one summer and I got a chance to ride with him to the camp grounds. We talked about being a lawyer and I mean I was at the point where I really made up my mind that I wanted to be a lawyer, just based on my conversation with him.

Shvonda Young: We've always had trouble with cabs. Cabs do not like comin' in the projects. Pizza places, they don't come over here either. They afraid the boys will take it or they think someone's setting them up, so with that you can understand....Now Chester's [Pizza] used to always come in here....We had a couple boys take our pizzas from us once, me and my brother went down to get our pizza and the boys took it. I ran to the police station in 364, [*laughing*] but the boys was gone by then so there was nothin' they could do.

Richard Blackmon: I mean, you can go anywhere in this country and say you're from Cabrini-Green and people know it. And they think they know you.

There's no other housing development in the country that has a reputation as notorious as Cabrini. That's notorious, it's not for the good stuff that happens. And there's a lot of good stuff that happens in this community, but it's the negative stuff that has given us that reputation.

You got people that won't even say they're from Cabrini. I was going to law school and when I got there, there was a girl there who I grew up with. She lived in 1230 Larrabee, and nobody [at law school] knew that she grew up in Cabrini. She told everybody she's from the West Side, until I said, wait a minute now, you and

I grew up together. Your family might have moved to the West Side when you were like 18, 19 years old, but you grew up in Cabrini you know. I had to kind of challenge her on it, because she had totally blocked out that she ever lived in Cabrini. Now, when it became popular, after everybody found out I was from Cabrini and I started espousing the more positive aspects of living in Cabrini, it was then okay to be from Cabrini-Green. And then she said, okay, I'm from Cabrini.

Tyrone Randolph: Right now I'm working with Urban Systems of Care, a program of Depaul University. We assist residents in Cabrini. We help with social problems, with getting their kids help, seeing therapists and whatever. Before that I was working at Winfield Moody Health Center with the youth pregnancy prevention program, and that put me in the realm of working with kids, and I still work with all the schools over here so I've gotten to know a lot of the kids.

There are some bright kids, but I'm not sure if it's because they don't like school or what that they're not doing as well as kids when I was coming up. I think the problems are much worse today that I'm sure they can't just focus in on what's going on.

I know that the respect level is really low for some of them, due to being neglected by family members....A lot of kids don't have that respect, you'll see 'em walking down the street talking like drunken sailors. It's a lot different today. I think a lot of kids nowadays need a lot of therapy, and social rehabilitation. I think because a lot of parents are younger they need parenting classes on how to take care of kids. Sometimes I come home from the [music] studio at one or two o'clock in the mornin' and you see

kids out, and you know they have school in the mornin'. A lot of kids get hurt that way, hanging out at night. I have two kids so I'm tryin' to give them as much support as possible.

Richard Blackmon: The thing that complicated our situation even more than the physical confinement was the financial confinement. The fact that the majority of people living in the buildings were on welfare. So you have this generational thing going on....And then I'd just sit and see people taken advantage of, like the educational and academic opportunities we were being given. And that frustrated me, because something inside of me just knew that that was the real way out and that people didn't take advantage of that.

I can remember going to school and coming back home, and people would be standing in the exact same place that they were standing when I left. It was like I stepped into a time warp and people had not changed, and I think that was the most frightening thing for me on everything that I experienced in Cabrini; the fact that I could go away to school for three or four years, and come back and people would be standing and doing the exact same thing as they were doing when I left.

Yeah, I'm not talking months, I'm talking years. They would be standing in the exact same place they were standing when I left. So even now I go back and I still see people that I know, that I grew up with, and they look different, they look harder and it's just, it just pains me.

Sugar Ray Dinky: To me, this is how I feel, when people move out of Cabrini-Green, all my friends and family that got moved out of here, it's like six, seven months later, I hear about them getting killed or shot in the new neighborhood that they went to. I mean that's why I was saying I was going to funerals left and right, you know. And sometimes, at the funerals they were shooting. Man, I've been trapped in a funeral where a guy shuts the door and we can't go outside 'til the police come and escort us out of the funeral home. I been to a couple of those.

Shvonda Young

Shvonda Young: I think that in the red buildings they still deal drugs on the first floor and in the whites they on the third floor, the fourth and the fifth floor...so when the kids come in the white buildings they can't see them sellin' drugs to somebody. I know in the reds they have school hours they try not to work and stuff but...it's just not as open in the white buildings.

Really, I don't care what they do, but when my son gets big I gotta look out for him gettin' into the gangs, 'cause he's a boy.

Sugar Ray Dinky: To me, everybody gets a fair chance. We all started the same. It's up to you to do something with your education. I mean I don't see nobody trying to kick you out of grammar school. It's up to you. You do what you want to do. If you want to sit around and mess around in school, that's on you. I'm really concerned about the kids that go, or drop out, 'cause if I had a chance to start all over, I don't know. I probably would have been a doctor or something, you know, anything. But, man, once you blow that chance, it's like you don't get it back. You don't get it back. That's what I try to tell my children. You got to take advantage....Opportunity knocks on the door only so much.

Richard Blackmon: No question about it, there are leaders that come from Cabrini and leaders who are still there. I think we inspired each other as kids. One of the things that all of us found very powerful about Cabrini was, you hear people talk about ethnic pride and that kind of thing. One of the things that it did for us, because it is all African-American, was that you never had to wonder who you were. It's almost like going to a black college. People talk about the benefits of going to an historically black college. Well, in this instance, you got kids that are in a historically black community. I mean we don't look at it like that. but if you look at what happened in the '70s and '80s, Cabrini was basically 100% African-American. And with that comes a certain degree of pride.

The other thing is that the educators, I think the schools played a difference. The educators that we had in this community at that time didn't allow us to make excuses about our environment and our community. So you were pushed, because everybody was in the same situation.

That's why I get so frustrated now with schools that say, well, these kids can't learn because they're poor, they're black, their parents are single parents. They aren't involved, there's no parent involvement. I grew up in a community where that was the case, and yet, we were still able to get a quality education. I've got classmates that are writers for the *New York Times*, you know, the *Wall Street Journal* and that kind of stuff. So I just don't buy into the fact that those excuses can keep a child from learning. So, I'm constantly demanding that people not tell kids that....Let's say okay, these kids, they're in a terrible economic, social, cultural situation. They still have to learn despite that. And so, that was sort of the attitude of the educators that we had in this community, and that carried over to us as kids. We were not allowed to make excuses. It was just unacceptable.

And the other thing is that you never doubted the fact that people cared about you. I don't care if you were the worst kid in the school, you always knew that the people in that school and in this community cared about you. The people at the park district cared about you, the people at the YMCA cared about you, and they were going to protect you. And I don't know if they still have that any more.

Everywhere you went there were people pushing you to do your best. So you got pushed at the Y, you got pushed at the park, you got pushed at school. Everywhere you went, and nobody cared that you lived in Cabrini 'cause everybody lived in Cabrini. It didn't matter. It was not acceptable to use that as an excuse.

Tyrone Randolph: In a lot of cases it's true that kids are lookin' to the gang for belonging. Even with the protection thing, a lot of them might not feel protection at home or self-worth within the family and so they have friends who say, hey, come on and make this money with us, hey, we love you.

When it comes down to that, they look to the outside. They try to comfort those wounds with the outside, and they're not necessarily thinkin' about the consequences, 'cause the consequences at home may be even worse.

Shvonda Young: The only building that had a different gang was 500-502 and 1150-1160, and they both closed down. All the rest was Gangster Disciples. So, sometimes they'll have conflicts but not as much as before.

I know they nervous about the police station they building at Division and Larrabee. Them boys don't want the police station there because it's real close.

Some say the guys in the buildings protect the community better than the police. And, the boys from the buildings, they give out toys to the little kids on Christmas, and on Halloween they decorate the building for the kids.

Tyrone Randolph: Things are different now 'cause back then you could walk past the police and say hello and they say hello, and now it's more like they're lookin' at you as a threat, so you have to worry about that. I'm kinda stuck in the middle because I look younger than I am, and I always get taken as a young guy....It's common for me to be stopped. You just have to be aware of your surroundings, and hopefully nothing happens around you that you don't get pointed out as one of those threats, ya know, and you just have to be aware of that.

Richard Blackmon: I remember when we first moved in, the supervisors and managers for the CHA would come around and ask you how things were. They were much more visible. You knew who they were. I think as times changed they became more and more distant from the people. It became administrators not really caring about the people.

The other thing that I never really thought I saw was the connection between the schools and the development and the park district. I mean, there was never that coalition. Everybody kind of worked independently of one another, and I always thought that hurt us a little bit. They should have had a better working relationship.

As for the police, they were terrible. They used to beat us, they'd take us places and beat us....I can remember one time me and my friend, there used to be a coal factory right across the street on Halsted. It was coal, and we used to go play in the coal. They caught us one day over there playing in the coal and beat us with these hoses. They had these rubber hoses they kept in the truck. The theory was, they beat you with the hose because it didn't leave marks. They took us over behind the coal factory and roughed us up. Another time they caught us breaking windows out of one of the factories over there. They took us over there and beat us up pretty good. They were to be avoided. And, you know, you learned at a very early age that you avoided the police. They were not your friend.

As I got older my brothers got gang involved, and was selling drugs, and probably doing God knows what else. So our house got raided on a pretty regular basis. That's when we'd get evicted.

And it was just amazing. They would come in and totally destroy our house, I mean just turn everything upside down, break stuff, pull bricks out of the wall, all kind of stupid stuff. No warrant or a fake warrant, or one they wrote up. And this was constant. It was like every other week. You'd get the house back together and they'd come back and do it again. So I don't have very fond memories of the police.

The most fond memory I have of them is, every year they'd give a Christmas party for the kids. They had pretty good gifts, they would make sure everybody at least got a coat and gloves and hats. I can't remember the sergeants name, but I can see his face. He did this every single year as long as I can remember. They'd put on a nice show for us and after the show was over they'd give everybody a Christmas present. That was my fond memory of the police. That was the only one.

Shvonda Young: The people I went to grammar school, they don't live over here anymore. People have gradually moved out. Some of the people from 1150-1160 and 500-502, when they closed a lot of those people left the neighborhood. So, it's already changed.

Richard Blackmon: The turning point for me personally was, well, of course when Dantrell Davis was killed. But I think the one that took the most steam out of me was Girl X. That whole situation just devastated me. But I can remember when the two police officers got killed in the '70s, and the trauma that we went through after that.

What really sticks out in my mind was the night my mom died. She actually died in my arms, and one of the reasons that she died was because the ambulance guys was afraid to come up that night 'cause they had been shooting early in the day.

My mom had lupus and she got sick that night. I had just come back from camp. I had gone to camp with some kids as a counselor. She just, she couldn't breathe. But it took them about two hours, two and a half hours to go upstairs and get her. She slipped into

a coma and just never came out of it, and I think that contributed to her passing, that they couldn't get to her quickly.

I realized then that the reason they didn't come up was because of the environment. They were afraid of the environment, and I think those are some of the things that kind of stick out, you know, about Cabrini. But, I don't care how far you get from this place it still is your neighborhood. It's always your neighborhood, and anything that happens there now, it affects you as much as the people that are still there.

Shvonda Young: I see Cabrini as one big neighborhood. Any where you go, there's nothing really different about it to me. I'd like to stay in this neighborhood 'cause they talkin' about takin' it down and they gonna be movin' people to the suburbs. How we gonna get from the suburbs to the city?

I'm waiting on my apartment now. I got my number, but they tell me it's 305 people in front of me, and that was five months ago so I don't know how long it will take.

You have to be 18 or just have a baby to get an apartment, so you get a number. If you younger than 18 and you got a baby your mama has to come to the office with you so you can get on the list for an apartment. That's how they do it now, you get an application from housing and they wanna know what kinda income you got to see what kind of rent you gotta pay and then they give you a number. So, you just have to wait, then you get an interview.

It's not only people here that's tryin' to get an apartment, but there's people out west and out south that's tryin' to get an apartment in Cabrini...so it's strange that all these people are tryin' to get in here but they talkin' about tearin' these buildings down. The only thing they gotta do is fix up the vacant apartments and then everybody would have an apartment.

chapter**TEN**
Living On a **GOLD** Mi

Gloria Cockrell-Smith **says she learned how to lie at an early age.** Sitting in the homey apartment she shares with her three children in one of the red high-rise buildings, she laughs in embarrassment at the idea of it all.

"I went to Walt Disney," she recalls. "It's a magnet grammar school in Chicago, and I remember a lot of kids from different ethnic backgrounds going there. The kids came from all over the city and I remember people asking me, ya know, where are you from? I knew what the TV was always sayin' about my neighborhood, and that the kids at school heard it on TV and were repeating it, so I would say I was from the North Side." Again she chuckles. "When they'd say, well, what neighborhood? I'd say, oh, I forgot. I bet they knew, but I was ashamed, so I lied."

Gloria says her shame didn't last. She became convinced her neighborhood wasn't the only one with problems. "As I got older I learned that the reason Cabrini was on the media so much was because we was sittin' on a gold mine. Really, you got the Gold Coast right there, Lincoln Park is right next door and downtown, the Magnificent Mile, is just blocks away. Oh, I was real proud after learning all that," she says with a smile. "Anybody ask me where I live and I say, 'Cabrini-Green! I live on that gold mine everybody wants.'"

With plans of the long rumored redevelopment finally taking shape, Gloria admits she's unsure how those plans will affect her and her family. "I don't know how long we'll live in this area," she says. "But I know one thing, I'm proud of my kids. I'm proud of who they are and what they can be."

Gloria insists that despite the painful and destructive events that may have forever labeled Cabrini-Green as infamous and notorious, and no matter what becomes of this modern-day gold mine, she's raising children who will one day say they are proud to have been raised in Cabrini-Green.

Gloria Cockrell-Smith

Rachella Thompson: I just got one question. Where are they going to put all these people?

What's the point of them closing these building, because they're gonna have to open some of them back up. They can't put all of these people out like that. And for them to just, you know, remodel, and then give these people what they're remodeling...

Then again, I wouldn't want some of these people living in nothing new either because they don't even know how to take care of what they have.

But they do have people living in the new houses on Larrabee. Some of the people they have living over there, it's like, okay, you lived in Cabrini. Okay, I saw your house when you lived in Cabrini and they gave you a new house. I mean this one girl I know she showed a picture of her new house and it looked the same exact way it did when she lived in Cabrini. I'm like, you are not even taking care of this apartment, so they gave you all a new apartment?

Gloria Cockrell-Smith: Sometimes you just pray and find a way to kind of distract yourself from the [gangs] and the trouble around here. And sometimes it almost starts lookin' and feelin' the way it used to, when our whole building was really just like one big family. It really was. Every summer we'd all go somewhere together, to Great America, Fun Town or Kiddie Land....Part of me still thinks there's a chance it can be like that again.

Ramsey Lewis: When I go back to the community now, it's sad to look at the conditions people have to live in. I don't see a lot of optimism there....In some ways I think the changes are the best thing that could happen to the community. Overcrowding, I think, has had a helluva lot to do with the problems in Cabrini-Green. All low-income people shouldn't have to live together....Just because you don't have as much money as the next guy doesn't mean you don't want the same things for your children, the same things for your community...and when you put 20,000 people together who are struggling financially and then you have the few bad apples that 'cause problems, things can't get any better.

The way the system is set up hasn't been any help. I think low income people should be sprinkled throughout the city....The big picture, to me, looks better if they make some changes in Cabrini.

Jesse White: I went to Washington, D.C., and I spoke on behalf of the residents of Cabrini-Green. I want the redevelopment to go forward for them. I want there to be housing for the residents, but I want them to be selective about who they provide housing for, and I want them to be able to move expeditiously to get rid of those individuals who can't live in peace and harmony with their neighbors.

We want them to be good neighbors. We want the kind of people who you don't mind having next to you and I don't mind having next to me. But, the people who are on the wrong side of the ledger of good citizenship, they should not be considered for an opportunity in this community.

Things are already moving forward, with the new Jenner school, a new police department, a new shopping center, a redeveloped park at Seward, the new Walter Payton High School...and some new housing that is already there. We want this community to be one of the finest communities in the city. We want the residents of Cabrini-Green to live in harmony with the rest of the community. As far as relocating all of them, no, but the ones who are not good citizens, they have to go.

People who pay their rent on time, don't create problems, they're going to be fine, but the other ones, they have to go.

Henry Johns: If they had kept the rules from the beginning, it would still be okay. For example, we keep tellin' them we smell gas or the stove goes out on us, they don't send somebody until the fire jump out and burn some body. That's the only way you get somethin' done around here, after someone gets hurt.

That started a long time ago. The CHA has been doin' that a long time, but not in the early days. I think the city, they wanna do everything they can against us so they can go right ahead and take this land. They won't fix anything, that's the reason they let it go down so they could have an easy way to put us out. But, they gonna put us out after we get through fightin' and I don't care what it takes, we gonna march and have meetings and we gonna do whatever we can.

Viola Holmes: I been around here all these years so I hate to see them buildings comin' down. There ain't much left now. It used to be nothin' but houses way back. It was real nice.

Jerry Butler: I think every neighborhood goes through the process of evolution and retraction. For a while this community has been retracting, and so I think the changes might be good. I just think it depends on how they go about it.

Paulette Simpson: People can walk to work, walk to the beach, to Lincoln Park. I remember thinkin' this area got too many conveniences, they gonna get it. They just gonna take it one day.

But, if you're gonna complain, you shoulda' been protesting 25 years ago, or tryin' to do better 25 years ago. Now, it's too late, but I think a lot of people over here don't believe it. They just don't see it.

Jesse White: All you have to do is stand on the corner of Oak and Larrabee, on the southwest corner, and you'd understand exactly what I'm talking about as far as the changes that need to be made. You know what I'm talking about, where they have a liquid breakfast, liquid lunch and a liquid supper. And then further down the street you have them practicing pharmacy without a license. They have not earned the white coat. Those are the people that have to go.

All in all I love the community. I love the people in it. Yes, in a way you're changing the neighborhood back to what it once was, yes, you have to make sure to have the same type of good people that we had before.

Thelma Randolph: Oh, it's gone....You see it all around. It's only a matter of time 'cause they're building fast. Most of the residents, they ain't concerned, just waiting to see what happens. They should be at some of these meetings inquiring about it, stating what they feel because as long as they sit back, they're going to take it over. And that's exactly what's happening.

Debra Wilson: A lot of people think the changes around here aren't for us. It's just for when they move in....Even the homes that they built down there on Larrabee, we figure it's not for us. They're just building all around us and they know in a matter of time they're going to snatch it. My father used to tell us all the time, you all better keep yourselves together because you're living on a gold mine.

Lillian Swopes: People are concerned, yeah, but then I don't sympathize with them. No, because about 25 years I've been trying to preach to them...but they didn't want to hear. They didn't want to organize. They'll say they don't want to know anything about it, but now there's a rush because they see those buildings coming up. They read the paper, and hear that they're gonna have to move, so now it's a rush.

There is some good because the redevelopment is going to integrate people with each other. The housing situation, I think, it's gonna be better. The only thing about it, I hate to see the type of housing they puttin' up. If you scratch a match on one, they're gonna all end up going down. They're very poorly structured and the attitude is very poor, that's because they haven't been allowed to intermingle, ya know, the new people and the people from Cabrini. I can understand why that's true due to the fact that the prices they payin' for decent housing they don't figure they have to intermingle.

Oh, we have some good, and kind-hearted people here. We've got some religious people here. We've got some people here that would like to see this change-over become realistic. But, uh, they're gonna have to do a little more integrating than they have.

I don't have too much faith in the city. I think the percentage of people [from Cabrini] who gonna stay here is so low that it's gonna be just like an auction. It'll never be a mixed community again. Who can afford those houses?

Thelma Randolph: I love the vicinity, not necessarily the community. There is not community to me anymore. That's why I go to work, come home and shut the door. But, yeah, I'd move across the street...if they give me a chance to get in one of these. It's the vicinity, the access to downtown. They just realized what they did, built this property on a gold mine so they've been talking about tearing this down for a long time.

My mom can remember, she said far as she knows the plan goes back 30 years. Yeah, they've been trying to figure how to get this back, you know. They realized what they did. It's one of the richest plots of land in the United States.

Rochelle Satchell: In 1954, I was educated that this community was not built to stand. This community was built temporarily and they had a plan down for that. It's finally happening.

Zora Washington: The redevelopment is a nice thing but I believe it's a lie because the people that's living here, they are not the ones that are going to be living in the reconstituted Cabrini-Green. Let's get real.

We all know that's not going to happen. They can talk all they want to — they being the people with the power. I just don't believe it.

Angie Smith: I think it's too early to tell what's gonna go on with the neighborhood. I wouldn't be sad. As long as they don't mess with the row houses, I won't be sad at all.

The new playground at Seward Park is beautiful. It's really nice up there, but I don't think it's really for the kids around here. If it was for them they should have did it a long time ago.

Gerald Washington: I've been tellin' people Cabrini's gonna be a memory in the next 20 years, so you better hold on to a lot of this stuff....We've been talkin' about this for about five years, and we're supposed to go over and take a picture of the Cabrini-Green sign at Division Street and Larrabee before it's gone, because it's happening right now.

Another sad thing about this redevelopment is that people in this community don't even know what's going on, and there's maybe about 30% that really care....I went to a town hall meeting discussing this neighborhood and I'd say about 85% of the people at this meeting were not living in this area. That was crazy to me. It was people like myself who don't live here anymore, but there was not too many residents.

Rosalind Kirkman-Bey: I recently saw Seward Park and I think they're doin' good. I know they're building a lot of condos around here but I'm surprised they're doin' everything so quick. A lot of people are now trying to figure out somewhere else to live. There's been nothing mentioned about the row houses yet, but I'm sure they're going to get to us. This is a prime spot, a prime spot. You can't help but to see that.

Marsha Crosby: Things have gotten better around here. They have gotten better thank God. It's a little too late as far as what they might want to do to the neighborhood because all that's been decided. It's going to happen.

Not a lot of people are ready for it because to have to move to places you may not choose to go to, like way out in the suburbs or whatever, to be told to take this or take that is not right.

No matter how bad Cabrini is or was or whatever, inside your home, that's your home. To be told that you got to get up and leave, that's a bad feeling. That's a bad feeling there....I don't care how bad it is, that's still your home.

Richard Blackmon: Cabrini is about people. You know, and it's people that are no different than the people in your neighborhood, people that want better lives for their kids and themselves. That's all Cabrini has ever been about.

Gerald Washington: Some people are excited about moving, and I think that's good. It gives people a different environment and I think that should happen, but I think we have ownership on this property, some kind of ownership, squatters rights or whatever you wanna call it, some kind of ownership...but I think it's a little late because a lot of this land is gettin' bought up.

Now people are beginning to get a little more concerned, especially when "the castle," as they called 1117-1119 [building], came down a couple years ago. When that building came down people were like, uh oh, maybe something is gonna go on over here. Too late, it's gone. People out there trying to keep them from tearing it down, all they have to do is just call the police and move you out the way and let the demolition go on through.

Walter Burnett: I think the main thing is to make sure that the people don't get lost in the shuffle. I think [redevelopment] can be a good thing. You got to make sure that it is, and that part is going to be very challenging. I'm going to do as much as I can to try to make it that way.

There is a lot of greed out there. People are greedy and when they're greedy, they disregard not only people in Cabrini-Green, but in other areas too.

Gloria Purifoy: I look at the new Seward Park and it's so beautiful yet disgusting. What they're doing for this community now pretty much says that the people who lived in the community before were not worthy of it.

Remember, you still have people livin' in this community, right? You have a new park, a new library and things, and do you see people tearing up those new things? They are still there and they aren't being destroyed.

If you build neighborhoods that look like neighborhoods, people will not destroy it. They built that library over there on Division Street and even I thought oh, a library for the new white people moving in, but the times I've walked into that library kids from

the neighborhood are in there by the droves. They go in there to do their homework and stuff, and we never had that before. We used to have a little pocket hole library in 1169 [building]....It was a little apartment that they made into a library. So, to put all this new stuff here now says that we weren't worth it...so when you hear people say the new Seward Park looks disgusting, it's because they think that wasn't built for them.

Marsha Crosby: I thank God I was spared that feeling of being forced to move....It really weighed on my mind because, being that things was so terrible there, I didn't want to raise up my child in Cabrini. Ya know, bullets comin' through our living room windows and everything, but I felt like I was in a Catch 22 situation. I didn't want to live over there, but with my illness I'm unable to work. I can't afford to move any place else. That was bad in itself, then when they started talking about they was going to tear it down, it was okay, what am I going to do and where am I going to go?

I used to just worry so much about that, until one day I just said, I can't worry about it anymore. I prayed on it that when it comes down for the building to be torn down God will make a way, find some place for us to go. And then last year, in June, they told me that my name had been pulled out from many names to move down here [to the new houses]. So that was the answer to my prayers. They said that when they build their things, that they set aside 15 or 16 units for low income families to be mixed in. I think they called it a Hope VI Program or something like that, which I knew nothing about. I remember because I used to get so angry every time we would be driving down Larrabee that they was building all these new things. I said, they just building up all around here and in Cabrini we don't have opportunity to get anything good, but you never know what God has in store for you.

Everybody in our building, they said like they was so happy for us, but who knows really deep down inside....I'm sure some wished it was them, but I don't even know how the program came about. I don't know how they came about pulling my name. I have to say I guess God was just watching out for us.

Rosalind Kirkman-Bey: More opportunity for people around here would be great. There is some opportunity but they don't want to work for minimum wage...but at the same time they do want the government basically to take care of them and their children for free. I can relate because when I was in that position other tax payers were payin' for me and my children. Now, me being a tax payer, I want my taxes to come down. So I think if I can do it other people can do it.

Marsha Crosby: This sounds so crazy, you really want to move but in a way you do have bittersweet memories, because after you've been at some place for so long....Everything wasn't all bad. I had some friends that always looked out for me; like when I was sick, I just called my friend and tell her and she would look out for my son. I had friends and I guess childhood memories and everything. So it was bittersweet for me when I moved. Don't get me wrong, I was glad to go. I was so glad to go.

Richard Blackmon: I'm happy for the community and the people if they are going to get what the rest of us should have gotten.

Despite things that have happened, it is a great community. It is a great place to live, but it can be made so much better. I can't believe the stuff that's already changed. I see a new library, new Dominick's, I mean it doesn't even look like the same place.

I think that sense of isolation is going to disappear. In some ways we always felt isolated, like cut off from the rest of the city. I'm hoping that now these changes help take away some of that sense of isolation so that people feel more a part of, you know, the rest of the city. But, it's going to be tough because nobody likes change. And, you're talking about wholesale, massive change. It's going to be hard for some people to stomach.

I remember when my mom worked at Goldblatt's, she would bring home strollers or play pens, anything that she thought the girls in the neighborhood needed to take care of their babies. This was when they started to have babies younger, and she had a discount from working at Goldblatt's. She would bring it home and give it to them, just to make sure they had it. You know, these were real families. That's what it was about. It was just about family trying to get a better life, that's all. So there has always been a sense of community.

I guess that's why it infuriates me when people who would leave the community and then try to pretend like they were never a part of Cabrini. There was always this sense of community so, you know, how dare you deny that we didn't have that?

Gloria Purifoy: There was violence going on all around, but it was highlighted in our community. It was basically because that community sits on the richest property in the city of Chicago, so why would you ever wanna make it seem like anything good is happening there if you got a plan, which has been in place for years, that was called gentrification.

On top of that, the buildings were built like prisons. They look like prison, and if people are part of something that looks like a prison, then it's gonna feel like prison and make them feel like they're prisoners. It makes them feel like they are a problem others need to be protected from. So how else are they gonna treat that? They're gonna rebel against it. That's the nature of the human being, but not everybody gets it.

So I think those buildings need to come down because they have held a lot of people captive for a long time. But, I am not sure of the opportunities [the redevelopment] is going create for the masses over there. There's just far too many people in need, period.

Jan Morgan: Our world here is just gettin' tighter and tighter. Pretty soon, it's gone. Pretty soon it's poof, and we outta here. By 2010 Cabrini-Green's gone. It's prime real estate. It's right here and they want it. They've wanted it a long time. They wanted it, they just didn't know how to get us outta here...but we helpin' them get rid of us, ya know, by the things that we doin'.

If we just unite, and that's one of the things that's wrong with this community, they will not unite until it's too late. And it's too late. It's not gonna be affordable for anyone from Cabrini to live here anymore.

C'mon, $200,000 and up for a one-bedroom condo [*laughing*]. Okay, everybody over here's got two or three kids...plus a quarter of a million dollars for housing? If everybody over here put all their money together, we couldn't find that quarter million, ya know what I'm sayin?

Rochelle Satchell: When I moved out of Cabrini, I had to make up my mind that I had to look at it in a positive way. If I'm paying them $650 a month, I could be using that as a mortgage payment.

But I was still working in Cabrini and so my goals was, if I could succeed I would stay here and organize women and families so they could do it too. That was the component built in to my program; to work with the whole family instead of just working with the teen parents.

Erick Moore: Some people are like, I'm glad they're tearing this thing down. Some people, like me, born and raised in Cabrini, it hurts. Because right before your eyes you're seeing Cabrini change. It's sick because the change is not changing for us, it's changing for other people.

Probably about ten years, 15 years down the line you come down to see Cabrini and it probably be called William Hallberg III Townhomes or some shit....I can see it. I'm seeing Cabrini change right before my eyes.

Wanda Hopkins: I don't have their opinion about the Cabrini high-rises. I believe it was a fantastic idea. If you can build Presidential Towers downtown, and they have more floors than our building, then you can have a Cabrini-Green housing development and the only thing that you have to do is to make sure that the maintenance there do their job.

And when there are organizations in the community who are supposed to be getting money for counseling for low income parents, when they begin to start doing their job for people and help them to learn how to do this transition and teach them how they can get out of these buildings, this could have worked as the temporary housing it was meant to be.

I hear people all the time say they shouldn't of stacked us on top of each other. My mother never had a problem. We had a beautiful apartment. We didn't have a problem with being stacked on top of each other, that is not the truth. It's just like the apartments on our lake downtown, all you do is make sure it's maintained. You call the maintenance to come up and take care of it, right? See, it's not a problem.

Richard Blackmon: I mean, think about it, you got 16 stories. Let's say ten apartments on each floor, that's 160 families. If each family has three kids, the number is astronomical. You're talking about more than 500 people in a space that's probably the equivalent of what five families would live in. That's too much.

That's too many people in too small a space, and I don't care who the people are. If you put people in that kind of space, and you throw on top of that economic struggles and issues of poverty, you're going to have problems. I don't care who it is.

Marsha Crosby: They say they're going to tear down Near North High School. They building a new high school. That high school is a college preparatory high school that they're building. How many kids from Cabrini that were going to Near North, which is a good school, but how many kids you think are going to pass the test to get over in that new school? So, where's the new Near North?

They trying to make it seem like they're doing everything that's there to help people in Cabrini and to me, they're not. They're doing it to help the city, bring a lot of people from the suburbs into the city, make it more comfortable and desirable for them to live in the city....So, most of it's not for the people in Cabrini. They only going to take so many people.

Gloria Purifoy: To be honest, I don't know what opportunity there will be for the working people most of all. People who make okay money and work hard, they can't live over there. You have to either be dirt poor and hope someone will pick you, ya know, you have to be able to not stand on your own feet at all and a few will be chosen, or you have to be very well off. But for people in the middle, there's nothin' for them. There's nothin' for them, so who is it really creating opportunity's for? And that's not just this community, that's a problem all over this city.

Rochelle Satchell: No, you can't recapture the past, but if they can come back not with the old laws but with a system that monitors the buildings a little bit more it would help. Make people responsible for their actions and their kids' actions, then it would be better here.

And, I don't think that the process they're using for transition is working. The people still have the same mentality. This is just my opinion. I would think that okay, the conditions here have deteriorated real bad. So, you're taking people from here and you're putting them in a new house, what's going to change them?

There needs to be education of sorts. That screening process needs to be put back in place. You have some people here that would love the screening process. If you have behavior problems, the process needs to be back. And family counseling, if you can't get a hold of that, then you have to go because we're not going to have it here. It needs to be something in place for the change or it's not going to work.

Debra Wilson: I hear the rent will be so high that it will force us to just move out. They've got Section 8, which I heard was going in debt. I had applied for Section 8 before...and I waited 14 years. When I got back in low income housing they was renovating the building, 1234. They moved me four times in 1234, from apartment to apartment four times. I was pregnant. Then my Section 8 comes through. I had to write to tell them, I'm tired, I'm pregnant, I can't go look because I didn't have a car. I just can't do it.

Evelyn Turner: A lot of the people are stuck in the rut that they're in because they don't like change. And it's not that you can't change, or you can't do better, it's just that you have this view, and you're just stuck there, you know, and sometimes motivation just won't help you out if you're not willing to accept change. You've got to be able to accept a challenge. Because right now, that's exactly what it is, it's a challenge, you know, day to day, you never know what's going to happen. And the bad part about it is, as I said, they're stuck.

People who live there don't own it, and that's what the tenants seem to forget. You don't own it. That's not a piece of property

that's for sale. That's not something that you've actually paid a mortgage on, or you rented with the option to purchase. They can do with those buildings what they please. They can offer you some place to live, and that's what people seem to forget. That's not a development that's owned by a Realtor, you know, taxes pay for that.

It's just so sad that all those people are still there. And a lot of them, like the folks on the first floor, you know, the first floor, those are the biggest apartments. Where would you find a place big enough for a family who's now occupying a five bedroom apartment? I don't think they thought about that, I think they just came in and said, well, this is what we need to do. And they just started it.

But, to be perfectly honest, is that going to stop those kids from being shot while they walk to school, or little old ladies catching stray bullets? I say, tear them all down. I mean, innocent people don't deserve to suffer at the hands of some other ignorant person. So, I mean, you say you're being wronged now, well, maybe you were a part of the problem, you know. Not everybody over there is a part of the problem, it's just that there's so many bad people until you can't see the good ones, you know.

Every body is not smoking crack tonight, you know, you've actually got some people who return home and just want to cook a nice dinner, sit down, enjoy dinner and maybe watch a little TV and go to bed. But then you've got those who slept until one, two in the afternoon, and they get up to come out on the prowl so they can stay out 'til three, four in the morning, you know, to do the drug thing. So, I mean, you know, you've got two worlds over there.

Runetta Thompson: I'm not depending on what somebody else is going to offer me. I'm fortunate enough to be in a position where I can go out here and try and pay my own bills without them trying to offer me something. But I know I have four kids, so if they do offer me something, it will be worth it...because I don't want to be going and trying to pay seven and nine hundred dollars in rent when I know I still got three kids that are home and they're going to college and I can use, you know, that subsidized income.

But what kills me is they'll give that to somebody that really don't appreciate it. When I inquired [about the new housing], they denied me this. I don't know if they feel like I made too much money, but if I did I would have moved. I mean, I'm trying to make it just like the next person. I'm not asking them for no

handouts either, but why would you deny me an opportunity when you're talking about that you want to put people in them that really want to maintain them?

Rochelle Satchell: I have an attraction here. I know where everything is and when it's gone, I'll miss it. I always felt like if I was blind, I would never be lost here, but if I was blind in the community I live in now I would be lost.

I can sense the people, I can hear the voices. I know the voices. Somewhere else, I would be totally lost.

When I'm walking down the street, I feel good on the inside here, because I know everybody. I feel like a person. You live somewhere else, nobody knows your name. You might get a good mornin' but here it's like, "Hey, Rochelle, how's it goin'!" I know everybody and I know whatever happens to me, I still would be accepted here.

Debra Wilson: I'm on disability now because of my illness. I've been off five years and I'm looking for something better. I have a child and I have to look for something better. I don't want to have this nonchalant attitude like I don't care about the community, because I'm still here. But, it's like my hands are tied.

Richard Blackmon: We all know there's too many people in too small a space. So some of the buildings would have to come down. We knew that.

Come on let's face it, I mean this is not the best design for housing people. So, what are we fighting for? None of us have been that thrilled about what we've got here...and all the designs about changing Cabrini and making it more habitable, making them like Presidential Towers and that kind of stuff you know, it's just been talk....They always talked about putting stores on the first floor, a Laundromat, a daycare and that kind of stuff. That stuff would have been great if we ever did it. That's frustrating.

You know there was always some outside force dictating to us about, you know, what life would be like in Cabrini-Green. So I just never really felt like we had a chance.

Evelyn Turner: Another bad thing was when they started to board up the units. After the people vacated the units, the CHA would board them up. Well, quite naturally, you invite any and everybody in there when you board it up. You don't know if somebody's crawled in through a window or what. So, that was another thing, and the place just literally deteriorated.

I don't really think they wanted to pay too much attention to it. They were trying to force as many people out of there as they could, so that they would have less to relocate when they tore them down.

Walter Burnett: I used to live in 714 and then I got to 534 and then the row houses. I think God gave me the opportunity to live all over Cabrini, you know, in all the different areas and identify with the cultures. Like I said, each area has a different culture so to speak, and I think all that happened in my life for a reason, even to the point where I had my challenges in life and got in trouble and came back.

My family still lives over in Cabrini, so I got an investment in the community. I want to make sure they get the best that they can get. I enjoy seeing the two schools that I went to, Byrd and Jenner, becoming a brand new school. And I know a lot of folks who think the police station coming over there will help people to have better protection. I also know a lot of folks think the police station is just for the white folks, because the rich folks are moving to the neighborhood, but I think it's better. There's a lot of folks in Cabrini that need service.

Rochelle Satchell: Some people are saving and looking. What I'm doing is working with the ones that are looking into buying a home. What I'm saying to them is you can go anywhere you want to go, but you have to plan. We talk about it. They come in and I tell them about the down payments they would need. What a lot of them are doing right now is building up their credit so that they can be prepared for that day, rather than buying the things that they would need in their new home right now. Those that want it are saving. It's in their own hands.

Runetta Thompson: I have a feeling they're going to rehab some of these buildings and make them into condos...but I'm not going to worry about it. Everybody keeps asking me, well, when are they going to come and tear it down? Well, I'm not concerned when they're going to tear down my building. That's not my concern. My concern is what I'm going to do for my family. I'm not concerned when CHA is going to make me move, or about what they're going to do with the property over here. I don't care.

It may sound callous, but I have more important things to worry about, like supporting my family. I'm not worried about what they're going to do. I'm worried about what I'm going to do and how I'm going to make it.

Debra Wilson: It's water under the bridge now because they've spent thousands of dollars, millions of dollars and what do we have to show for it? Broken elevators, cabinets pulled out, doors off the hinges and messed up houses. They needed to keep on overseeing those who were in control. I don't know, America must got this kind of money to keep throwing away because they sure throw away a lot of it.

Richard Blackmon: I'm almost hysterical about the police station they're building at Division and Larrabee. That is, I couldn't believe it. Why now? You know, why couldn't they do it, like, in 1970. That would have been one that would have changed the community dramatically. You put the police station on the corner. The firemen have been there since the day that we moved here. They never had any problems.

They would always be sitting out in summertime, sometime they would come out and join people out in front of the buildings, for a barbecue or something. You know, they would spray people with the hoses — in a loving kind of a manner.

Rachella Thompson: The young people that are talking about it, they're concerned because they know either that their mother is not going to take responsibility because she's either strung out on drugs or she just don't care, so their mother isn't gonna take responsibility so they need to be worried about what's gonna happen to them. So that's why they're really talking about the changes.

And the other young people, they are talking about it because they have a child of their own and they need to worry about, ya know, where am I going to take my child? They can't afford to go anywhere else.

The people who are really worried are the people who don't have anywhere to go, I mean, can't afford anything else, don't have any education, nothing, you know. It's like my mother, I can see her moving anywhere, but maybe somebody like another person who lives upstairs from me or something I can see them being worried, like where will they take me?

Especially like in 364, it's a big senior citizen, handicapped building, and where are you going to put those people? A lot of them, they have been in Cabrini all their lives, and you're going to just throw them out of the neighborhood? This is all they know. It's like people that have been in jail, that's all they knew was jail, and you're going to just kick them out and tell them you're free to go. Where you gonna go? You gotta know where to go.

Richard Blackmon: Certainly those of us that survive are strong, you know, but what about the ones that don't survive? So 25% or some of us make it, what happens now to the 75% of the ones that get stuck?

Debra Wilson: It just wasn't always like this. Authority figures is why it has become what it has become. Their negligence in maintenance, in inspecting houses and screening tenants, they just created something that was sure to fall. In a matter of time it couldn't do nothing but fall, because they're the ones overseeing the community, not the tenants. So they can't blame the tenants for what's happening.

Dwayne Ford: For a couple years now we pretty much had the idea that they was going to make changes here. When I was away at college, I used to come home for a weekend or a week break, and every time I come home something is different. This building was gone, they building something new here. It was just a change. Not necessarily bad, not necessarily good, it was just something different.

I think it's been kind of nice to see white people jog through the neighborhood, walking their dogs or whatever. A few years ago

you couldn't imagine that. It's nice to see that, I'm all for it....And I think people would be all for it if they were getting out of here to a better home. But people here can't afford it.

From what I see, people are pretty much in denial, like 75% are in denial and 25% are concerned, so you do find some concerned people around. But the majority is in denial with everything, that's pretty much how their life is. Everything is denial, they don't want to try anything new, they're scared of the unknown, and they think nothing bad can happen to them.

Wanda Hopkins: I still believe part of the plan to destroy these buildings was not to have them cleaned any more because back then they stayed clean, the elevators worked all the time. I never remember as a young child having to walk up to our apartment.... It's when I came back the second time to live here with my children, in 1976, that I found the dirtiness in the buildings and the no elevator services, and the gangs taking over and all of that.

That was the designed plan, I think. We stop cleaning the buildings, then it will look like they just don't know how to take care of where they live and they'll have to tear it down.

Richard Blackmon: It always amazed me. I used to deliver papers on the Gold Coast to Sandburg Terrace. I delivered the old Daily News. It was the first job I ever had. I was 11 years old. It just always amazed me the contrast in wealth. I mean here you are you've got the richest one mile right next door to the poorest one mile. You know, I never understood that part of why we were so close [*laughing*]. But we never ventured beyond Wells Street....So I knew that it wouldn't be long before somebody came in, and just extended Sandburg Terrace.

Richard Parker: If you notice anything bad that happens here now, they don't want the media to find out because they want people coming here and thinking it's safe...and nine times out of ten it is. But the city wants to keep it toned down.

Tyrone Randolph: Along with the renovations, how they're building up around the community, it makes it difficult these days to even walk where you used to walk. Now, when you walk to the store you've been going to all your life, you have to worry about the police stopping you. If they do stop you, you have to have identification, for sure, because if they don't know who you are then they wanna take you to the station and check it out. You're sittin' waiting there, eight, nine, ten hours, ya know, until they decide you are who you say you are.

They have a totally different presence now. It's serve and protect but it's also harass and demean and put people down....In a way I kinda understand where they're coming from, but in a way I think they should find another way to handle those situations, because not everybody's a gang banger and not everybody has drugs or weapons on them.

Runetta Thompson: I feel like my mom, she was all about taking care of her family...especially living in a place where we lived. My mother worked. She supported us. I have the most respect for my mother. Had it not been for her, where would I be now?

My mother enabled me to go to school. I went on and went to college. And I mean without her, all that would not have been possible. It's not whether she was strict or not. She did the right thing by me. That's all that matters.

She taught me right. I never have been in jail. I don't know what handcuffs feel like because my mother taught me that's not how I want your life to be. Now, I have four kids. I'm divorced. But I feel like even with that, my mother taught me one thing. Once you make your bed, you lay in it and you do the best by it. So now that you're a mother, be a good one.

That's how I look at the [redevelopment]. We have to do what's best for our family. I would love to stay right here, right here in this area, but if we don't, we don't.

But I can't see them just putting out all this stuff around us without somebody getting something good out of it. Somebody's going to get something, and I hope that somebody does because there are some people that are worthy of it over here.

Steve Pratt: It should be like a wake up call to everybody. My attitude is we already sittin' on a valuable piece of land, all right? And, these [gang] guys is out here doin' all this nonsense and they ain't payin' attention to that, they ain't lookin' at that, and they ain't makin' it no better.

It's like, if they are tryin' to get rid of us or whatever, the stuff the gangs is doin' is just speeding up the process. And from that standpoint, the city or police have that attitude, like it just makes it easier for us to get them outta there.

Thelma Randolph: Really, Cabrini-Green is no different than any other neighborhood or community to me. You have good ones, you have bad ones, you know, and that's everywhere you go. Shootin' happens all over, you know. Now there's people goin' crazy about their job and shootin' up the workplace and shootin' in restaurants, you know.

So, Cabrini ain't as bad as people portray it to be. Just by them rebuilding around here, they say white folks was afraid to come over here. White folks jog through here. They ride the carriages through here, you know. Don't nobody bother them. It's not about black and white. It's not about that. You don't bother them. They're not going to bother you.

Wanda Hopkins: The new Walter Payton High School is just down the street and even though there is a new mandate that 20 percent of the community must go to the school, you still have to meet the requirements. Our children are not at that level of requirement, so our children may not reap the benefits, if any of them are still living here.

I think it's important that if they're going to redevelop the community like they say they're going to, then do it. But, I don't know that we're really a part of the plan. If it's supposed to be a racially mixed community and a mixed income community, then a lot of people from Cabrini should be part of the future here.

I don't think gang members or drug dealers should be in Cabrini, now or later, but some of us are good people, some of us should be able to stay in Cabrini at a rent that we could afford.

Richard Parker: I think a lot of residents are still in la-la land. They're still thinking, this is our property. No, it's not your property. It's not even your house. It's not even Cabrini property. This is River North. This is now River North.

Zora Washington: I've seen the new little park in front of the Seward Park fieldhouse, and it's very nice. When we were growing up Seward Park was a ramshackle, thrown-together building and I guess on the inside the building is still not all that great. They fixed up all the outside, so why haven't they done anything inside?

Because these little children from Cabrini are still going over there, and once they move out and the other people move in, then they will rehab the inside.

That tells the story right there. They fix it up so it looks good on the outside, but it's still raggedy on the inside. And once these people are gone they're going to fix it up on the inside. To me that says it all.

Henry Johns: The only thing the media would focus on in Cabrini is tragedy....Something happens on Wells Street, they'd say it was Cabrini, but that's when they wanted everyone else to leave this area....Now, since they got all these new houses, something did happen, this boy got shot over in 412, and we didn't see anything on the news at all. They used to build everything up, but now they don't because they want people to buy these houses over here...and they want us out.

Noreen Rhodes: I want people to come together and do what we can. Within the next two years, if they don't realize what's happening and wake up then it's over....We gotta all come together and do this. We have to come together as one group...because, to me, this is home. And it's worth fighting for.

Debra Wilson: If there was some wins that we could see, some chance of victory I believe people would come together, they would come together and do whatever they had to. But you don't see no win. I mean you can't even walk outside the house now at night without having some fear, so there's really nothing to hold on to but your memories.

It's just not there no more. The flowers are concrete. The bars on the porches go all the way up. The windows that are not boarded up are Plexiglas. The elevators are broke, so you really have nothing to hold on to.

They put all this money in and it doesn't look like they're going to do it all over again. I wouldn't. I wouldn't even suggest it. So what I think people should do is clean up their own house. Act like they're concerned about their lives and maybe God will grant them a blessing. That's where I'm standing right now.

Steve Pratt: As far as them talkin' about puttin' people outta here, you just can't do that unless you got some place for people to go. You can't kick people out in the street...but if people don't wake up and come together then it's gonna be like we don't have no say so.

It's like they say, divided we fall united we stand. I wish everybody would wake up to it. This is like a part of our history, especially people that was born and raised here. It's like our roots, so it will be real messed up to just lose it like that.

Viola Holmes: I don't really wanna go nowhere else. I ain't got long to live so why am I gonna go somewhere else? They say they gonna tear it down, I don't know, but I got my little bag packed. I'll just walk out when they start bangin' it. That's it.

theEND!

I was about halfway through my pitch when his eyes brightened and his forehead wrinkled. I knew he was in.

Jimmy Biggs was essentially the first person I brought the idea to because I knew that without him this would be a tough assignment to pull off. At 23, he was already a wily old character of the community, well-known and widely-respected in social circles that ranged from church-goin' grandmas to coin-pitchin' teens. Born and raised in Cabrini-Green, Jimmy already possessed a unique sense of his own history. He was already a reliable resource, already a trusted friend.

So when I told him I'd like to put together a book that tells the story of Cabrini-Green through the eyes of its current and former residents, I wasn't surprised how quickly the concept hooked him.

For five years Jimmy has worked at Cabrini Connections, a not-for-profit tutor/mentor program serving seventh through twelfth grade students who live in the area. Jimmy is a graduate of the program as well. As a long-time volunteer to the organization, I and others often talked with Jimmy about Cabrini's struggles, its upsides, its reputation, its people, its past and its prognosis. With this book, we've turned that conversation over to Cabrini residents — and former residents — of various ages. And, of course, Jimmy knew right where to start. "We've got to talk to Mother Vassar."

Since the historic Mother Vassar interview, Jimmy served heroically in a supporting role that included tracking down and scheduling potential interview subjects, guiding me through the streets and buildings of Cabrini, consulting on neighborhood landmarks and protocol, assisting in interviews, building team morale and much, much more. I truly can't thank him enough.

As much time as Jimmy put in on the project, he still had a full-time job to attend to at Cabrini Connections. That's where I found my reinforcements. Anita Gunartt, another graduate of the tutoring program, led a group of Cabrini Connections students that included Tasheeka Conley, LaShaun Crosby, Tamicka Garner, Keyana Jackson, Monique Kirkman-Bey, Sabrina Nelson, and Shakea Truss. These students set up interviews and, after preparing for them, they helped conduct interviews. I am grateful to each of them.

The students of this organization not only contributed to the book's production, they served as inspiration, which is why author royalties of this book will be donated to Cabrini Connections. Having gotten to know dozens of students over the years, some who have moved on to college or work, I am continually struck by their collective strength, spirit, warmth and sense of humor. I'm even more impressed by the traits that set each one of them apart. I especially salute Bradore Thompson, who I have had the pleasure of tutoring and mentoring for ten years. We would also would like to remember Jamar Barnes, Carlos Chambers and LaToya Chambers, former students who died too young.

I thank the staff and volunteers at Cabrini Connections, who continually serve as inspiration to the students. Specifically, my thanks to Gena Schoen, Jackie Rubert, Beth Galantha, Alicia Hall and Sheridan Enomoto. They, along with Dan Bassill, the organization's executive director, were supportive of the book idea from the start. They often went out of their way to be of help.

Many times our interview subjects suggested others to interview. "Oh, you should go talk to so-and-so…" was a line we heard

ac**KNOWLEDGE**ments

again and again. I owe a special thanks, and a sincere apology to those who were interviewed but do not appear in the book.

For various reasons, not every interview subject could be included, but I do warmly thank Ruby Boclair, Diane Brooks, Paulette Clay, Eric Cotton, Donell Gunartt, Pastor Charles Infelt, Ora Jones, Father Sebastian Lewis O.S.B., Ester Moore, Pernecie Pugh, Bernice Thompson, Eliza Truss, LaTrese Truss, Tammie Truss, Juanita Williams, Jessie Visinaiz, and Priscilla Nelson for spending the time and sharing their memories. I do wish I was able to include them all, and the many other residents who have a story to share.

We couldn't have asked for a better production team than photographer Blair Jensen and design-man John Bistolfo of Bark Design. I thank them for contributing their tireless work and reliable talent.

I also thank my wife, Jill, and daughter, Grace, for their patience and love during the production of this book.

Thanks to Peggy Parfenoff and Jay Clark of the LPC Group for getting the book on store shelves, and for enthusiastically spreading the word.

I owe a great debt of gratitude to David Weinberg and David Wilk for embracing the idea, getting it off the ground and seeing to it that this book be professionally produced and handsomely printed, ensuring that the passionate voices inside be given proper presentation. Without these two men, this book might still be just an idea.

Finally, we thank residents — past and present — of Cabrini-Green. Ultimately, it is the residents who made this book possible. They welcomed us into their homes. They welcomed us into their lives. The openness and honesty of all those we interviewed was overwhelming, which says a lot about this community's true character.

Above all, perhaps, it says that after 58 storied years, Cabrini-Green still **is** a community. This book is dedicated to those who worked so hard trying to keep it that way.

— *Dave Whitaker*

Pictured left to right: *Jimmy Biggs, Tasheeka Conley, Monique Kirkman-Bey, Tamicka Garner, Keyana Jackson, Sabrina Nelson, Bradore Thompson, Anita Gunartt*